Carlos Martyn

The Pilgrim Fathers of New England

Carlos Martyn

The Pilgrim Fathers of New England

ISBN/EAN: 9783337293475

Printed in Europe, USA, Canada, Australia, Japan

Cover: Foto ©ninafisch / pixelio.de

More available books at **www.hansebooks.com**

THE
PILGRIM FATHERS

OF

NEW ENGLAND:

A HISTORY.

BY W. CARLOS MARTYN,

AUTHOR OF THE LIFE AND TIMES OF JOHN MILTON, A HISTORY
OF THE ENGLISH PURITANS, ETC.

> "What sought they there, whose steps were on the dust
> Of the old forest lords? Not summer skies,
> Nor genial zephyrs, nor the amenities
> Of golden spoils. Their strength was in the trust
> That breasts all billows of the abyss of time,
> The Rock of Ages, and its hopes sublime."
> —AMERICAN SOUVENIR.

PUBLISHED BY THE
AMERICAN TRACT SOCIETY,
150 NASSAU-STREET, NEW YORK.

ENTERED according to Act of Congress, in the year 1867, by the AMERICAN TRACT SOCIETY, in the Clerk's Office of the District Court of the United States for the Southern District of New York.

PREFACE.

Lord Bacon assigns the highest meed of earthly fame to the builders of states, *conditores imperiorum*. The Pilgrim Fathers were members of that guild, and their story belongs to the heroic age of America. "No other state," remarks Stoughton, "can boast of such an origin, and adorn its earliest annals with a tale as true as it is beautiful, as authentic as it is sublime."

But aside from the honor which attends the Forefathers as the founders of empire, they march down the ages crowned with richer and more fragrant laurels; for they built not for themselves or for posterity alone, in imitation of Romulus, and Cyrus, and Cæsar, and Ottoman; they planted also for justice and for God.

Therefore they are the rightful heirs of the benedictions of mankind; while to Americans they are doubly precious as "the parents of one-third of the whole white population of the Republic."

Of course, the career of the Pilgrim Fathers has been often painted: but the interest of the story is inexhaustible, and its thrilling incidents exhibit the wisdom, the benevolence, the faithfulness of God in so many glorious and delightful aspects, and are so replete with facts whose inevitable tendency is to inflame the love, strengthen the faith, and awaken the wondering gratitude of the human heart, that it is impossible to wear the "twice-told tale" threadbare by repetition. Besides, a thoughtful scholar, who has himself laid his garland of everlasting upon the altar of the Pilgrims, has reminded us that, "however well history may have been written, it is desirable that it should be re-written from time to time by those who look from an advanced position, giving in every age to the peculiar and marked developments of the past, a simple, compact, and picturesque representation."

This sketch runs back to the cradle of Puritanism; summarily rehearses the causes of which it was begotten; accompanies the Pilgrim Fathers across the channel, and depicts the salient features of their residence in Holland, and the reasons which pushed them to further removal; sails with them in the "Mayflower" over the stormy winter sea; recites in some detail, the incidents which accompanied the settlement at Plymouth and the kindred colonies throughout New England; and closes in the sunshine of that league between the New England colonies which was the prophecy of the Republic; and the crowning glory of those who are distinctively called the *Pilgrim Fathers*.

The volume has been carefully written, and it is fortified by copious marginal notes and citations from a wide range of authoritative authors, from the humblest diarist to the most pretentious compiler who struts in the rustling satin of history.

This is "a round unvarnished tale," and aims at fairness of statement, not copying that dealer in history whom Lucian derides for always styling the captain of his own party an Achilles, and the leader of the opposition a Thersites. Nor does it enter the "debateable ground" of sectarian polity; but avoiding alike the Scylla of indiscriminate encomium, and the Charybdis of controversy, it merely reproduces the broad and unquestioned facts of an emigration whose purpose and whose result was to

"Win the wilderness for God."

NEW YORK, January, 1867.

CONTENTS.

CHAPTER I.

Spiritual Forces and the Motors of Materialism—English Puritanism—Its Conflicts with the Dramatic Religion of the Popes—Aspiration—The Modern Era—The Recast Ecclesiasticism—Two Parties in the New-modelled English Church—The Puritans—The Conformists—The Error of the Church-and-state Reformers—The Epic of our Saxon Annals—Britain, emancipated from the Pope, hugs the *Popedom*—Persecution—The Separatists—Their Disappointment—The Separatists of the North of England—Division in the Protestant World—The Philosophy of Luther—Calvin's *Rationale*—The Separatists adhere to Calvin—The Raid for Exact Conformity—The PILGRIM FATHERS prepare to quit the Island—Pilgrim Traits—Obstacles—The Attempted Exodus—Treachery—The Pilgrims "rifled by the Catchpole Officers"—Imprisonment—The Second Attempt—The Rendezvous—A Midnight Scene by the Sea-shore—Arrival of the Ship—The Stranded Barque—The Captain's Alarm—The Ship sails—The Deserted Dear Ones on Shore—A Woful Picture—Captured—The Storm—Holland at last—Reunion ---------------------------------------PAGE 17

CHAPTER II.

The Quays of Amsterdam—Quaint Aspect of the City—Its History—The Pilgrims and the Dutch Burghers—Strange Characteristics of Dutch Social Life—The Pilgrims go to Work—Their Employments—The Removal to Leyden—Reason of the Change of Residence—Leyden—Its Thrilling Story—The Exiles "raise a Competent and Decent Living"—They "enjoy much Sweet Society and Spiritual Comfort together in the Ways of God"—John Robinson—Elder Brewster—The Pilgrims grow in Knowledge and Gifts—Their Discipline—Robinson's Wisdom—The Exiles win the Cordial Love and Respect of the Dutch—An

Illustration—Testimony of the Leyden Magistrates—The Controversy—Robinson and Episcopius—The Debate—"Famous Victory" of the English Divine—Reformed Churches of the Continent—Catholicity of the Pilgrims—Their Bias towards Religious Democracy—*Peregrini Deo curæ* 37

CHAPTER III.

Many Circumstances conspire to render the Exiles anxious and uneasy in Holland—They "know that They are but Pilgrims"—The Projected Removal from the Low Countries—Their "Weighty Reasons"—A Grand Germ of Thought—The New World—Career of Maritime Discovery—The Pilgrim Council—The Debate—The Argument of the Doubters—The Apostles of the Future—Ho, for America—The Decision 52

CHAPTER IV.

Pilgrim Prayers—"Where shall we plant our Colony"—"Large Offers" of the Dutch—Determine to settle in "the most Northern Part of Virginia"—The two English Emigration Companies—The Envoys—Their Return—The Letter of Robinson and Brewster—The Virginia Company and King James—Two Questions—The "Formal Promise of Neglect"—The "Merchant-adventurers"—Terms of the Compact—Republicanism of the Pilgrims—Robinson's Sermon—Who shall sail with the "Forlorn Hope?"—The Past—Robinson's Farewell—The "Speedwell" and the "Mayflower"—"Good-by, Leyden"—"Adieu, Friends"—The "Yo hoy" of the Seamen 61

CHAPTER V.

At Southampton—The Abortive Departure—The Number of *Voyageurs* "winnowed"—Final Embarkation—The "Floating Village"—On the Atlantic—Opening of Robinson's Letter of Advice—The Seaborn Government—All Hail, Democracy!—Carver elected Governor—The Pilgrims propose to land—The Captain's Mistake—Geography of the Wilderness—The Unseaworthy Shallop—The Sixteen Scouts—Miles Standish—On Shore—First Drink of New England Water—The Mysterious Mound—The Hidden Corn—Pilgrim Conscientiousness—Return of the Explorers—In the Shallop—The Dawn of Winter—Renewed Search for a Landing Spot—First Encounter with the Indians—"*Woath wach haha hach woach*"—The Breakers—First Christian Sabbath in the New World—PLYMOUTH ROCK ... 77

CHAPTER VI.

The Pilgrims decide to settle at Plymouth—The Landing—The First Law—The Pioneers at Work—Plan of the Town—The Weather—Satisfaction of the Pilgrims with the Site of their Colony—The Journal—Pilgrim Traits—A Page from Cotton Mather—The Frenchman's Prophecy—Social Arrangements—Standish chosen Captain—Births and Deaths—The Block Citadel—Isolation of the Pilgrims—Combination of Circumstances which produced the Settlement of Plymouth in 1620 ----- 90

CHAPTER VII.

The Early Spring of 1621—The Pilgrims Buoyant and Hopeful—Planting—In the Woods—The Tyro Hunters—A Forest Adventure—The Storm—On the Skirts of the Settlement—"Welcome, Englishmen"—The Solitary Indian—His Entertainment—Samoset's Story—Valuable Information—The Kidnapper—The Nausets—Pilgrim Description of Samoset—"What shall we do with our Dusky Guest?"—Samoset's Embassy—His Return—Squanto—His Romantic History—Massasoit—The Redman and the Pale-face—Negotiations—The Treaty—Its Faithful Observance—A Picture of Massasoit—Billington's Offence—The Lackey-duelists—Death—Frightful Mortality—Burial-hill—Death of Governor Carver—Bradford elected Governor—Departure of the "Mayflower"—Feeling of the Pilgrims—The "Orphans of Humanity" ----- 98

CHAPTER VIII.

The Pilgrim Panacea—The Summer—The Prospect—Wild Fowl, Shell-fish, and Berries—A Glimpse at Plymouth in 1621—The Pioneers open the Volume of Nature—Lessons in Woodcraft—Bradford and the Deer-trap—Explorations—The Embassy to Massasoit—Its Object—The Indian Guide—The Pause at Namasket—A New "Kind of Bread"—The "Deserted Village"—The Wigwam "Palace" of Massasoit—Presents—The Sachem and the Horseman's Coat—The "Pipe of Peace"—The Sagamore's Cordiality—Massasoit's Housekeeping—A Full Bed—Indian Games—The Feast—The Return—Honorable and Amicable Treatment of the Indians by the Pilgrim Fathers—Advantages of this Course—Barbarism makes an Obeisance to Civilization—End of the Indian's Lease of Ages of the Forest—The New Tenant takes Possession in the Name of God and Liberty ----- 110

CHAPTER IX.

The Lost Boy—The Searching Party—In the Shallop—The Water spout—The Bivouac—Visitors at the Camp-fire—The Indian Hag—Her Strange Emotion—The Riddle solved—*En Route* again—The Lost Boy found—His Adventures—A Startling Rumor—The Hasty Return—Intrigues—The Narragansetts—Squanto, Tokamahamon, and Habbamak—Corbitant's Wiles—The Runner's News—Departure of Standish and his "Army" of Fourteen Men—The Forest March—On the War-trail—The Sleeping Village—The Bloodless Assault—"Friend, Friend"—Flight of Corbitant—Safety of Squanto and Tokamahamon—Homeward—Good Effect of the Bloodless Raid—Heroism and Kindness of the Pilgrims—The Midnight Expedition of Miles Standish—Boston Bay, and the River Charles—The "Harvest Home"—"New England's First Fruits"—Building at Plymouth—The Variety of Game—The First THANKSGIVING—"Free Range" 121

CHAPTER X.

The Strange Sail—"Is it a Frenchman, or a Buccaneer?"—Warlike Preparations—The English Jack—Joy of the Pilgrims—Arrival of the "Fortune"—News from Home—The Reinforcement—A Moment of Sadness—The Letter Budget—The London Company under a Cloud—Course of the King—A Technical Difficulty—The New Patent—Weston's Complaint and Bradford's Reply—Departure of the "Fortune"—Cushman's Sermon—The Bane of Plantations—Winslow's Letter Home—Hilton's Missive—Social Life and Wants of the Pilgrim Fathers—The "Fortune's" Mishap 134

CHAPTER XI.

Provisions for the New-comers—Danger of Famine—Hardships—Patient Spirit of the Pilgrims—Brewster's Submission—*Morale* of the Colony—Some "Lewd Fellows of the Baser Sort" get "shuffled" into the "Mayflower's" Company—Character of the Recent Reinforcement—Bradford's Government—The Laws—Bradford and the "Tender Consciences"—The Controlling Element—Homogeneity 144

CHAPTER XII.

The Salient Features of the Colonial Government—The "Proper Democracy"—The Course of England—The Governor—The Council—The Legislative Body—Test of Citizenship—Reasons and Excuses for It—Early Decrees—The Jury Trial—First Laws—The Digest—Provision for Education—The Old Statute Book of the Colony—Unique Legislation—First Marriage in New England—Marriage a Civil Contract.................. 149

CHAPTER XIII.

Second Winter in the Wilderness—Faith as a Motor—Anxiety—The Indian and the Package—A Prisoner—The Riddle Solved—The Mysterious Rattlesnake Skin—Defensive Measures—First "General Muster" in New England—The Expedition and the Alarm—Habbamak's Confidence—The Squaw-scout—No Danger—The Expedition resumed—Squanto's Freaks—The Boast of a Travelled Indian—The Buried Plague—The Cheat uncloaked—Hunger—The Boat and the Letter-bag—Cold Comfort—Dissensions among the Merchant-adventurers in London—Bradford's Comments 156

CHAPTER XIV.

Arrival of the "Charity" and the "Swan"—The News—Weston's Desertion—The Situation in England—In a Quandary—The Pilgrims entertain Weston's Rival Colony—Word brought of a Massacre in Virginia—Winslow's Mission to the Coast of Maine—The Double Benefit—*Morale* of the Westonians—They finally settle at Wessagusset—Their Lazy Mismanagement—Bradford's Rebuke—The Forayers—Bradford's Walk of Fifty Miles—Death of Squanto—The Lean Harvest—The English Trading Ship—Progress in Building at Plymouth—How the Pilgrims went to Church............................ 168

CHAPTER XV.

Affairs at Wessagusset—Expostulations and Appeals of the Pilgrims—An Anecdote—Reported Sickness of Massasoit—Pilgrim Embassy to visit Him—On the Way—The Death Song—Corbitant's Lodge—At Massasoit's Wigwam—The Pow-wows—Winslow and the Sachem—The Cure—Massasoit discloses a Conspiracy—The Return—The Envoys and Corbitant—A Shrewd Sagamore—How the Pilgrims communicated Religious Truth—Deliberation at Plymouth—A Frightened Messenger from Wessagusset—The Expedition of Miles Standish—Standish and the Westonians—Sad Condition of that Colony—The Plot disclosed—Indian Braggadocio—The Two Knives—The Little Man and the Big Man—Patience of Standish—The Death-grapple—Habbamak's Comment—The Skirmish—The "Capital Exploit" of Miles Standish—The Westonians abandon Wessagusset—End of a Colony whose "Main End was to catch Fish"—Wetawamat's Head—A Liberation—News of the Baffled Conspiracy reaches Leyden—Robinson's Fine Comment—Strength and Weakness------178

CHAPTER XVI.

The Mysterious Blacksmith—Weston at Plymouth—A Favor—Ingratitude—Continued Famine at Plymouth—The Community of Interest—How it worked—Its Partial Abandonment—Facts brain Plato's Theory—Bradford's Argument against the Communal Idea—The Pilgrims rest on Providence—Their Shifts to live—The Drought—The Fast—The Answered Prayer—Rain at last—Habbamak's Remarks—Five Kernels of Corn—A Package of Home Letters—Pierce's Patent—He "vomits it up"—Captain Francis West—New Recruits—The "Annie" and the "Little James"—Feeling among the New-comers—Cushman's Epistle—A Prescient Scribe------193

CHAPTER XVII.

The Lading of the "Anne"—Winslow departs for England—Plenty once more—Social Arrangements—Robert Gorges—Birth and Death of Another Colony at Wessagusset—Morrel's Latin Poem—Prosperity of Plymouth—An Election—The Mishaps of a Fishing Expedition—Preparations for Planting—Winslow's Return—What he brought—The Purpose and *Animus* of the London Company of Merchant-adventurers—John Lyford—Circumstances of his Advent—John Oldham—The Pernicious League—Onslaught upon the Pilgrim Government—Wolves in the Sheepfold—The Intercepted Letters—An Explosion—"Oldham "tamed"—Lyford's Trial—The Sentence—Winslow's *Exposé* in England and America—Running the Gauntlet—Banishment of Lyford and Oldham—Effect of the Lyford Troubles—Brewster's Ministry—An Exception to the Indian Doctrine of "Poor Pay, Poor Preach"—Tenets of the Plymouth Church—"Brown Bread and the Gospel is Good fare"—Liberty------205

CHAPTER XVIII.

The Pilgrims initiate Measures to buy out the Merchant-adventurers—Standish sails for England on this Errand—His Narrow Escape from Capture by a Turkish Rover—His Partial Success and Return—Sad News—Death of Cushman in England—Death of Robinson at Leyden—Last Hours and Character of the Moses of the Pilgrims------227

CONTENTS.

CHAPTER XIX.

Progress of Population at Plymouth—Smith's Report—A Leaf from Bradford's Journal—Romulus and Rome; Plymouth and the Pilgrims—The Winter of 1626-7—Allerton's Embassy to England—His Success—The "Undertakers"—The New Organization—Plan of Division—Habbamak's Grant—First Coveted Luxury of the Emancipated Colony—Allerton's Second Mission—Provision made for the Transportation of the Remainder of the Leyden Congregation—Patent for Land on the Kennebec—The New Trading Station—A Crazy Clergyman—Catholicity of the Plymouth Church—Wide Range of the Pilgrim Enterprise—Commerce opened with the Dutch at New Amsterdam—Isaac de Rasières at Plymouth—Wampum—The Pilgrim Settlement as seen through the Eyes of a Dutchman—Joyous Arrival of the Leyden Exiles—How They were received—Mount Wollaston—Thomas Morton turns it into a Den of Riot and Debauchery—Grief of the Pilgrims—Expostulation—Affront—End of an *Experimentum Crucis* of Immorality—The Pilgrims find "All Things working together for their Good" ------ 232

CHAPTER XX.

English Politics—The Puritans and the Pilgrims—Multitudes in Britain prepare for Emigration—Roger Conant—Old John White of Dorchester—The *Point d'Appui*—White's Message—Conant's Determination—Agitation at London—A New Scheme for Puritan Emigration—It is patronized by Men of Substance and "Gentlemen born"—The Lock opened by the Silver Key—A Patent—John Endicott leads a Colony into New England—Salem settled—The English Hermit—Individuality of the Saxon Race—The Explorers colonize Charlestown—News of Endicott's Success in England—Incorporation of the Massachusetts Company—Its Powers—An Old Legend -------- 249

CHAPTER XXI.

Organization of the Massachusetts Company—A Unique Letter of Instruction to Endicott—The Soil ordered to be purchased of the Indian Owners—A Blast against Tobacco—The Colonial Seal—Preparations for the Embarkation of Fresh Emigrants—Buckingham—Strafford—Laud—Puritans Eager to Emigrate—The Flotilla—The Plentiful Provision of "Godly Ministers"—Bright—Smith—Higginson—Skelton—"Farewell, Dear England"—Britain does not know her Heroes—The Landing at Salem—Higginson's Impressions—The Pilgrims plant a Church at Salem—Cordial Relations opened with the Plymouth Colonists—Endicott's Letter to Bradford—An Additional Link in the Chain of Friendship—Ordination of Higginson and Skelton—The Ceremony—Bradford's Tardy Arrival—The Confession of Faith—Birth of the Theocracy—Dissatisfaction of the Church of England men at Salem—The Brothers Brown—Breach of the Peace imminent—Endicott sends the Browns home to England—Endicott cautioned by the Massachusetts Company 260

CHAPTER XXII.

The New Colony outstrips Plymouth—Intense Interest in the Colonies felt in England—Higginson's Tract—Men of Wealth and Position prepare to emigrate—One Thing makes Them Hesitate—Character of the Charter—The "Open Sesame"—Alienation of the Government of the Company—A Daring Construction changes a Trading Corporation into a Provincial Government—Joy of the Would-be Emigrants—The Election—An Extensive Emigration set Afoot—The Fleet of Ten Vessels—In the Cabin of the "Arbella"—Winthrop—Dudley—Humphrey—Johnson—Saltonstall—Eaton—Bradstreet—Vassall—The Women of the Enterprise—The Lady Arbella Johnson—The Farewell at Yarmouth—On the Atlantic 274

CHAPTER XXIII.

"Land ho!"—The Supper at Salem—Sickness—Explorations—The Settlement at Cambridge—Busy Days—Death—The Last Hours of Francis Higginson—Death of Arbella Johnson—Grief and Death of her Husband—The Mortality List—Cambridge partially Deserted—Settlement of Boston—The Original Occupant of Shawmut Peninsula—Blackstone's Oddities—The "Lord Bishops" and the "Lord Brethren"—Activity of the Colonists—The View from Beacon Hill—Winthrop's Cheery Letter to his Wife 286

CHAPTER XXIV.

Fundamental Law of the Colonies of Massachusetts Bay—Earliest Legislation—First General Assembly—The Democratic Tendency—The Test of Citizenship—Reflections—Animadversions on the Theocratic Plan—The Acorn and the Oak 293

CHAPTER XXV.

Life in the Wilderness—Winthrop's Adventure—The False Alarm—The Settlers and the Wolves well frightened—The Courtship of Miles Standish—Alden's Wedding—Morton once more at

"Merry Mount"—An Execution—Radcliff, and his Punishment—The Mysterious Stranger—A Knight of the Holy Sepulchre astray in the Wilderness—The Three Wives—The Pursuit—An Unmasked Jesuit—The "Italian Method" tabooed in New England—Satan's Ill-manners—Utopia—A Sentence from Demosthenes—Great Combat between a Mouse and a Snake—Its Significance—Fresh Arrivals—Eliot—Roger Williams—Attachment of the Pilgrims to their Rocky Refuge—How New England looked to a Puritan—How it looked to a Churchman—A Difference of Standpoint—The Brood of *Townlets*—The Western Wilds no longer Tenantless ------------------- 299

CHAPTER XXVI.

The Advance of Civilization—Growth of Plymouth—Ralph Smith—Winthrop visits Bradford—Gubernatorial Civilities in the Olden Time—Leaves from Winthrop's Note-book—The Primitive Ferry-boat—Bradford's Mare—The Empty Contribution-box—Boundary Quarrel with the French—The Compliments of the Gentlemen from the Isle of Rhé—How They were answered—The Valley of the Connecticut—Efforts to colonize those Bottom Lands—Bradford solicits Winthrop to organize a United Effort for that Purpose—The Sachem's Offer—Winthrop's Refusal—The Plymouth Pilgrims determine to enter Connecticut unassisted—The Dutch attempt to balk Them—The Pilgrims colonize Windsor—A few Dutch Oaths—A War-path which ended in a Hug—An Infectious Fever at Plymouth—Consequent Mortality—Some "Strange Flies"—Ebb and Flow of the Tide of Emigration—Attempted Emigration of Hazlerigge, Pym, Hampden, and Cromwell—They are stopped by an Order in Council—The King's *Faux Pas*—Three Famous Men embark for New England, and supply The Great Necessities of the Colonists—Haynes—Cotton—Hooker—Title by which the Settlers hold their Lands—Progress towards Democracy—Cotton's Sermon against Rotation in Office—Its Non-effect—Colonial Authority divided between Two Branches—Law against Arbitrary Taxation—Representative Republicanism—A Dream broken --- 314

CHAPTER XXVII.

The Pilgrim Fathers and the Mosaic Code—Toleration in the Seventeenth Century—American and European Thinkers alike reject it—Arrival of Roger Williams at Boston—His Motives for Emigration—His Hopes and Views—Speedily attracts Attention — His Devotion to the Principle of Toleration — His Advocacy of it places Him in Direct Opposition to the System on which Massachusetts is founded — Under the Frown of the Authorities — Williams refuses to join the Boston Church — His Declaration — Statement of his Idea of Toleration — The Pilgrims regard Him as a Dangerous Heresiarch with "a Windmill in his Head" — Consternation at Boston on the Rumor of Williams' Instalment in the Place of Higginson at Salem — Winthrop's Letter of Expostulation — The Salem Church does not heed it — Williams begins to preach — Quits Salem for Plymouth — Bradford's Estimate of the Young Welchman — Williams cements a Lasting and Cordial Friendship with the Indians — Returns to Salem on Skelton's Death — Recommencement of his Struggle with the Colonial Government — His Pamphlet on the Charter — His Retraction — Ought Women to appear Veiled at Church? — Williams says Yes, Cotton says No — Cotton convinces the Ladies — The English Commission for the Regulation of the Colonies — The Pilgrims decide to "avoid and protract" — Endicott cuts the Cross out of the English Flag — Williams speaks against the "Freeman's Oath" — Trouble — Williams' Democracy — Points of Variance between the Reformer and the Colonists — The Citation — Williams before the Court — His Frank Defence — Banishment — The Flight through the Winter Woods — Animadversions — Months of Vicissitude — Settlement of Providence — Williams bases his Colony on Toleration and Democracy — Mather's Epigram — Williams makes a Distinction between Toleration and License — Williams' First Visit to England — Intimacy with Vane and Milton — The Second Visit — Cromwell and Marvell added to his List of Trans-atlantic Friends — Elected on his Return President of the Providence Plantations — Excelsior — Williams and the Indians — An Incident — Reflections on the Work and Character of Roger Williams -- 334

CHAPTER XXVIII.

Progress of New England in Material Prosperity — Arrival of Three Thousand Settlers in a Single Year — An Illustrious *Trio* — Hugh Peters — The Younger Winthrop — Sir Harry Vane — A Long Smouldering Feud placated — Value which the Pilgrims set on Education — Good and Bad Universities — A Public School planted at Cambridge — Harvard College — Relations between Learning and Manners — Enlarged Colonization of New England — The Plymouth Pilgrims at Windsor — The Younger Winthrop at Saybrook — Hooker's Parishioners at Cambridge — Petition for "Enlargement or Removal" — The Advance Guard of Civilization—The New Hesperia of Puritanism—Hooker and Haynes lead a Colony into Connecticut and settle at Hartford—Pilgrimage from the Seashore to the "Delightful Banks" of the Inland River—Liberality of the New-born Colony—New Haven planted by English Puritans—Colonization of Guilford, Milford, and Long Island—Character of these Settlers—Commerce and Agriculture as the Basis of New States—Constitution of New Haven—The First Political Paper ever cradled in a Manger—The Connecticut Colonists and the Dutch at New Amsterdam quarrel over their Boundary Line — A Yankee Ruse—The Dutchmen and the Onion Rows—Isolation of the New Settlements—The War-whoop 357

CHAPTER XXIX.

The Pilgrims and the Indians—Stern Justice with which the Forefathers treated the Aborigines—An Illustration—Murder in the Woods—Its Punishment—End of the Epoch of Peace—Reason Why—The Pequods—Uncas—The Pequod Embassy to the Narragansetts—The Forests pregnant with Insurrection—Vane solicits the Intervention of Roger Williams—The Solitary Canoe—Williams in the Wigwam of Miantonomoh—The Pequod Diplomats at Work—Williams pushes his Dangerous Opposition—Old Friendship prevails—The Narragansetts refuse to dig up the Hatchet—The Pequods take the War-path alone—Sassacus—First Patter of the Coming Storm—A Thrilling Scene on the Connecticut River—The Captured Pinnace—Border Gallantry—A Unique Naval Battle—How News travelled in the Olden Time—Endicott on the Trail—A Pilgrim Friar Tuck—Failure—Pandemonium—New England trembles on the Verge of Death—Energy of the Colonists—Mason's Expedition—The Council of War—The Chaplain's Prayer—Off Point Judith—The Landing—The Seaside Bivouac—The Midnight March—The Pequod Village—A "Sound of Revelry by Night"—The Indian Fort—The Night Attack—Scenes of Horror—The Flight of Sassacus—The Pursuit—The Swamp Battle—The Sagamore's Escape—The Gory Scalp-lock—"Sachem's Head"—Death, and Servitude of the Survivors—Civilization Victorious 370

CHAPTER XXX.

Pilgrim Exclusiveness—The Old Alien Law—Dissenters swarm into Massachusetts Bay—Agitation—The Two Parties—Anne Hutchinson—A Commendable Practice—Mrs. Hutchinson's Week-day Lectures—The "Covenant of Works" and the "Covenant of Grace "—Heady Current of Dissension—Horror of the Pilgrims — Antinomianism — Familism — The Female Heresiarch—The "Legalists"—Mutual Exasperation—Vane's Disgust—Wreck of Vane's Administration—Winthrop's Law—Vane's Reply—The Founders of the Colony regain their Influence—Trial of Anne Hutchinson—Cotton and his *Protegé*—"Immediate Revelations"—Banishment of the Antinomians—Roger Williams welcomes the Exiles to Providence—Purchase and Settlement of Rhode Island—A Happy Result from an Unhappy Cause 388

CHAPTER XXXI.

Law as the Reflection of National Character—Pilgrim Legislation—The Homes of New England—Origin of Towns—Town Meetings—Duty of voting—"Prudential Men"—An Odd Trait—Pilgrims fined for refusing to hold Office—High Character of the Early Governors — Bradford — Edward Winslow and Thomas Prince—Winthrop — Dudley—Vane—Endicott—Other Pivotal Men—God's Benediction on New England 400

CHAPTER XXXII.

New England in 1641 — Inhabitants — Villages — Churches — Houses — Agriculture — Commerce — Trade — Manufactures — Foreign Influence of the Pilgrims—The Tone of New England in treating with the Long Parliament during the Civil War—Two Rejected Invitations—Consolidation of Colonial Liberty—The Oppressed made Guests of the Commonwealth—The Germ of Union—The UNITED COLONIES OF NEW ENGLAND—Character of the League — Reflections — Colonial Union the Crowning Service of the Pilgrim Fathers to Humanity—The Second Generation—The Work and the Lesson of the Pilgrim Fathers 415

THE PILGRIM FATHERS

OF

NEW ENGLAND.

CHAPTER I.

THE EXODUS.

> "Nothing is here for tears; nothing to wail
> Or knock the breast; no weakness, no contempt,
> Dispraise or blame; nothing but well and fair."
>   MILTON, *Samson Agonistes.*

THE influence of that mysterious triad, the gold eagle, the silver dollar, and the copper cent, has been overestimated. Spiritual forces are more potent than the motors of materialism. The Sermon on the Mount outweighs the law of gravity. Ethics make safer builders than stocks. Two hundred years ago, commercial enterprise essayed to subdue the New World in the interest of greedy trade, hungering for an increase; but though officered by the brightest genius and the highest daring of the age, backed by court favor and bottomed on the deepest bank-vaults of London, the effort failed.

Where physical forces balked, a moral sentiment bore off a trophy. The most prosperous of the American colonies were planted by religion. New England is the child of English Puritanism; and yet, paradoxical as it may seem, antedates its birth. Men say that the history of New England dates from 1620. 'T is a mistake. New England was in the brain of Wickliffe when, in the infancy of Britain, he uttered his first protest against priestcraft and pronounced the Christianity of Rome a juggle. New England, *in esse*, was born in that chill December on Plymouth Rock; New England, *in posse*, was cradled in the pages of the first printed copy of the English Bible.

Soil does not make a state; nor does geographical position. That spot of ground which men call Athens does not embrace the immortal city. It bears up its masonry; but the Athens of Socrates and of Plato exists in the *mind* of every scholar. The intellectual and moral elements which enter into and shape it, these are the real state. In this sense, New England was in the pages of the Puritan publicists, in the psalms of the Lollards, and in the prayers of Bradwardine, centuries before that winter's voyage into the dreary wilderness.

Society, government, law, the graces of civility, the economic formulas, are growths. "Books, schools, education," says Humboldt, "are the scaffolding by means of which God builds up the human soul." There are no isolated facts. Events do not occur at hap-hazard. Each effect has its cause; it may lie buried beneath many blinding strata, so that it must be dug for, but it exists.

Puritanism was not a sudden creation. It did not crop out of the sixteenth century unexpectedly, and begin to impeach formalism without a cause. It was a growth. "It was as old as the truth and manliness of England. Among the thoughtful and earnest islanders, the dramatic religion of the popes had never struck so deep root as in continental soil."* Chafed and weary, the people had long demanded a purer and more spiritual faith. The strong repressive hand of the Vatican was not able to stop the mouth of unwearied complaint. Thinkers were convinced that Rome had paganized Christianity. Christ was banished from all active influence. He could only be reached and "touched with the feeling of our infirmities" through the intercession of saints, who were constantly invoked. The popes professed to possess a fund of supererogation, which they might dispense at will; and this became their stock in trade. Salvation by meritorious works was preached. Brokers in souls hawked their celestial wares in every market-place. Rome, an incarnate Pharisee, made broad its phylactery, and hid beneath it a dead religion and a corrupt church.†

From Wickliffe to Tyndale, a few earnest, devout men had impeached this cheat. But the influ-

---

* Palfrey, Hist. of New England, vol. 1, p. 101.

† Perhaps this whole chapter of history is nowhere more graphically treated than in D'Aubigné's Hist. of the Ref. in the Sixteenth Century. See also, Ranke's Hist. of the Popes.

ence of these teachers was at best but local. They were barely able to keep the gospel torch aglow, and to pass it down from hand to hand through the dusky centuries. The masses were affrighted from the pursuit of knowledge by the jingle of the rusty and forged keys of St. Peter, which locked the storehouse of divine revelation, and barred the investigations of the human mind.

The modern era dawned in the sixteenth century. The invention of printing was the *avant courier* of reform. The reformers gained a fulcrum for their lever. Scholars might shake the dust from their mouldy folios, and by opening the early records, convict Rome of heresy. Their conclusions might then be scattered broadcast on the wings of the press. Well might the perturbed ghost of Latin Orthodoxy exclaim,

> "Ah, fatal age, which gave mankind
> A Luther and a Faustus."

Bibles were everywhere opened. Reform swept from the mountains of Bohemia into Germany; crossing the Saxon plains, it entered the Netherlands; thence it passed the channel into England. In the island it was received with enthusiasm. The government, from personal motives, extended to it the hand of fellowship; the people adopted it, because they felt the inadequacy of Romanism to meet their religious wants.*

Rome did not strike its flag without a struggle. As Demetrius was shocked when Paul, a wandering

---

* Uhden, New England Theocracy, p. 15.

preacher from Tarsus, impeached his Diana, so the Vatican professed to be horrified when the reformers inveighed against the popedom. "Socrates"—so runs the old Grecian indictment—"is guilty of crime for not worshipping the gods whom the city worship, but introducing new divinities of his own."* The adherents of the ancient faith tacked a similar indictment upon the front of the reform. Where they dared, they invoked the thumb-screw and kindled an *auto-da-fé*. When they could not fight with these congenial weapons, they made faces at their opponents, and hurled epithets. The iconoclasts were called "infidels." Hooker and Hales, Stillingfleet, and Cudworth, and Taylor were thus stigmatized.† And indeed, " this is a cry which the timid, the ignorant, the indolent, and the venal are apt to raise against those who, faithful to themselves, go boldly forward, using the past only to show them what the present is, and what the future should be."

These men recast the ecclesiasticism of their age. The essence of Romanism was extracted from their creed, but many of its forms were retained. Then, within the new-built temple of the English church, there arose two parties. The *Puritans* demanded the complete divorce of the reformed church from Rome, in its ceremonies and in its belief. They strove to inaugurate the purity and simplicity of what they conceived to be the primitive worship. They esteemed the retained forms

* Grote, Hist. of Greece.
† Preface to Warburton's Divine Legation.

to be pregnant with mischief, in that they were the badges of their former servitude, and because they tended to bridge over the chasm between Rome and the Reformation.*

At the outset, the Puritans did not quarrel with the English Establishment; they all claimed to be within its pale,† and many of their leaders were men of high ecclesiastical standing, of the truest lives, and of the loftiest genius; but they held to the spirit rather than to the letter; to the substance of the church, not to its forms.‡

The *Conformists* considered the ceremonies to be non-essential; but they desired to retain them, partly because they were enamoured of those old associations which they symbolized, but chiefly because they dreaded the effect of too sudden and radical a change upon the peace of the island. Besides, to facilitate the passage from Romanism to the reformed church, they were willing to step to the verge of their consciences in the retention of the old forms, and in the incorporation of those features of the ancient faith into the outward structure of the new theology which were not intrinsically bad.§

---

* Neale, Hist. of the Puritans. Collier's Church Hist. Hallam, Const. Hist. of Eng.

† See "An Account of the Principles and Practices of Several Non-conformists, wherein it appears that their religion is no other than that which is professed in the Church of England," etc. By Mr. John Corbet; London, 1682.

‡ Elliot, Hist. of New Eng., vol. 1, p. 43.

§ Fuller, Church Hist. Strype, Life of Parker. Heylin, Life of Lord Clarendon.

Unquestionably honest minds might differ in this policy. "But certainly the doctrine of the Puritans concerning the connection and mutual influence between forms and opinions, so far from being fanciful or fastidious, had foundations as deep as any thing in moral truth or in human nature. A sentiment determined their course; but it was more cogent than all the learned argument which they lavished in its defence. A man of honor will not be bribed to display himself in a fool's cap; yet why not in a fool's cap as readily as in any apparel associated in his mind, and in the minds of those whom he respects, whether correctly or not is immaterial, with the shame of mummery and falsehood? To these men the cope and surplice seemed the livery of Rome. They would not put on the uniform of that hated power, while they were marshalling an array of battle against its ranks. An officer, French, American, or English, would feel outraged by a proposal to be seen in the garb of a foreign service. The respective wearers of the white and tricolor cockades would be more willing to receive each other's swords into their bosoms than to exchange their decorations. A national flag is a few square yards of coarse bunting; but associations invest it which touch whatever is strongest and deepest in national character. Its presence commands an homage as reverential as that which salutes an Indian idol. Torrents of blood have been poured out age after age to save it from affront. The rejection of the cope and mitre was as much the fruit and the sign of the great reality of a religious revolution, as a political revolution was betokened and effected when the cross of St. George came down from over the fortresses along fifteen degrees of the North American coast"* in '76.

The contest which ensued between nascent Puritanism and the entrenched Conformists was prolonged and bitter. It deeply scarred the history of the contemporaneous actors; and it has shaped the ethics and the politics of two centuries; nor is its force yet spent. Indeed, it may be fitly called the epic of our Saxon annals.

"On the one side, in the outset, were statesmen desiring first and mainly the order and quiet of the realm. On the other side were religious men desiring that, at all hazards, God might be worshipped in purity and served with simplicity and zeal. It is easy to understand the perplexities and alarms of the former class; but the persistency of their opponents is not therefore to be accounted whimsical and perverse. It is impossible to blame them for saying, 'If a man believes marriage to be a sacrament in the sense of the popes and the councils, let him symbolize it by the giving of a ring; if he believes in exorcism by the signing of the cross, let him have it impressed on his infant's brow in baptism; if he believes the bread of the Eucharist to be God, let him go down on his knees before it. But we do not believe these things, and as honest men we will not profess so to believe by act or sign

* Palfrey, Hist. of New England, vol. 1, p. 113, note.

THE EXODUS.

any more than by word.' Theirs was no struggle against the church, but against the state's control over it."*

The fatal error of the church-and-state reformers was, that they strove to coerce unwilling consciences into exact conformity with a prescribed formula of worship by penal legislation. No latitude was even winked at. It was a new edition of the old story of Procrustes and his iron bed. Britain, emancipated from the pope, still hugged the *popedom*. The rulers of the island clutched the weapons and enacted the *rôle* of the Hildebrandes, the Gregorys, and the Innocents of ecclesiastical history. Dissent was "rank heresy." Liberty was "license." The measure of a conscience was the length of a prelate's foot.

"An act was passed in 1593," says Hoyt, "for punishing all who refused to attend the Established Church, or frequented conventicles or unauthorized assemblies. The penalty was, imprisonment until the convicted person made declaration of his conformity; and if that was not done within three months after arrest, he was to quit the realm, and go into perpetual banishment. In case he did not depart within the specified time, or returned without license, he was to suffer death."†

In 1603, when James I. came down from Scotland to ascend the English throne, so stood the law. Nor did it rest idle in the statute-book. The parch-

---
* Palfrey, Hist. of New England, vol. 1, p, 114.
† Hoyt, Antiquarian Researches.

ment *fiat* was instinct with vicious life. Hecatombs of victims suffered under it.* "Toleration," remarks Goodrich, "was a virtue then unknown on British ground. In exile alone was security found from the pains and penalties of non-conformity to the Church of England."†

During the pendency of the dissension between the Puritans and the Conformists within the bosom of the church, many honest thinkers, feeling hopeless of success in that unequal conflict, broke from their old communion, and set up a separate Ebenezer.‡ Even so early as 1592, Sir Walter Raleigh, speaking in the House of Commons, affirmed that these "Come-outers" numbered upwards of twenty thousand.§ Since that date, every year had added new recruits to their ranks, until, in 1603, they had expanded into a wealthy, influential, and puissant party in the state.‖

Though socially tabooed and politically ostracised—though shackled by fierce prohibitory legislation and by governmental ill-will, the Separatists, as they were called, still prayed and hoped, walking through persecution with faith in their right hand and with patience in their left. At one time they thought they could discern a ray of light on the sullen horizon which gloomed upon them. James

---

* Fuller, Ch. Hist., vol. 3. Rymer's Fœdera, vol. 16, p. 694.
† Goodrich, Ch. Hist.
‡ Neale, History of the Puritans, vol. 1. Rushworth, Clarendon, etc. § Parliamentary History.
‖ Strype, Life of Whitgift. Bradshaw, English Puritanism, 1605.

I. had been educated in Presbyterian Scotland.* He had often hymned the praises of the polity of stout John Knox.† When he crossed the Tweed, jubilant Puritanism cried, "Amen," and "All hail." Ere long, however, the weak and treacherous Stuart deserted his Scottish creed. From that moment he hated his old comrades with the peculiar bitterness of an apostate. No epithet was vile enough by which to paint them. He raked the gutter of the English language for phrases. "These Puritans," said he, "are pests in the church and commonwealth—greater liars and perjurers than any border thieves."‡

At the Hampton Court Conference—an intellectual tournament between the representatives of the opposing religious parties—the royal buffoon affirmed his determination to make the Puritans "conform, or harry them out of the land, or else worse."§

It has been truly said that "the friends of religious reform had never seen so hopeless a time as that which succeeded the period of the most sanguine expectation. In the gloomiest periods of the arbitrary sway of the two daughters of Henry VIII., they could turn their eyes to a probable successor to the throne who would be capable of more reason or more lenity. Now nothing better for them ap-

---

* Calderwood, True Hist. of the Ch. of Scotland. Perry, Ch. Hist., vol. 1. † Ibid.

‡ Fuller, Ch. Hist., vol. 3. Hume, Hist. of Eng., etc.

§ Barlow's Account of the Hampton Court Conference. A copy of it is in Harvard college library. Harrington, Nugæ Antiquæ.

peared in the future than the long reign of a prince wrong-headed and positive alike from imbecility, prejudice, pique, and self-conceit, to be succeeded by a dynasty born to the inheritance of the same bad blood, and educated in the same pernicious school. It is true that, as history reveals the fact to our age, almost with the reign of the Scottish alien that nobler spirit began to animate the House of Commons which ultimately" checkmated tyranny beneath the scaffold of Charles I. But this astounding blow was then remote. "As yet the steady reaction from old abuses was but dimly apparent, even to the most clear-sighted and hopeful minds; and numbers of devout and brave hearts gave way to the conviction that, for such as they, England had ceased for ever to be a habitable spot."*

Towards the close of Elizabeth's reign, a number of yeomen in the North of England, some in Nottinghamshire, some in Lincolnshire, some in Yorkshire, and the neighborhood of these counties, "whose hearts the Lord had touched with heavenly zeal for his truth," separated from the English church, "and as the Lord's free people joined themselves, by a covenant of the Lord, into a church estate in the fellowship of the gospel, to walk in all his ways made known or to be made known unto them, according to their best endeavors, whatsoever it should cost, the Lord assisting them."†

The Protestant world was at this time divided

---

* Palfrey, Hist. of New England, vol. 1, p. 131.
† Bradford, Hist. of the Plymouth Plantation, p. 9. '

between two regal phases of reform. "Luther's *rationale*," says Bancroft, "was based upon the sublime but simple truth which lies at the bottom of morals, the paramount value of character and purity of conscience; the superiority of right dispositions over ceremonial exactness; and, as he expressed it, 'justification by faith alone.' But he hesitated to deny the real presence, and was indifferent to the observance of external ceremonies. Calvin, with sterner dialectics, sanctioned by his power as the ablest writer of his age, attacked the Roman doctrines respecting the communion, and esteemed as a commemoration the rite which the papists reverenced as a sacrifice. Luther acknowledged princes as his protectors, and in the ceremonies of worship favored magnificence as an aid to devotion; Calvin was the guide of Swiss republics, and avoided in their churches all appeals to the senses as crimes against religion. Luther resisted the Roman church for its immorality; Calvin for its idolatry. Luther exposed the folly of superstition, ridiculed the hair-shirt and the scourge, the purchased indulgence, and the dearly-bought masses for the dead; Calvin shrunk from their criminality with impatient horror. Luther permitted the cross, the taper, pictures, images, as things of indifference; Calvin demanded a spiritual worship in its utmost purity."*

The Separatists were ardent Calvinists. They esteemed the "offices and callings, courts and can-

* Bancroft, Hist. United States, vol. 1, pp. 277, 278.

ons" of the English church "monuments of idolatry." Those of the North of England, though "presently they were scoffed and scorned by the profane multitude, and their ministers urged with the yoke of subscription," yet held "that the lordly power of the prelates ought not to be submitted to."*

In this northern church was "Mr. Richard Clifton, a grave and revered preacher, who by his pains and diligence had done much good, and under God had been the means of the conversion of many; also that famous and worthy man, Mr. John Robinson, who afterwards was their pastor for many years, till God called him away by death; and Mr. William Brewster, a reverent man, who afterwards was chosen elder of the church, and lived with them till old age."†

In the year 1607 these reformers seem to have received the vindictive attention of the government, for Bradford makes this record: "After that they could not long continue in any peaceable condition, but were hunted and persecuted on every side. Some were taken and clapped up in prison. Others had their houses beset and watched night and day. The most were fain to fly and leave their houses and goods, and the means of their livelihood. Yet these things, and many more still sharper, which afterwards befell them, were no other than they looked for, and therefore they were better able to bear them by the assistance of God's grace and

* Bradford, Hist. Plymouth Plantation.
† Ibid., Morton's Memorial, Founders of New Plymouth, etc.

spirit. Nevertheless, seeing themselves thus molested, and that there was no hope of peace at home, by joint consent they resolved to go into the Low Countries, where, they heard, was freedom for all men; as also how sundry from London and various parts had been persecuted into exile aforetime, and were gone thither, sojourning at Amsterdam and in other cities. So, after they had continued together about a year, and kept their meetings every sabbath in one place and another, exercising the worship of God despite the diligence and malice of their adversaries, seeing that they could no longer continue in that condition, they prepared to pass over into Holland as they could."*

The Pilgrims were preëminently men of action. They were not dreamy speculators; they were not *dilettanti* idealists. They never let "I dare not" wait upon "I would." With them decision was imperative, and meant action. They had dropped two words from their vocabulary—doubt and hesitation. Instantly they prepared for exile; and they accepted it as serenely when conscience beckoned that way with her imperious finger, as their descendants would an invitation to attend a halcyon gala.

Still, in the very outset they met obstacles which would have unnerved less resolute men. But the heart of their purpose was not to be broken. In 1607,† the Pilgrims made an effort to quit the shores

---

* Bradford, Hist. Plymouth Plantation, pp. 10, 11. See also Neal's Hist. of New England, vol. 1, p. 76.

† Some authorities say 1602. Newell, for instance, p. 348, citing the British Quarterly Review. But so competent an author-

of this inhospitable country. They had appointed Boston, in Lincolnshire, the rendezvous, and a contract had been made with an English captain to convey their persons and their goods to Amsterdam. The Pilgrims were punctual; the seaman was not. Finally, however, he appeared. The eager fugitives were shipped; but they were taken aboard only to be betrayed. The recreant master had plotted with the authorities to entrap the victims. The unhappy Pilgrims were taken ashore again in open boats, and there the officers "rifled and ransacked them, searching them to their shirts for money."* Even the women were treated with rude immodesty.† After this thievish official raid, they were "carried back into the town and made a spectacle and wonder to the multitude, which came flocking on all sides to behold them. Being thus first, by the catchpole officers, rifled and stripped of their money, books, and much other goods, they were presented to the magistrates, and messengers were sent to inform the lords of the council of the matter; meantime they were committed to ward. The magistrates used the Pilgrims courteously, and showed them what kindness and favor they could; but they were not able to deliver the prisoners till order came from the council-table. The issue was, that after a month's imprisonment, the greater part were dismissed, and sent to the places from which they

---

ity as Bradford gives the date in the text. See also Young's Chronicles, etc.   * Bradford, p.12.
 † Ibid. Young's Chronicles of the Pilgrims.

came; but seven of their chiefs were still left in prison and bound over to the next assizes."*

In the spring of 1608, these same indomitable Pilgrims, together with some others, resolved to make another effort to quit the house of bondage. Dryden says that

> "Only idiots may be cozened twice."

This time they made a compact with a Dutch captain at Hull—they would not trust an Englishman.† The plan now was, that the men should assemble on a wild common, between Grimsby and Hull, a place chosen on account of its remoteness from any town; the women, the children, and the property of the exiles were to be conveyed to that part of the coast in a barque. The men made their way thither, in small companies, by land. The barque reached its destination a day sooner than the foot travellers; it was also some hours ahead of the ship.‡ As the short, chop-sea of the channel caused the passengers in the barque to suffer acutely from sea-sickness, the sailors ran into a small creek for shelter. Here the night was passed. How comfortless! The deep roar of the sullen breakers smote heavily upon their ears; and while the chill winds swept over them, the ceaseless pulsing of the sea and the hollow moaning of the waves at midnight, for the sea continued rough, deepened the melancholy feelings which could not but agitate their breasts. So

---

* Bradford, p. 12.
† Stoughton, Spiritual Heroes, p. 72.
‡ British Quarterly Review, vol. 1, p. 15.

huddled on the weird, strange shore, they counted the hours till dawn.*

In the morning the longed-for ship arrived; but through some negligence of the sailors, the vessel containing the women, their little ones, and the property, had run aground. The men stood in groups on the shore; and that no time might be lost, the captain sent his boat to convey some of them on board, while a squad of sailors were detailed to help get the grounded barque once more afloat. But alack, by this time so considerable a gathering in such a place, and at an hour so unusual, had attracted attention; information was conveyed to the neighboring authorities; and as the boat which had already taken the great part of the men to the ship, was again returning to the shore, the captain espied a large company, some on horseback, some afoot, but all armed, advancing towards the spot where the hapless barque still lay aground with the few remaining men grouped about it. Alarmed, the mariner put back to his vessel, swore by the sacrament that he would not stay, and deaf to the importunities of his sad passengers, he spread his sails, weighed anchor, and was soon out of sight.†

We may imagine with what aching hearts the poor exiles in the ship looked towards the receding shore, to their disconsolate companions, and to their precious wives and children, who stood there "crying for fear and quaking with cold." Those on board

* Stoughton, Young, Bancroft.
† Young's Chronicles, Stoughton, Bradford, etc.

the ship had no property, not even a change of raiment; and they had scarcely a penny in their pockets. But the loss of their possessions was as nothing to the cruel stroke which had severed them from those they best loved on earth.*

"Robinson—honest and able general as he was in every sense—had resolved to be the last to embark. He was therefore a witness of the scene of distress and agony which ensued on the departure of the ship. The outburst of grief was not to be restrained. Some of the women wept aloud; others felt too deeply, were too much bewildered, to indulge in utterance of any kind; while the children, partly from seeing what had happened, and partly from a vague impression that something dreadful had come, mingled their sobs and cries in the general lamentation. As the sail of the ship faded away upon the distant waters, the wives felt as if one stroke had reduced them all to widowhood, and every child that had reached years of consciousness felt as one who in a moment had become fatherless. But thus dark are the chapters in human affairs in which the good have often to become students, and from which they have commonly had to learn their special lessons."†

On the approach of the officers some of the men escaped, others remained to assist the helpless. These were apprehended and "conveyed from constable to constable, till their persecutors were weary

* Stoughton.
† British Quarterly Review, vol. 1, p. 15.

of so large a number of captives and permitted them to go their way."*

As to the voyagers, the very elements seemed to war against them. They soon encountered foul weather, and were driven far along the coast of Norway; "nor sun, nor moon, nor stars, for many days appeared." Once they gave up all for lost, thinking the ship had foundered. "But when," says a writer who was himself on board, "man's hope and help wholly failed, the Lord's power and mercy appeared for their recovery, for the ship rose again, and gave the mariners courage once more to manage her. While the waters ran into their very ears and mouths, and all cried 'We sink! we sink!' they also said, if not with miraculous, yet with a great height of divine faith, 'Yet, Lord, thou canst save! yet, Lord, thou canst save!' And He who holds the winds in his fist, and the waters in the hollow of his hand, did hear and save them."†

Eventually the storm-tossed ship dropped anchor in Amsterdam harbor; and "in the end," says Young, "notwithstanding all these tortures, the Pilgrims all got over, some at one time and some at another, and met together again, according to their desire, with no small rejoicing."‡

* Stoughton, p. 74.
† Young, cited in Stoughton, p. 74.
‡ Young's Chronicles, p. 29.

CHAPTER II.

THE HALT.

"Weep ye not for the dead, neither bemoan him; but weep sore for him that goeth away: for he shall return no more, nor see his native country." JER. 22 : 10.

WHEN the Pilgrims stepped from the deck of their vessel upon the quays of Amsterdam, they felt that sad, aching sense of utter desolation which always smites exiled hearts in a strange country. But there was much about Amsterdam which tended to increase this natural homesickness, and to make the blood pulse still more coldly through their veins. Every thing was novel; the manners, the costume, the architecture, the language of the people. Their first steps were involved in an apparently inextricable maze; they were confounded by the bewildering confusion of land and water. Canals, crawled with their sluggish water, before them and behind them, to the right and to the left. Indeed, the town was so much interwoven with havens, that the oozy ground was cut up into ninety-five islands or detached blocks, connected with each other by two hundred and ninety fantastic bridges. The principal havens, called grachts, were from a hundred to a hundred and forty feet wide, and extended in semicircular curves one after the other through the town.

In order to reach the interior of the city, it was necessary to cross a number of these broad harbors; and in making the necessary deflections in passing from gracht to gracht, all recollection of the points of the compass vanished from the minds of the bewildered Englishmen, so that they received the impression that they were wandering in a labyrinth from which it was impossible to escape by their own unaided efforts.

The houses were built of brick, and were generally four or five stories high, with fantastic, pointed gables in front. Some of them were elegantly constructed; but the larger number of the citizens seemed desirous of making their dwellings look as like warehouses as possible. Almost every house had a piece of timber projecting from the wall over the uppermost window in the gable, and this was used for hauling up fuel or furniture to the top story. All the residences were erected upon piles of wood driven into the soft, marshy ground; but so insufficient was this precaution in giving stability, that many of the buildings leaned considerably from the perpendicular, and seemed as if about to topple over into the street or splash out of sight through the mud. The roadway between the houses and the water was so narrow, that in some of the finest streets a coach could not conveniently turn round.

Such were some of the strange sights which greeted the wondering eyes of the Pilgrims as they hurriedly trod, on the day of their arrival, from the quay where they had landed, into the interior of the quaint old town in search of lodgings.

A brief residence sufficed to familiarize the exiles with the peculiarities of the city. They soon discovered that Amsterdam stood upon the southern bank of the Ai, a neck of the sea which possessed the appearance of a navigable frith. They examined the quays and piers which rose sheer out of the water, so as to afford the greatest facility for the shipment of goods from the abounding warehouses. They wondered at the peculiar form of the town, which was semicircular, with its straight side on the Ai, while the bow swept several miles inland. The canals were fed by the river Amstel, from which the town was named. An immense exterior belt of water, which the Dutch termed "the cingel," pursued a zig-zag line round the sites of ancient bastions, which were then crowned with windmills, whose long arms and tireless fingers were incessantly employed in snatching up the ever-encroaching water, and casting it far out into the sea.

From the condition of a fishing-village on the Amstel, in the thirteenth century, Amsterdam had risen, under the fostering privileges of the counts of Flanders, to be a commercial town of some importance even in the fourteenth century. The establishment of the Dutch independence so greatly accelerated its prosperity, that in the beginning of the seventeenth century it had attained the first rank as a maritime city. Antwerp, the old El Dorado, was eclipsed. Amsterdam became the entrepôt of commerce; ships visited it from all nations; its merchants were famed for their honesty and frugality; and its great bank enabled it to take the lead in the pecuniary concerns of Europe. The city was inhabited by a quarter of a million of souls; and seated in its swamp, it was the freest town in the world. It was a city of refuge to the oppressed of all nations; and therein, perhaps, lay the secret of its wonderful prosperity.

Amsterdam was the Venice of the Netherlands. It was literally a spot which had been wrung from the grasp of the unwilling and ever-protesting sea. A perpetual Waterloo conflict was waged between the persistent Hollander and old Neptune for the possession of the soil which man's skill had usurped. The city, and indeed the Netherlands at large, formed the "debatable ground" of this unique struggle between humanity and the elements. The whole country was a morass, whose buildings were constructed on huge piles; and it was this that gave rise to the saying of Erasmus, that "multitudes of his countrymen were like birds, living on the tops of trees." Across the forehead of the Netherlands brains and persistence had written their motto, "*Labor omnia vincit.*"*

---

* The facts in the above description of Amsterdam are taken from Motley's Rise of the Dutch Republic, from various accounts of travels in the Low Countries, and particularly from the very interesting and instructive "Tour" of W. Chambers. London, 1837.

Such was the city in which the Pilgrims now found themselves domesticated. In some things they found it easy to assimilate with their new neighbors: a common faith was one strong bond of union; a passion for liberty was another. But there were not lacking strong points of dissimilarity. The Pilgrims were orderly and staid; yet they never could reconcile themselves to that spirit of system, or precise, long-authorized method, which formed one of the most remarkable traits in the manners of the Dutch. In all departments of their social economy they seemed to act upon established rules, from which it was esteemed a species of heresy to depart. There were rules for visiting, for sending complimentary messages, for making domestic announcements, for bestowing alms, for out-of-door recreations—every thing was required to be done in a certain way, and no other way was right. Society was an incarnate rule.

Another thing which puzzled the Pilgrims was, that in their various walks they observed that every house was provided with one or more mirrors in frames, fastened by wire rods on the outsides of the windows, and at such an angle as to command a complete view both of the doorway and of all that passed in the street. They afterwards found that these looking-glasses were universal in Holland, and were the solace of the ladies while following their domestic avocations.

But the exiles were too grateful for toleration to be hypercritical. "They knew that they were

Pilgrims, and looked not much on these things, but lifted up their eyes to heaven, their dearest country, and quieted their spirits."* They spent no time in idleness, but with stout hearts went to work. They had been bred to agricultural pursuits; but in Holland they were obliged to learn mechanical trades. Brewster became a printer;† Bradford learned the art of dyeing silk.‡ Some learned to weave, and found employment in the cloth guilds and at the looms. But though grim poverty often pinched them, and their temporal circumstances were never very prosperous, they yet praised God for what they had; and exile and the bond of a common misfortune knit their hearts close together, so that their spiritual enjoyment in each other's society was precious and full.§

Amsterdam was not altogether a city of strangers. There were some there already, who, like themselves, had left their native island for conscience' sake.‖ But though they had formed a church, its vitals were torn by fierce dissension. The feud blazed when Robinson and his friends reached Holland; since nothing could placate the resentment of the hostile parties, the Pilgrims, fearful of the baleful effect of the quarrel upon themselves, decided, after a sojourn of twelve

---

* Bancroft, Hist. United States, vol. 1, p. 303.
† Ibid. Bradford, Young, Stoughton, etc.
‡ Bradford, Hist. Plymouth Plantation.
§ Stoughton, p. 82. Young's Chronicles.
‖ Morton's Memorial, Prince, Bradford.

months, to remove from Amsterdam to the neighboring city of Leyden.*

. "While Amsterdam was rising into mercantile wealth, Leyden was acquiring literary reputation. By a singular but honorable preference, the citizens, on being offered by William the Silent, in 1575, as a reward for their valor during the famous siege, either a remission of taxes or the foundation of a university, at once chose the university. The city had obtained the appellation of the Athens of the West. But with its scholastic cloisters it combined busy manufactures: while in one street the student was engaged with his books, in another the weaver was seated at his loom. But all breathed quietude and liberty; and it is difficult to imagine a more inviting home than that which Leyden presented to these weary, sore-footed Pilgrims as they trod along the pleasant road from Amsterdam, 'seeking peace above all other riches.'

"If the history of the city they had left was calculated to stimulate them to industry, the story of the town they were entering was adapted to keep alive their love of liberty. Traces might still be seen of the effects of the heroic deed performed by the citizens of Leyden, when, contending for their freedom, they preferred to inundate their city and give it to the sea, rather than submit to the cruel tyranny of Spain."†

Here, as before at Amsterdam, they fell to work.

* Bradford, Cotton Mather, etc.
† Stoughton, p. 82.

"Being now pitched," says Bradford, "they fell to such trades and employments as they best could, valuing peace and their spiritual comfort above any other riches whatsoever; and at length they came to raise a competent and decent living, but with hard and continual labor."*

In Leyden the Pilgrims remained for many years, " enjoying much sweet society and spiritual comfort together in the ways of God, under the able and prudent government of Mr. John Robinson. Yea, such was the mutual love and respect which this worthy man had to his flock and his flock to him, that it might be said of them, as it once was of the famous emperor Marcus Aurelius† and the people of Rome, that it was hard to judge whether he delighted more in having such a people, or they in having such a pastor. His love was great towards them, and his care was always bent for their best good, both for soul and body; for besides his singular ability in divine things—wherein he excelled—he was very able to give direction in civil affairs, and to foresee dangers and inconveniences; by which means he was very helpful to the outward estates of the exiles, and so was in every way a common father to them."‡

Mr. William Brewster was Robinson's assistant, and "he was now called and chosen by the church"

---

* Bradford, Hist. Plymouth Plantation, p. 17.

† Golden Book of Marcus Aurelius; first printed in English in 1534. Debley's Typog. Antiq., vol. 3, p. 289.

‡ Bradford, pp. 17, 18.

to fill the place of elder.* The Pilgrims "grew in knowledge and gifts and other graces of the Spirit of God, and lived together in peace and love and holiness; and as many came unto them from divers parts of England, they grew to be a great congregation. If at any time differences arose or offences broke out—as it cannot be but sometimes there will, even among the best of men—they were ever so met with and nipped in the bud betimes, or otherwise so well compassed, as still love, peace, and communion, were preserved; or else the church was purged of those that were incorrigible, when, after much patience used, no other means would serve—which seldom came to pass."†

Though strict in their discipline and strongly attached to their distinctive principles, the Leyden exiles were far from being bigots. Robinson, though, in Cotton Mather's phrase, "he had been in his younger time—as very good fruit hath sometimes been, ere age hath ripened it—soured by the principles of rigid separation,"‡ was now developed into a man of large-hearted benevolence and enlightened catholicity. Over his flock he breathed this heavenly spirit. Nothing more offended him than the conduct of those "who cleaved unto themselves, and retired from the common good."§ Nothing more provoked him than to witness undue rigid-

---

* Bradford, pp. 17, 18. Young, etc.
† Bradford, pp. 17, 18.
‡ Cotton Mather's Magnalia, vol. 1, p. 47.
§ Bradford, p. 18. Stoughton.

ity in the enforcement of subordinate matters, especially when sternness on points of outward order was associated, as is often the case, with laxity in the critics. Robinson knew how to estimate " the tithe of mint and anise and cummin" in their relative value to the weightier matters of the law. Schism he condemned; division he deplored. From the government and ceremonies of the English Establishment his conscience compelled him to dissent, but he was prepared to welcome the disciples of that and of all other Christian communions to the fellowship of the Lord's table. "Our faith," said he, "is not negative; nor does it consist in the condemnation of others, and wiping their names out of the bead-roll of churches, but in the edification of ourselves. Neither require we of any of ours, in the confession of their faults, that they renounce or in any one word contest with the Church of England."*

It is not strange that such a teacher should have won the reverent regard of his Pilgrim flock. They could not fail to hold him "in precious estimation, as his worth and wisdom did deserve." And "though they esteemed him highly while he lived and labored among them," says Bradford, "yet much more after his death,† when they came to feel the want of his help, and saw, by woful experience, what a treasure they had lost; yea, such a loss as they saw could not be repaired, for it was

* Cited in Stoughton, p. 84.
† Robinson died at Leyden, March 1, 1864-5.

as hard for them to find such another leader and feeder in all respects, as for the Taborites to find another Ziska.* And though they did not, like the Bohemians, call themselves orphans after his death, yet they had as much cause to lament their present condition and after-usage."†

Characterized by so much unity, peacefulness, consistency, and true-hearted love, the Pilgrims could not fail to win the sincere respect of the Leyden citizens. Though most of them were poor, yet there were none so poor but if they were known to be of the English congregation, the Dutch tradesmen would trust them in any reasonable amount when they lacked money, and this because they had found by experience how careful they were to keep their word, while they saw them painful and diligent in their respective callings. The Leyden merchants even strove to get their custom; and when they required aid, employed the honest strangers and paid them above others.‡

The city magistrates testified to the sobriety and peacefulness of their guests on the eve of their departure from Holland. "These English," said they, in reproving the exiled Walloons§ who were

---

* For an interesting account of Ziska, or Zisca, the blind Hussite leader of the Bohemian insurgents, who was never defeated, see Mosheim's Eccles. Hist., cent. XV., Hallam's Hist. of the Middle Ages, vol. 1, p. 463, or the Encyclopædia Americana, article "Zisca."

† Bradford, pp. 18, 19.   ‡ Ibid., pp. 19, 20.

§ The Walloons inhabited the southern Belgic provinces bordering on France. As they spoke the French language, "they were

attached to the French refugee church, "have lived among us now these twelve years, and yet we never had any suit or action against any one of them; but your strifes and quarrels are continual."*

The reputation of their pastor for sanctity and learning no doubt tended to raise the respectability of the English church in the estimation of the Dutch.

Circumstances afforded him ample scope for the display of his talents. A heated discussion between the Arminians and the Calvinists raged in Leyden during his residence in the city, and in that far-famed controversy the great English divine was finally persuaded to take part.†

In the schools there were daily and hot disputes. Scholars were divided in opinion. The two professors or divinity readers of the Leyden university were themselves ranged on opposite sides; one of them, Episcopius, teaching the Arminian tenets; the other, Polyander, proclaiming the Calvinistic creed.‡

Robinson, though he taught thrice a week, besides writing sundry pamphlets,§ went daily to listen

---

called *Gallois*, which was changed, in Low Dutch, into Waalsche, and in English into Walloon." Many of them were Protestants, and being subject to relentless persecution by the Spanish government, they emigrated in great numbers into Holland, carrying with them a knowledge of the industrial arts. See Bradford's Hist. Plym. Plantation, p. 20, note.

* Bradford, p. 20. Stoughton, Young, Ashton's Life of Robinson. † Stoughton, p. 85.

‡ Bradford, Young, Neal, Mather, etc.

§ A collection of the Works of John Robinson was printed in

to the disputations, hearing first one side, then the other. In this way he became thoroughly grounded in the controversy, saw the force of the opposing arguments, and became familiar with the shifts of the inimical disputants. Some sermons which he delivered in the English church on the contested issues attracted public attention. Episcopius had just published certain theses which he had affirmed that he was prepared to maintain against all opponents. Polyander and the chief preachers of the city waited upon Robinson, and urged him to pick up the gauntlet. He was loath, being a stranger; but they beat down the rampart of his objections, and finally Robinson consented to dispute. Episcopius and the Pilgrim pastor met, and in this public tilt the English champion is said to have achieved "a famous victory."*

Ever after this verbal tournament, Robinson was held in the highest esteem by the learned men of the university, by the Dutch preachers, and by the republican government of Holland.† Indeed, it is said that nothing but the fear of offending the English king prevented the bestowal upon him of some mark of national favor.‡

On their part, the English refugees always treated the reformed churches of the Continent with honor and fraternal kindness. "We acknowl-

London in 1851, with a memoir and annotations by Mr. Robert Ashton.

* Bradford, p. 21. Cotton Mather's Magnalia, vol. 1, p. 47.
† Bradford, Mather, Stoughton.
‡ Ibid., Young, Ashton's Life of Robinson.

edge," remarked Robinson, "before God and man, that we harmonize so perfectly with the reformed churches of the Netherlands in matters of religion, as to be ready to subscribe their articles of faith, and every one of them, as they are set forth in their confession. We acknowledge these churches as true and genuine; we hold fellowship with them as far as we can; those among us who understand Dutch, attend their preaching; we offer the Supper to such of their members as are known to us and may desire it."*

Yet the Pilgrims did not indorse the system of church government which received the *imprimatur* of the Synod of Dort. They steadfastly maintained that each single church or society of Christians possessed within itself full ecclesiastical authority for choosing officers, administering all the ordinances of the gospel, and settling its discipline; in a word, they held to the perfect independence of the individual churches, and framed their ecclesitical polity on the purest democratic model.†

"They conceded," observes Uhden, "that synods and councils might be useful in healing divisions between churches, and in imparting to them friendly advice, but not in the exercise of judicial authority over them, or in the imposition of any canon or any article of faith, without the free assent of each individual church."‡

---

* Robinson's Apology for the Romanists.

† Uhden, New England Theocracy, p. 42. Robinson's Works, etc. ‡ Uhden, p. 42.

Sheathed in the panoply of their principles, busied in the multifarious activities of their daily employments, and solaced by faith, the Pilgrims "made shift to live in these hard times." *Peregrini Deo cura*, runs the old Latin phrase; and this exiled band of worshippers proved that strangers are indeed peculiar objects of God's care.

CHAPTER III.

THE DECISION.

"Can ye lead out to distant colonies
The o'erflowings of a people, or your wronged
Brethren, by impious persecution driven,
And arm their breasts with fortitude to try
New regions—climes, though barren, yet beyond
The baneful power of tyrants? These are deeds
For which their hardy labors well prepare
The sinewy arms of Albion's sons."

DYER.

ALTHOUGH the Pilgrims resided at Leyden in honor, and at peace with God and their own consciences, many circumstances conspired to render them anxious and uneasy. The horizon of the Netherlands grew gloomy with portents of war. The famous truce between Holland and the Spaniard drew near its conclusion.* The impatient demon of strife stood knocking at the door. Homesickness gnawed at their hearts. Dear, cruel England filled their thoughts. The language of the Dutch had never become pleasantly familiar.† Frequently "they saw poverty coming on them like an armed man." Many of their little band were taken from them by death. "Grave mistress Experience hav-

---

* This "famous truce," so long desired, embraced a period of twelve years. It was signed in April, 1609, and expired in 1621. Grattan, Hist. Netherlands.

† Bancroft, Hist. United States, vol. 1, p. 303.

ing taught them many things," some of their "sagest members began both deeply to apprehend their present dangers and wisely to foresee the future, and to think of timely remedy." They inclined to removal, "not out of any newfangledness or other such like giddy humor, by which men are oftentimes transported to their great hurt and danger, but for sundry weighty and solid reasons."*

These have been often recited, and they completely vindicate the project to remove.

The Pilgrims "saw, and found by experience, the hardness of the place and country to be such that few in comparison would come to them, and fewer would bide it out and continue with them; for many that joined them, and many more who desired to be with them, could not endure the great labor and hard fare, with other inconveniences which they underwent and were content to bear. But though they loved the persons of the exiles, approved their cause, and honored their sufferings, yet they left them weeping, as Orpah did her mother-in-law Naomi, and as those Romans did Cato in Utica, who desired to be excused and borne with, though they could not all be Catos.† For many, though they desired to enjoy the ordinances of God as the Pilgrims did, yet, alas, chose bondage, with danger of conscience, rather than to endure these hardships. Yea, some preferred the prisons of England to this liberty in Holland, with these afflictions.

---

* Bradford, Hist. Plymouth Plantation, pp. 22, 23.
† See Plutarch's Life of Cato the Younger.

The Pilgrims thought that if a better and easier place of residence could be had, it would draw many to them, and take away these discouragements. Yea, their pastor would often say that many of those who both wrote and preached against them there would, if they were in a place where they might have liberty and live comfortably, practise as they did."*

Then again, "they saw that, though the exiles generally bore all these difficulties very cheerfully and with resolute courage, being in the best and strength of their years, yet old age began to steal upon them—and their great and continued labors, with other crosses and sorrows, hastened it before the time—so it was not only probably thought, but apparently seen, that within a few years more they would be in danger to scatter by necessities pressing them, or sink under their burdens, or both. Therefore, according to the divine proverb, that 'a wise man seeth the plague when it cometh, and hideth himself,'† so they, like skilful and tried soldiers, were fearful to be entrapped and surrounded by their enemies, so as they should neither be able to fight or fly; so they thought it better to dislodge betimes to some place of better advantage and less danger, if any such could be found."‡

It was furthermore perceived that, "as necessity was a task-master over them, so they were forced to be such, not only to their servants, but in a sort to their dearest children; the which, as it did not a

---

* Bradford.   † Proverbs 22:3.   ‡ Bradford.

little wound the tender hearts of many loving fathers and mothers, so it produced likewise sundry sad and sorrowful effects; for many of their children, who were of the best disposition and most gracious inclinations, having learned to bear the yoke in their youth, and being willing to bear part of their parents' burden, were oftentimes so oppressed by their heavy labors, that though their minds were free and willing, yet their bodies bowed under the weight, and became decrepit in early youth, the vigor of nature being consumed in the bud. But that which was more lamentable, and of all sorrows most heavy to be borne, was, that many of the children, by these means and the great licentiousness of youth in those countries and the manifold temptations of the place, were drawn away by evil example into extravagant and dangerous courses, getting the reins off their necks, and departing from their parents. Some became soldiers, others made far voyages by sea, and some walked in paths tending to dissoluteness and the danger of their souls, to the great grief of their parents and the dishonor of God. The Pilgrims saw that their posterity would be in danger to degenerate and be corrupted."*

Still again—" and this was not least"—they were inclined to remove by the "great hope and inward zeal they had of laying some good foundation, or at least of making some way thereto, for the propagation and advancement of the gospel of the kingdom of Christ in remote parts of the world; yea, though

* Bradford, p. 24.

they should be but even as stepping-stones unto others for the performance of so great a work."*

These and some other kindred reasons† pushed the Pilgrims to further emigration. The question which each began to ask the other was, "Whither shall we go?" Soon this query stared all other considerations out of countenance, and became the all-engrossing topic of discussion at the hearth-stones and in the chapel of the exiles.

At this juncture a germ of thought was developed which proved to be the seed of a mighty empire. All Europe stood a-tip-toe gazing across the misty and chilling waste of waters towards that new continent by whose discovery the genius of Columbus had rounded the globe into perfect symmetry. The glories of the New World flashed in the brilliant eloquence of Raleigh. Marvellous tales were told of the fertility of the soil and of the healthful beauty of the skies; while old sailors, who had gazed with their own eyes upon the legendary shores, passed from city to city depicting to eager and credulous crowds the terrors of the wilderness and the wild ferocity of the Western savages.

Meantime "the career of maritime discovery had been pursued with daring intrepidity and rewarded with brilliant success. The voyages of Gosnold, and Smith, and Hudson, the enterprise of Raleigh, and Delaware, and Gorges, the compilations of Eden, and Willes, and Hakluyt, had filled the com-

* Bradford, p. 24.
† For additional reasons, see Young, p. 385.

mercial world with wonder. Calvinists of the French church had already sought, though vainly, to plant themselves in Brazil, in Carolina, and, with De Monts, in Acadia;"* and now, in 1617, some bold thinker and unshrinking speaker among the Leyden Pilgrims, perhaps Brewster, perhaps Bradford, perhaps Robinson himself, proposed to colonize "some of those vast and unpeopled countries of America which were fruitful and fit for habitation, but devoid of all civilized inhabitants; where there were only savage and brutish men, who ranged up and down little otherwise than as wild beasts."†

At the outset the Pilgrims listened to this proposal, some with admiration, some with misgiving, some openly aghast. Bradford's quaint pages afford us some glimpses of their debates. The doubters said, "It is a great design, and subject to inconceivable perils; as besides the casualties of the seas, which none can be freed from, the length of the voyage is such that the weak bodies of many worn out with age and travel, as many of us are, can never be able to endure; and even if they should, the miseries to which we should be exposed in that land will be too hard for us to bear; 't is likely that some or all will effect our ruin. There we shall be liable to famine, and nakedness, and want of all things. The change of air, diet, and water, will infect us with sickness; and those who escape these evils will be in danger of the savages, who are cruel,

---

* Bancroft, Hist. United States, vol. 1, p. 303.
† Bradford, p. 24; Young's Chronicles, etc.

barbarous, and most treacherous in their rage, and merciless when they overcome; not being content only to kill, but delighting to torment men in the most bloody way, flaying men alive with the shells of fishes, cutting off the joints by piece-meal, broiling them on coals, and eating collops of their victims' flesh while they yet live, and in their very sight."

As these horrors darkened in their imaginations, the deeply-interested exiles who thronged the council-chamber shuddered with affright. Mothers, hearing the shrill war-whoop in advance, strained their babes yet closer to their breasts. "Surely it could not be thought but the very hearing of these things must move the very bowels of men to grate within them, and make the weak to quake and tremble."

But the opponents of the project urged still other objections, "and those neither unreasonable nor improbable." "It will require," they said, "more money than we can furnish to prepare for such a voyage. Similar schemes have failed;* and our experience in removing to Holland teaches us how hard it is to live in a strange country, even though it be a rich and civilized commonwealth. What then shall we do in the frozen wilderness?"

Fear chilled the hearts, doubt paralyzed the nerves of the assembled exiles. Then the more resolute stood up, and, fixing their eyes on the sky,

---

* In allusion, probably, to the plantation project at Sagadahoc, in 1607. See Bancroft and others.

exclaimed, "God will protect us; and he points us on. All great and honorable actions are accompanied with great difficulties, and must be both undertaken and overcome with answerable courage. We grant the dangers of this removal to be tremendous, but not desperate; the difficulties are many, but not invincible; for though many of them are likely, all are not certain. It may be that sundry of the things surmised may never happen; others, by provident care and the use of good means, may be prevented; and all of them, through the help of God, by fortitude and patience may either be borne or overcome. True it is that such attempts are not to be undertaken without good reason; never rashly or lightly, as many have done, for curiosity or hope of gain. But our condition is not ordinary; our ends are good and honorable; our calling lawful and urgent; therefore we may invoke and expect God's blessing on our proceeding. Yea, though we should lose our lives in this action, yet may we have comfort in it, and our endeavor would be honorable. We live here but as men in exile; and as great miseries may befall us in this place, for the twelve years of truce are now nigh up, and here is nothing but beating of drums and preparations for war, the events whereof are always uncertain. The Spaniard may prove as cruel as the savages of America, and the famine and pestilence as sore here as there, and our liberty less to look out for a remedy."*

* This debate is copied from Bradford, pp. 25-27.

It was thus that the undaunted apostles of the future pleaded; and now as always, the policy of active, trustful, and religious courage overbore the timid pleas of the undecided, the plausible doubts of the skeptical, and the wailing dissent of the croakers who paused distrustful of the unknown future and enamoured of the anchored past. The Pilgrims announced their decision to follow in the wake of Columbus, and launch boldly across the Atlantic, trusting God.

CHAPTER IV.

FAREWELL.

> "Like Israel's host to exile driven,
>   Across the flood the Pilgrims fled;
> Their hands bore up the ark of heaven,
>   And Heaven their trusting footsteps led,
> Till on these savage shores they trod,
>   And won the wilderness for God."
>
> PIERPONT.

HAVING decided to settle in America, the Pilgrims, "after humble prayers unto God for his direction and assistance," held another general conference, and in this they discussed the location of their proposed colony. Some were ardent for Guiana,* whose tropical climate and immeasurable mineral wealth Raleigh had painted in dazzling colors, and whose fertility was such that it was only necessary to "tickle it with a hoe, and it would laugh with a harvest." The Spaniard was already there. It has been well said that the golden dreams which deluded the first European settlers of America were akin, alike in object and results, to the old alchymists' search after the philosopher's stone. The painful alchymist lost not only the gold he sought, but the wealth of knowledge and of substantial commercial treasure which the researches of modern chemistry have disclosed; and so the Spanish colonists slighted

---

* Bradford, Young, Elliot, Bancroft, etc.

the abounding wealth of a genial climate and a fertile soil, while chasing the illusive phantom of "a land of gold."*

Yet, despite the apparent opening in Guiana, the Pilgrims would not go thither, partly because the pretensions of England to the soil were wavering, but chiefly because a horde of intolerant and ubiquitous Jesuits had already planted themselves in that vicinity.†

"Upon their talk of removing, sundry of the Dutch would have had them go under them, and made them large offers;" but "the Pilgrims were attached to their nationality as Englishmen, and to the language of their fatherland. A deep-seated love of country led them to the generous purpose of recovering the protection of England by enlarging her dominions. They were 'restless' with the desire to live once more under the government of their native land."‡

This feeling led them to reject the proposal of the Holland merchants; and, since they had also given up the idea of colonizing Guiana, they determined to essay a settlement in "the most northern parts of Virginia," hoping under the provincial government "to live in a distinct body by themselves," at peace with God and man.§

There were in 1617 two organized English companies which had been chartered by James I. to

---

* Wilson's Pilgrim Fathers, p. 341.
† Bancroft, vol. 1, p. 204. ‡ Ibid.
§ Ibid., Bradford, Young.

colonize America, and empowered to effect regular and permanent settlements, extending one hundred miles inland. The headquarters of one of these was in London, of the other in Plymouth.* The Leyden Pilgrims were impelled to sail under the auspices of one of these merchant-companies by a double consideration—a lack of means to effect an independent settlement, and a desire to emigrate in such shape that they might live under English protection.† Hence on selecting Virginia as the site of their intended settlement, the exiles at once despatched two of their number to England, at the charge of the rest,‡ to negotiate with the Virginia company.§ They "found God going along with them;" and through the influence of "Sir Edwin Sandys, a religious gentleman then living," they might at once have gained a patent; but the careful envoys desired first to consult "the multitude" at Leyden.‖

In their interview with the Leyden merchants, the envoys had expressly stipulated for freedom of religious worship.¶ On their return to Holland they told the Leyden congregation that they "found the Virginia company very desirous to have them go out under their auspices, and willing to grant them a patent, with as ample privileges as they could bestow; while some of their chiefs did not

* Wilson's Pilgrim Fathers, p. 356.
† Ibid., Bradford, Bancroft. ‡ Bradford, p. 29.
§ Ibid. ‖ Bancroft, vol. 1, p. 304.
¶ Bradford, p. 28.

doubt their ability to obtain a guaranty of toleration for them from the king."*

The Pilgrim agents carried back with them a friendly and sympathizing letter from Sir Edwin Sandys;† and to this a formal answer was returned. "We verily believe," wrote Robinson and Brewster, "that the Lord is with us, unto whom and whose service we have given ourselves in many trials; and that he will graciously prosper our endeavors according to the simplicity of our hearts therein. We are well weaned from the delicate milk of our mother-country, and inured to the difficulties of a strange and hard land, which yet, in a great part, we have by patience overcome. Our people are, for the body of them, industrious and frugal, we think we may say, as any company of people in the world. We are knit together as a body in a most strict and sacred bond and covenant of the Lord, of the violation whereof we make great conscience, and by virtue whereof we do hold ourselves strictly tied to all care of each other's good, and of the whole. It is not with us as with other men, whom small things can discourage, or small discontentments cause to wish themselves at home again. We know our entertainment in England, and in Holland; we shall much prejudice both our arts and means by removal; but once gone, we should

---

* Bradford, p. 28.

† For some account of Sir Edwin Sandys, one of the most prominent members of the Virginia company, see Hood's Athenæ Oxon., vol. 2, p. 472.

not be won to return by any hope to recover even our present helps and comforts."*

While these negotiations were pending the Virginia company found much greater difficulty than they had apprehended in winning from the silly and pedantic king an assent to the tolerant clauses of the Pilgrims' patent; "and though many means were used to bring it about, it could not be effected."† When the Pilgrims asked that liberty of worship might be confirmed under the king's broad seal, they were asked two questions: "How intend ye to gain a livelihood in the new country?" The reply was, "By fishing, at first." "Who shall make your ministers?" was the next query. The Pilgrims answered, "The power of making them is in the church;" and this spoiled all. To enlarge the dimensions of England James I. esteemed "a good and honest motive; and fishing was an honest trade, the apostles' own calling," yet he referred their suit to the decision of the prelates of Canterbury and London.‡

The exiles were advised not to carry their suit before the bishops, but to rely upon events and the disposition which his majesty had shown to connive at their enterprise under "a formal promise of neglect."§ Besides, it was considered that if James had confirmed their titles, nothing could bind him. "If afterwards there should be a purpose to wrong

---

* This letter, as also that of Sandys which occasioned it, may be found *in extenso* in Bradford, pp. 30, 31, 32, 33.
† Bradford, p. 29,   ‡ Bancroft, p. 305.   § Bancroft.

us," said they, "though we had a seal as broad as the house floor, it would not serve the turn; for there would be means enough found to recall or reverse it."* So they determined in this, as in other things, to rest on God's providence.

New agents were at once despatched to England to urge forward the lagging preparations. But dissensions in the Virginia company "ate out the heart of action." At last, in 1619, a patent was granted,† and only "one more negotiation remained to be completed. The Pilgrims were not possessed of sufficient capital for the execution of their scheme. The confidence in wealth to be derived from fisheries had made American expeditions a subject of consideration with English merchants; and the agents from Leyden were able to form a partnership between their friends and the men of business in London. A company called the 'Merchant-Adventurers' was formed. The services of each emigrant were rated as a capital of ten pounds, and belonged to the company; all profits were to be reserved till the end of seven years, when the whole amount, and all houses, lands, gardens, and fields, were to be divided among the shareholders according to their respective interests. A London merchant who risked one hundred pounds would receive for his money tenfold more than the penniless laborer

---

* Bradford.
† Ibid. "Being taken in the name of one who failed to accompany the expedition, the patent was never of the least service." Bancroft, vol. 1, p. 303.

for his entire services. This arrangement threatened a seven years' check to the pecuniary prosperity of the colony; yet as it did not interfere with civil rights or religion, it did not intimidate the resolved."*

It is peculiarly interesting to us of this generation to notice how prominent a trait republicanism was in the intellectual character of the Pilgrims. It crops out constantly. Nothing must be done without the assent of "the multitude." When any important matter was broached, the pastor did not presume to dictate, nor did the elders assume to control; the decision rested with the majority vote of the community. Their council was the ideal model of a pure democracy.

So now, when their envoys returned, "they made a public recital," and the Pilgrims "had a solemn meeting and a day of humiliation to seek the Lord for his direction."† Robinson preached, "teaching many things very aptly and befitting their present occasion and condition, strengthening them against their fears and perplexities, and encouraging them in their resolutions."‡

This fine incident was at once an illustration and a prophecy; it illustrated the rugged, self-centred, yet devout independence of the exiles, and it prophesied from this the twining laurels of success. The Pilgrims were invincible; and the secret of their

---

* Bancroft, pp. 305, 306. The title of the company thus formed was "The Merchant Adventurers." See Elliot, vol. 1, p. 49. † Bradford. Winslow in Young's Chronicles.
‡ Ibid.

strength was religious democracy. If in their right-hand they held an open Bible, signifying faith and hope, in their left they clutched tenaciously the fundamental but still crude principles of organized liberty—the now open secret of later Saxon progress.

At length, in July, 1620, "after much travail and debate, all things were got ready and provided."* It had been previously decided who and how many should sail with "the forlorn hope;" "for all that were willing to have gone could not get ready on account of their other affairs; neither if they could, had there been means to have transported them all together. Those that stayed being the greater number, required the pastor to tarry with them; and indeed for other reasons Robinson could not then well go, so this was more readily yielded unto. The others then desired elder Brewster to sail with them, which was assented to. It was also agreed by mutual consent and covenant, that those who went should be an absolute church of themselves, as well as those who remained; seeing that, in such a dangerous voyage, and removed to such a distance, it might come to pass that they should, for the body of them, never meet again in this world; yet this proviso was inserted, that as any of the rest crossed the water, or any of the Pilgrims returned upon occasion, they should be reputed as members without any further discussion or testimonial. It was also promised to those that went first, by the body of the rest, that if the Lord gave

* Bradford. Winslow in Young's Chronicles.

them life and means and opportunity, they would come to them as soon as they could."*

On the eve of departure a solemn fast was held. "Let us seek of God," said these disciples so shortly to be severed by the sullen sea, "a right way for us and for our little ones and for all our substance." Is it strange that New England is moral and well-ordered and devout, when it was begotten of a fast and a prayer?

Robinson gave the departing members of his exiled flock "a farewell, breathing a freedom of opinion and an independence of authority such as then was hardly known in the world;"† and this he intermixed with practical directions for the future guidance of the Pilgrim voyagers. He chose that beautiful text in Ezra, "And there, at the river by Ahava, I proclaimed a fast, that we might humble ourselves before God, and seek of him a right way for us, and for our children, and for all our substance."‡

Unhappily, "but a brief outline of that remarkable sermon has been preserved. We would gladly give whole shoals of printed discourses in exchange for that one homily. While, however, the larger part is lost in the long silence of the past, the fragments of this great man's farewell utterances are gathered up and preserved among our richest relics."§

* Bradford, p. 42. † Bancroft.
‡ Ezra 8:21. This is the version in Bradford's Narrative.
§ Stoughton, Spiritual Heroes—The Pilgrim Fathers.

Never was there a more affecting occasion. A Christian congregation, welded together alike by a common faith and a common misfortune, was about to be rent asunder. Some of their number, thrice exiled, were soon to essay the settlement of an unknown and legendary wilderness. These dear wanderers they might never see again with their mortal eyes; and even should they meet them once more on the shores of time, years must intervene before the greeting. Strange thoughts and anxious chased each other across the troubled mirror of each countenance. All eyes were dim with tears; all hands were clasped; the pastor's heart was full. Amidst the painful silence, broken by a frequent sob, the low, sweet voice of Robinson was heard quivering upon the sympathetic air : " Brethren, we are now ere long to part asunder, and the Lord knoweth whether I shall live ever to see your faces more. But whether the Lord hath appointed it or not, I charge you before God and his blessed angels to follow me no farther than I have followed Christ. If God should reveal any thing to you by any other instrument of his, be as ready to receive it as ever you were to receive any truth of my ministry, for I am very confident the Lord hath more truth and light yet to break forth out of his holy word. Miserably do I bewail the state and condition of the reformed churches, who are come to a period in religion, and will go no farther than the instruments of their reformation.

"Remember your church covenant, in which

you have agreed to walk in all the ways of the Lord, made or to be made known unto you. Remember your promise and covenant with God and with one another to receive whatever light and truth shall be made known to you from his written word; but withal, take heed, I beseech you, what you receive for truth, and compare it and weigh it with other scriptures of truth before you accept it; for it is not possible the Christian world should come so lately out of such thick antichristian darkness, and that full perfection of knowledge should break forth at once."*

Much is said nowadays about the development of Christianity. The clatter of *pseudo*-philosophers is deafening. We have the German rationalistic school; the worshippers in the "broad church" of the humanitarians; the idolaters of a mystic pantheism; the devotees of the Socinian tenets; the bold blasphemers who reject all faith, and form a creed in epigrammatic sneers; and the apostles of two churches, one of which believes that God is too good to damn men, while the other holds that man is too good to be damned. All this divinity is quite adrift; it floats rudderless, and rejects the anchorage of God's word. Robinson was wiser. He was no friend of stagnant Christianity; but in all his voyaging after truth he clung to his Bible anchorage. Inside of that he saw ample room for the completest development. "The Bible, not the fa-

---

* Neale; Winslow in Young; Belknap, Stoughton, etc.

thers, formed his text-book; he discerned there the depths of truth and glory, into which he was persuaded that thoughtful minds might plunge farther and farther as time rolled on. The Bible was to him like the universe, a system unchangeable in its great facts and fundamental principles, but ever opening wider and wider upon devout and studious intellects. He knew there would be no change in God's word, no addition to or subtraction from its contents; but he looked for beautiful and improving changes in men's views—for broader, clearer, and grander conceptions of God's truth."* This was Robinson's idea of "the development of Christianity," and it was surcharged with profound philosophy as well as with sound practical direction and Christian pathos. The great Puritan teacher was neither a Socinian, a Pantheist, a Rationalist, nor a Mystic; he claimed no kinship with the money-changers who scourge Christ out of the temple of his divinity; least of all did he sympathize with those who reject the sufficiency of the Scripture text, and found their schemes of progress upon material bases. No; Robinson favored the most radical Christian progress, but he based his idea upon the Bible, and knew how to guard his notion of development from misconception and abuse. The evangelical believers of our day owe the famous Leyden exile a lasting debt of gratitude for the clear distinction which he has drawn between the progressive "liberty of the sons of God," and

* Stoughton, p. 97.

the earth-born whims which materialism baptizes with the name of "progress."

In this same sermon Robinson pressed one other thing, exhibiting, in a bigoted and narrow age, rare catholicity of spirit. "Another thing I commend to you," he said; "by all means shake off the name of *Brownist*.* 'T is a mere nickname, a brand to make religion odious, and the professors of it, to the Christian world. To that end I should be glad if some godly minister would go over with you before my coming; for there will be no appreciable difference between the Puritans who have not renounced the church of England and you, when you come to the practice of the ordinances out of the British kingdom. By all means close with the godly party of England, and rather study union than division; in how nearly we may possibly, without sin, close with them, than in the least measure to affect division or separation from them. Nor be ye loath to take another pastor or teacher; for that flock which hath two shepherds is not endangered, but secured thereby."†

---

* The first separatists were so called after Robert Brown, who, in the latter part of the sixteenth century, propounded a system of church government which contained many of the features of modern Congregationalism. Brown was born in 1549, and was a relative of Elizabeth's lord-treasurer, the famous Burleigh. In 1582 he published his book, "The Life and Manners of True Christians," and suffered persecution therefor. Eventually, after a roving life, he conformed to the church of England, and was made rector in Northamptonshire. Shortly after, he died very miserably in a jail. Strype's Annals, vol. 2. Collier's Eccl. Hist., part 2, book 7. † Winslow's account of Robinson's Sermon.

Thus abruptly ends this precious fragment; and it may justly be esteemed one of the rarest verbal gems in the trophied casket of our Saxon tongue.

Two vessels had been chartered for the voyage: the "*Speedwell*," a small ship of some sixty tons, and a larger vessel of a hundred and eighty tons, called the "*Mayflower*."* The "Speedwell" lay moored at Delft Haven, a little seaport in the vicinity of Leyden.† The Pilgrims were to sail in this ship across the Channel to Southampton, where the "Mayflower" would join them, and thence they were to launch in company across the Atlantic.‡

On the 21st of July, 1620, the exiles quitted Leyden, which had been their quiet resting-place for eleven years, and journeyed to Delft Haven. "When the ship was ready to carry us away," wrote Edward Winslow, "the brethren that stayed at Leyden, having again solemnly sought the Lord with us and for us, feasted us that were to go, at our pastor's house, a commodious building. Here we refreshed ourselves, after tears, with singing psalms, making joyful melody in our hearts, as well as with the voice, there being many of the congregation very expert in music; and indeed it was the sweetest melody that ever mine ears heard. After this our friends accompanied us to Delft Haven, where we were to embark, and there feasted us

---

* Wilson's Pilgrim Fathers. Bradford, Belknap.
† Elliot, Hist. of New England, vol. 1. Palfrey, etc.
‡ Ibid., Bradford, Young.

again. And after prayer by our pastor, when a flood of tears was poured out, they accompanied us to the ship; but we were not able to speak one to another for the abundance of sorrow to part."*

Only a part of the colonists went aboard the "Speedwell" on the day of their arrival at Delft Haven; the others tarried in the town over night, spending the hours in conversation and expressions of true Christian love.† "The morning light must have gleamed mournfully upon their eyes through the windows of the apartments where they assembled. It told them that the last days of their pleasant intercourse with old, endeared friends had come, for the wind was fair, and the vessel was ready to weigh anchor and sail. And so they went down to the shore, where the scene at Miletus was literally repeated, save that the people were the voyagers, instead of their apostolic father. Robinson 'kneeled down and prayed with them, and all wept sore, and fell upon his neck and kissed him, sorrowing most of all for the words which he spake, that they should see his face no more; then he accompanied them to the ship.' Even the Dutch strangers, who saw the parting, stood and wept."‡

Then came the shrill "Yo hoy" of the seamen; final caresses were exchanged; sail was hoisted; a salute was fired from the "Speedwell;" and while the friends on shore watched the receding vessel

---

* Winslow in Young's Chronicles.   † Stoughton.
‡ Ibid., p. 100.

and strained their eyeballs to retain their vision, she glinted below the horizon, and was gone.

Southampton was safely and speedily reached; "the *Speedwell* entered port to join the *Mayflower*—ships whose names have become hallowed, and are worthy of being placed, with the Argo of the ancients, amid the constellations of heaven."

CHAPTER V.

THE FROZEN WILDERNESS.

"Whoso shrinks or falters now,
Whoso to the yoke would bow
Brand the craven on his brow.
Take your land of sun and bloom;
Only leave to freedom room
For her plough, and forge, and loom."
WHITTIER.

AT Southampton the Pilgrims made no lengthened stay, pausing but to perfect some necessary final arrangements.* A fortnight later, on the 5th of August, 1620, the "Speedwell" and the "Mayflower" weighed anchor, and hoisting sail, set out in company for America. The English soil had scarcely dipped below the horizon, when the "Speedwell" made signals of distress; she was found to leak badly. After consultation, the voyagers wore ship, and put into Dartmouth harbor for repairs. Here the Pilgrims passed eight days, "to their great charge, and loss of time and a fair wind."†

On the 21st of August, a fresh start was made. This time a hundred leagues of sea were passed, and the vessels were just rounding Land's End, when lo, the "Speedwell" again bore up under

---

* Young's Chronicles. Bradford. † Bradford.

pretence of unseaworthiness. Once more the shores of England were regained, and anchor was dropped in Plymouth harbor. The captain of the recusant ship, backed by his company, was dismayed at the dangers of the enterprise, and gave out that the "Speedwell" was too weak for the voyage. "Upon this," says Bradford, "it was resolved to dismiss her and part of the company, and to proceed with the 'Mayflower.' This, though it was grievous and caused great discouragement, was put into execution. So after they had taken out such provision as the 'Mayflower' could stow, and concluded both what number and what persons to send back, they had another sad parting, the one ship going back to London, and the other preparing for the voyage. Those that returned were such as, for the most part, were willing to do so, either out of discontent or some fear conceived of the ill-success of a voyage pressed against so many crosses, and in a year-time so far spent. Others, in regard to their own weakness and the charge of many young children, were thought least useful, and most unfit to bear the brunt of this hard adventure; unto which work of God and judgment of their brethren they were content to submit. And thus, like Gideon's army, this small number was divided, as if the Lord thought even these few too many for the great work he had to do."*

But though Cushman wrote, "Our voyage thus far hath been as full of crosses as ourselves of crook-

* Bradford, pp. 69, 70.

edness,"* no dangers could appal the dauntless; and "having thus winnowed their numbers, the little band, not of resolute men only, but wives, some far gone in pregnancy, children, infants, a floating village, yet in all but one hundred souls, went on board the single ship, which was hired only to carry them across the Atlantic; and on the 6th of September, 1620, thirteen years after the first colonization of Virginia, two months before the concession of the grand charter of Plymouth, without any warrant from the sovereign of England, without any useful charter from a corporate body, the Pilgrims in the 'Mayflower' set sail for the New World, where the past could offer no favorable auguries."†

But these Christian heroes of a grander venture than that classic voyage which Virgil has sung of old Æneas,

> "Trojæ qui primus ab oris
> Italiam, fato profugus, Lavinaque venit
> Litora,"‡

unawed by the abounding perils of the sea and land, unchilled by the desertion of their comrades, kept on their solitary way, and "bated no jot of heart or hope."

The "Mayflower" was a small vessel, yet smaller ones had repeatedly explored the ocean. "Columbus' 'ships' were from fifteen to thirty-two tons burden, and without decks. Frobisher had traversed the watery waste with a vessel of twenty-five

---

* Dated Dartmouth, August 17, 1620. Cushman remained in England. Elliot, vol. 1, p. 57.   † Bancroft.

‡ Virgil's Æneid, book 1.

tons, and Pring had coasted along the shores of New England in a bark of fifty tons. Those were manned by hardy seamen, to whom the tempest was a play-fellow; but these men and women and children knew nothing of the sea; they only knew that ships sailed, and too often did not return; they had seen the sea, even along the coasts of England and Holland, lashed into fury. To trust themselves upon it on an uncertain voyage to a wilderness harbor" was no gala undertaking; yet serenely they accepted the situation, thankful to God for civil rights and untrammelled liberty to hymn his praises.

"The voyage of the pioneer ship," says Elliot, "was long, tempestuous, and monotonous, as what sea-voyage is not? yet, with a firm purpose, she opened a way through the buffeting ocean towards the setting sun. Already its rays came to them a little shorn; the autumn solstice was at hand, and winter not far away. In religious exercises, in hopeful conversation, the exiles passed the weary days. These were varied by storms, and once by a great danger. In the straining of the ship, a strong timber threatened to break. Then, among the lumber which they had brought, a large 'iron screw was found, and the ship was saved.' Their faces were turned westward, but who can wonder that a lingering look was cast behind, and that pleasant memories for a moment dimmed their recent sufferings and present hopes? Men, women, and children suffered the 'sickness of the sea,' that sickness which is inexorable, which weakens the knees, burdens the heart, and paralyzes the brain. The sailors laughed and scoffed; but to them it seemed that death was nigh. Yet it was not; one only of the whole number, William Butten, died during the voyage; and one was born to take his place, a son of Stephen Hopkins, named Oceanus, the son of the sea.

"Daily the Pilgrims turned their eyes westward, hoping for a sight of the new land. They had shaped their course for the Hudson river, of which the Dutch navigators had made favorable reports. As the voyage lengthened, their longings for the land increased. They had been tossed on the sea now sixty-five days, when, on the 9th of November, the long, low coast-line of the New World gladdened their eyes. They thanked God for the sight, and took courage. On the 11th of November they dropped anchor within Cape Cod. Sixty-seven days they had passed in the ship since their final departure from England, and one hundred and twelve since the embarkation at Delft Haven. They were weary, many were sick, and the scurvy had attacked some. They might well rejoice that they had reached these shores."*

On their departure from Holland, Robinson had handed them a long and pregnant letter of instruction and advice. In this he counselled, among other things, the early formation of a body politic, and the inauguration of a civil government. "As

* Elliot. Hist. New England, vol. 1, pp. 58, 59.

you are not furnished with persons of special eminence above the rest to be chosen by you into office of government," he added, "let your wisdom and godliness appear not only in choosing such persons as do entirely love and will to promote your common good, but also in yielding unto them all due honor and obedience in their lawful administrations."*

In obedience to this sage counsel, the Pilgrims now, before landing, met to consider how their government should be constituted; and they formed themselves into a body politic by this formal, solemn, and voluntary compact:

"In the name of God, Amen; We whose names are underwritten, the loyal subjects of our dread sovereign King James, having undertaken, for the glory of God, and advancement of the Christian faith, and honor of our king and country, a voyage to plant the first colony in the northern parts of Virginia, do, by these presents, solemnly and mutually, in the presence of God and of one another, covenant and combine ourselves together into a civil body politic, for our better ordering and preservation, and furtherance of the ends aforesaid; and by virtue hereof, to enact, constitute, and frame such just and equal laws, ordinances, constitutions, and offices, from time to time, as shall be thought most convenient for the general good of the colony: unto which we promise all due submission and obedience.'†

* See this whole letter in Bradford, pp. 64–67.
† Bradford, Young, etc.

"This instrument—under which John Carver was immediately and unanimously chosen governor for one year—was signed by the whole body of men, forty-one in number; who, with their families, constituted the one hundred, the whole colony, 'the proper democracy' that arrived in New England. This was the birth of popular constitutional liberty. The Middle Ages had been familiar with charters and constitutions; but they had been merely compacts for immunities, concessions of municipal privileges, or limitations of the sovereign power in favor of feudal institutions. In the cabin of the 'Mayflower' humanity recovered its rights, and instituted government on the basis of 'equal laws' for 'the general good.' "*

Law and order provided for, the Pilgrims next proceeded to select the precise spot for their settlement. "The first Virginia colony," remarks Bancroft, "sailing along the shores of North Carolina, was, by a favoring storm, driven into the magnificent bay of the Chesapeake. The Pilgrims, having chosen for their settlement the country near the Hudson, the best position on the whole coast, were conducted, through some miscalculation, to the most barren and inhospitable part of Massachusetts."†

It was a mooted question whether to plant a colony on this frigid coast, or to hoist anchor anew and set sail for the Hudson. The captain of the "May-

* Bancroft, vol. 1, p. 310. This compact was signed Nov. 11, 1620. † Ibid., p. 309.

flower" favored an immediate settlement;* and the voyagers, weary of the sea, and, perhaps, influenced by the fact that the winter began to breathe upon them, finally determined to send ashore a reconnoitering squad to sound the disposition of the natives, and to select a landing-spot.

In 1584, the settlers under Sir Walter Raleigh's patent had named the entire southeastern coast of North America Virginia, after Queen Elizabeth; but in 1614 the name of New England began to be applied to the more northern portion of this immense extent of territory;† and thus it happened that here, on this wild coast, the Pilgrims had a dear home word still wrapped around them.

On the 13th of November, the exiles unshipped their shallop. It was found to want repairs. Sixteen or seventeen days must elapse ere it could be gotten ready for service, so the carpenter said. Impatient of delay, sixteen men, "with every man his musket, sword, and corslet," went ashore, headed by stout Miles Standish, the military leader of the Pilgrims.‡

"Short of stature he was, but strongly built and athletic,
Broad in the shoulders, deep-chested, with muscles and sinews of iron;
Brown as a nut was his face, but his russet beard was already
Flaked with patches of snow, as hedges sometimes in November."§

* "Some have charged that the Dutch bribed the captain to deceive the Pilgrims. Bradford does not mention it, and the Dutch historians deny it.". Elliot, vol. 1, p. 59.
† Uhden, Wilson, Smith's Narrative, etc.
‡ Bradford, Elliot, Bancroft.
§ Longfellow's Courtship of Miles Standish.

"On account of the danger," the expedition "was rather permitted than approved." But Standish and his comrades had braved peril too often to yield it obeisance. They found the shore inexpressibly bleak and barren. Winter had already set his icy kiss upon the streams. Nothing greeted their eyes but heavy sand, a few stunted pines, and some sweet woods, as junipers and sassafras. They made this record in their journal: "We found the greatest store of fowl that ever we saw."*

Explorations were at once commenced. "They sent parties along the coast, and into the forests." "About ten o'clock one morning," says a member of the band, "we came into a deep valley, full of brush, woodgaile, and tiny grass, through which we found little paths or tracks, and then we saw a deer, and found springs of fresh water, of which we were heartily glad, and sat us down and drank our first New England water."† Continuing their march, they were perplexed by the frequent forest cross-paths. Once they struck a track "well nigh ten feet broad," which they thought might lead to some human habitation; but eventually they concluded that it was "only a path made to drive deer in when the Indians hunted."

Still they found no natives; and wearying of that path they took another, when, lo, they saw a mound "which looked like a grave, but was larger." "Musing what it might be," they finally determined to examine. "We found," says the old chronicler,

* Journal of the Pilgrims. † Ibid.

"first a mat, and under that a fair bow, and then another mat, and under that a board about three feet long, finely carved and painted; also between the mats we found bowls, trays, dishes, and such like trinkets. At length we came to a fair new mat, and under that two bundles—one bigger the other less. We opened the greater, and found in it a great quantity of fine and perfect red powder, and the bones and skull of a man. We opened the less bundle, and found the same powder in it, and the bones and head of a little child.

"Once, when examining one of these grave mounds, we found a little old basket full of fair Indian corn, and on digging farther, found a fine, great basket full of very fair corn of this year, with some thirty-six goodly ears of corn, which was a goodly sight; the basket was round and narrow at the top; it held about three or four bushels, which was as much as we could lift from the ground, and it was very handsomely and cunningly made."*

This corn was carefully preserved for seed. "We took it," says the conscientious narrator, "proposing, as soon as we could meet with any of the inhabitants of that place, to make them large satisfaction."† And afterwards this corn was mentioned to Massasoit, the Indian king, when the exiles proffered it back to the owners, and on their refusal of it, paid them in "whatsoever they might rather choose."‡

---

* Journal of the Pilgrims. † Ibid.
‡ Elliot, vol, 1, p. 61.

This exploration was unsuccessful; as was also the first expedition in the shallop, which had been at length repaired. "Some of the people that died that winter took the origin of their death" in this second enterprise; "for it snowed and did blow all the day and night, and froze withal." The men who were from time to time set on shore "were tired with marching up and down the steep hills and deep valleys, which lay half a foot thick with snow."*

Checkered by these adventures, the days passed away, and meantime the winter deepened. Nothing had yet been done, the captain was impatient to be gone, and he threatened to set his passengers ashore at hap-hazard under the cheerless skies and bitter winds of drear December.†

Pushed to renewed exertion by these considerations, the dauntless Pilgrims once more launched their shallop, and quitting their loved ones in the ship, again essayed to find some proper site for a settlement. This time Carver, Bradford, Winslow, and Standish, accompanied by eight sailors, made the coasting voyage.‡ Infinite were the hardships which this little band, sailing in December, in an open boat, were compelled to undergo. "Some of them were like to have swooned with cold." "The water, dashing in spray upon their clothes, froze, and made them like coats of iron." For fifteen leagues they held on their cheerless course upon the winter sea. They had quitted the "Mayflower"

* Bancroft.   † Bradford, Winslow.
‡ Ibid. Young. Elliot Bancroft.

on the 6th of December; two days later they landed. "Whereupon," says the old chronicler, "we espied some Indians, very busy about some black thing; what it was we could not tell, till, afterwards, they saw us, and ran to and fro as if they had been carrying away something." "It was the body of a grampus. Ere long a great cry was heard, and one of the company came running in, shouting 'Indians! Indians!' This was followed by a flight of arrows; but Captain Standish was ready, and quickly discharged his musket; and then another, and another, so that the Indians retreated, and, except for the fright, no harm was done." "The cry of our enemies," remarks the narrator, "was frightful. Their note was after this manner: '*Woath wach haha hach woach*,' sounds which we may now utter with safety—if we can."* This spot was afterwards known as "First Encounter."†

No convenient harbor had yet been found. But "the pilot of the boat, who had been in these regions before, gave assurance of a good one which might be reached before night; and they followed his guidance. After some hours' sailing, a storm of snow and rain began; the sea was swollen; the rudder broke; the boat had to be steered with oars. Every moment the storm increased; night was at hand; to reach harbor before dark, as much sail as possible was crowded on: then the mast broke into three pieces; the sail fell overboard. The pilot, in dismay, would have run the shallop on shore in a

---

* Elliot, vol. 1., pp. 62, 63. † Ibid. Bradford, Young.

cove full of breakers. 'About with her,' shouted a sailor, 'or we are cast away!' They got her about immediately, and, in passing over the surf, they entered a fair sound, and found shelter under the lee of a small rise of land. It was dark, and the rain beat furiously; yet the men were so wet, and cold, and weak, that they slighted the danger to be apprehended from the savages, and going ashore, after great difficulty kindled a fire. Morning, as it dawned, showed the place to be a small island without the entrance of a harbor. Time was precious; the season advancing; their companions were left off Cape Cod in suspense. Yet the day was required for rest and preparation. It was so spent. The following day was the 'Christian Sabbath.' Nothing marks the character of the Pilgrims more fully than that they kept it sacredly though every consideration demanded haste."*

On Monday, the 11th† of December, 1620, the exploring shallop quitted the island Patmos, and, proceeding up the harbor, landed the Pilgrim scouting party, on that same immortal day, at Plymouth Rock. There, in one sense, New England was born; and, as the Forefathers stepped upon the rock-ribbed shore, it uttered its first baby cry, a prayer and a thanksgiving to the Lord—an echo of the old Chaldean shepherds' song, "Glory to God in the highest; on earth peace, good-will to men."

* Bancroft, vol. 1, p. 312.
† According to the new style of reckoning time, it was the 22d of December, now kept as "Forefathers' Day."

CHAPTER VI.

THE PILGRIM SETTLEMENT.

> "Quit ye as men; be true then, who would fight
> In this so holy cause; think ye a soul
> Weighed down by beggarly lusts can have a right
> To urge God's ark of freedom to its goal?
> They must be holy who're ordained to be
> The high priests of a people's liberty."
>
> WILSON.

A SHORT survey of the surrounding country convinced the Pilgrim pioneers that the long-sought spot had at last been found. They determined to plant their settlement on Plymouth Rock, with no other seal than the broad one of the Divine sanction. Entering their shallop, they soon regained the "Mayflower." Carver recited the story of their adventures to the clustering voyagers; and when he said that a spot had been found where they might erect their Ebenezer, devoutly all thanked God.

At once the "Mayflower's" course was shaped for Plymouth harbor, where she dropped anchor on the 16th of December.* The first law on the Pilgrim statute-book was, that each man should build his own house.†

A few days after the arrival of the ship, "a party of colonists went ashore to fell timber, to saw, to rive, to carry, and prepare for the impor-

---

* Bradford, Winslow. † Ibid., Elliot, Bancroft.

THE PILGRIM SETTLEMENT. 91

tant work of building; and that day every man worked with a will, hopefully and heartily. A new home, a pleasant refuge, future security, was the aim of every one, and while each cheered the other, the axes rang out in harmony with their hopes; their strokes were as heavy as their hearts were light. The crowned oaks of the forest did homage, and yielded their riches to found the infant state." After sufficient timber had been secured for present want, "many went to work on an adjacent hill* to prepare fortifications; others measured the land, and allotted the lots for building."†

The houses were ranged in a double row along one street ;‡ and for economic reasons the community was divided into nineteen families, an arrangement which necessitated fewer buildings and less outlay.§ Yet despite the energetic labors of the settlers, they made haste slowly. At that inclement season it was almost impossible to build. Happily the weather was moderate for December ;‖ but rain fell incessantly, which was disastrous to the health of men already wasting away under consumptions and lung-fevers.¶ It was remembered that "a green Christmas makes a fat church-yard."

The Pilgrims were well satisfied with the site of their settlement, hard and sterile as it was. Indeed, they had a devout habit of looking on the good, rather than the evil of events, and this made

---

* Fort Hill, now Burial Hill. † Elliot, vol. 1, p. 66.
‡ Now called Leyden-street.
§ Elliot, Bradford, Young's Chronicles.
‖ Journal of the Pilgrims. ¶ Ibid., Bancroft.

even their crosses easier to be borne. "This harbor," they said, "is a bay greater than Cape Cod, compassed with goodly land; and in the bay are two fine islands,* uninhabited, wherein are nothing but woods, oaks, pines, walnuts, beech, sassafras, vines, and other trees which we know not. The bay is a most hopeful place, and has innumerable store of fowl and excellent food; it cannot but contain fish in their seasons; skate, cod, turbot, and herring, we have tasted of. Here is abundance of muscles, the greatest and best we ever saw, also crabs and lobsters in their time, infinite. The place is in fashion like a sickle or fish-hook. The land for the crust of the earth is a spit's depth, excellent black mould, and fat in many places; and vines are everywhere, and cherry-trees, plum-trees, and many others whose names we know not. Many kinds of herbs we find in winter hereabouts, as strawberry-leaves innumerable, sorrel, yarrow, carrot, brooklime, liverwort, water-cresses, great store of leeks, and an excellent strong kind of flax or hemp. Here is sand, gravel, an excellent clay, no better in the world, exceeding good for pots, and it will wash like soap; we have the best water that ever we drank, and the brooks will soon be full of fish."†

So runs the journal of the Pilgrims. Hopeful and thankful for what they had, they seemed anxious to be pleased, and to make the best even of

---

* One of these was Clarke's Island; the other was probably Saquish Peninsula.
† Young's Chronicles. Journal of the Pilgrims

their ills. It was in no sour and bitter spirit that they

> "Leaned their cheeks against the thick-ribbed ice,
> And looked up with devout eyes to Him
> Who bade them bloom, unblanched, amid the waste
> Of desolation."

After all, perhaps it was well even for their present safety that they had landed on the bleak New England strand. "Had they been carried, according to their desire, unto Hudson's river," says Cotton Mather, "the Indians in those parts were at this time so many and so mighty and so sturdy, that in probability all this feeble number of Christians had been massacred by the bloody savages, as not long after some others were; whereas the good hand of God now brought them to a country wonderfully prepared for their entertainment by a sweeping mortality that had lately been among the natives. 'We have heard with our ears, O God, our fathers have told us, what work thou didst in their days, in the times of old; how thou dravest out the heathen with thy hand, and plantedst them; how thou didst afflict the people, and cast them out.' The Indians in these parts had newly, even about a year or two before, been visited with such a prodigious pestilence, as carried away not a tenth, but nine parts of ten; yea, 't is said, nineteen of twenty among them; so that the woods were almost cleared to make room for a better growth.

"It is remarkable that a Frenchman, who, not long before the Pilgrim settlement, had by a shipwreck been made captive among the Indians of New England, did, as the survivors report, just before he died in their hands, tell these tawny pagans that 'God, being angry with them for their wickedness, would not only destroy them all, but also people the place with another nation, which would not live after their brutish manner.' Those infidels then blasphemously said, 'God could not kill them,' which was confuted by a horrible and unusual plague, whereby they were consumed in such vast multitudes, that our first ancestors found the land almost covered with their unburied carcasses; and they that were alive were smitten into awful and humble regard of the English by the terrors which the remembrance of the Frenchman's prophecy had imprinted on them."*

During the first few months of their wilderness life, little occurred of special public interest among the Pilgrims. The routine of their days was undisturbed. Engrossed by the pressing present duties of the hour, they labored to complete their preparations for the winter. Their existence was that which is common in all pioneer settlements, which has been led a thousand times since on our western prairies, and which is led to-day by the settler who rears his log-cabin under the shadow of the Rocky mountains.

The country seemed lonely and monotonous.†
"Among the few recorded incidents," says Elliot,

* Cotton Mather, Magnalia, vol. 1, p. 51.
† Ibid., Elliot, Felt.

" we gather here and there some facts which serve to illustrate the social and moral condition of the exiles during these initial months of their western life. On the 21st of January, 1621, they celebrated public worship for the first time on shore. On the 17th of February, Standish was chosen captain, and all were arranged in military orders. This may be called their first legislative act, the first communal life of men who believed in and were forced to act out the principle of self-government; every man could vote, and the ballot of the lowest colonist counted the same as Governor Carver's. Births and deaths varied the monotony of existence. Peregrine White, the first born in New England, had appeared in November, and six persons had died in December, among whom was Dorothy, Bradford's wife, who was drowned. This was the beginning of a mortality which carried dismay and destruction into the weakened ranks."*

Measures were taken for the military protection of the colony. "A minion, a saker, and two other guns, were mounted on Fort Hill," where a block-citadel had been erected.† Standish was the *beau ideal* of a soldier—alert, provident, tireless. The words which Longfellow has put into his mouth exhibit his genial humor and quaint wisdom:

" 'Serve yourself, would you be well served, is an excellent adage;
So I take care of my arms, as scribes of their pens and their ink-horns.

* Elliot, p. 67.
† Ibid. Journal of the Pilgrims. Young, Bradford.

> Then, too, there are my soldiers, my great, invincible army,
> Twelve men, all equipped, having each his rest and his matchlock,
> Eighteen shillings a month, together with diet and pillage,
> And, like Cæsar, I know the name of each of my soldiers.'
> This he said with a smile, that danced in his eyes, as the sunbeams
> Dance on the waves of the sea, and vanish again in a moment."*

The peculiar situation of the Pilgrims tended to increase that rugged individuality, that self-confident earnestness, that somewhat dogmatic vigor, which already characterized them, and which is still a salient trait of their descendants. There they stood on a bleak and desolate shore; bereaved of sympathy at home, without friends in the wilderness, "with none to show them kindness or to bid them welcome." The nearest French settlement was at Port Royal; it was five hundred miles and more of trackless forest to the English plantation of Virginia.† The exiles were obliged to be self-centred; cut off from the outer world and isolated, they could entertain no friends but God and each other.

We can hardly be sufficiently thankful for the singular combination of circumstances which produced the Plymouth settlement in 1620. "Had New England been colonized immediately on the discovery of the American continent, the old English institutions would have been planted under the powerful influence of the Roman religion; had the settlement been made under Elizabeth, it would

* Longfellow's Miles Standish, p. 11.
† Bancroft, vol. 1, p. 310.

have been before activity of the public mind in religion had conducted to a corresponding activity of mind in politics." God builded better than men knew; and when the time was ripe, he chose "the Pilgrims, Englishmen, Protestants, exiles for religion, men disciplined by misfortune, cultivated by opportunities of extensive observation, equal in rank as in rights, bound by no code but that of religion and the public will,"* and with these elements He planted a model state, and bade it grow into a democratic, Christian commonwealth, that it might be at once an exemplar and a benefactor to mankind.

The Pilgrims cheerfully accepted peril and discomfort to build such a state. Peace under liberty—*sub libertate quietem*—this was their aspiration, and they said,

> "We ask a shrine for faith and simple prayer,
> Freedom's sweet waters, and untainted air."†

* Bancroft, vol. 1, p. 308.
† "Exiguam sedem sacris, litusque rogamus
Innocuum, et cunctis undamque; auramque; patentem."
· Cotton Mather, Magnalia, vol. 1, p. 52.

CHAPTER VII.

PIONEER LIFE.

> "E'en the best must own,
> Patience and resignation are the pillars
> Of human peace on earth."
>
> Young, *Night Thoughts.*

HAPPILY, God blessed the Pilgrims with an early and mild spring.* By the middle of March the birds began to sing; the streams shook off their icy cerements; the rills ran laughing to the sea; Nature put on her gala drapery; the myriad wild flowers opened their drowsy eyes; the time had come for the ever-marvellous resurrection of the year. The forests seemed instinct with life. On every hill-side nature hymned her praise.

The settlers shared in the buoyant and joyous feeling. They had met and mastered the New England winter. Their houses were built. Their family arrangements were completed; and now "the fair, warm days" of spring, the idyl of the year, were a harbinger of hope.

Careful and provident, the Pilgrims improved this delightful weather in planting. "On the 19th and 20th of March," says the old chronicler, "we digged our grounds and sowed our garden-seed."† This done, individual members of the community

---

* Bancroft, Banvard, Elliot, Felt.
† Journal of the Pilgrims.

began to stray into the bordering forest, incited thereto partly by natural curiosity to familiarize themselves with the salient local features of their wilderness homes, and partly by the pursuit of game. Sometimes the tyro hunters were startled by strange sights and noises; for to them the dim, still woods were a mystery. "John Goodman was much frightened this day"—so runs the entry in the Journal on one occasion—"he went abroad for a little walk with his spaniel. Suddenly two great wolves ran after the dog, which ran to him and betwixt his legs for succor. He, having nothing with him, threw a stick at one of them, and hit him, and they presently both ran away; but they came again. He got a plain board in his hand, and they sat both on their tails grinning at him a good time. At last they went their way and left him. He could not move fast, as he had lame feet."*

On another occasion a storm is recorded: "At one o'clock it thundered. The birds sang most pleasantly before this. The thunder was strong, and in great claps, followed by rain very sadly till midnight."†

Thus far they had seen no Indians since landing at Plymouth. Traces of them abounded. Pale wreaths of smoke, which curled above the forest-trees, gave certain token that they lurked in the vicinity. The settlers knew that they must ere long meet the aborigines, and they awaited the event with mingled hope and apprehension.

* Young's Chron. of the Pilg's. Pilgrims' Jour.   † Ibid.

On the 16th of March, one of the warmest, pleasantest days of the early spring, a number of the Pilgrims—Bradford, Winslow, Hopkins, and Carver, among the rest—were gathered on the skirts of the settlement, chatting over their plans and projects for the coming days, when suddenly a guttural shout was heard, and the words "*Welcome, Englishmen!*" spoken in broken Saxon, fell on their ears.*

The astonished settlers started to their feet, and glancing in the direction whence the words had seemed to come, discerned on the edge of the forest a single dusky figure, waving a hand and advancing boldly towards them. In deep silence the Pilgrims awaited his approach. On reaching the group, the Indian greeted them warmly, repeating his welcome. Reassured by his friendly gestures and hearty repetition of the familiar English phrase in which only kindness lurked, the settlers cordially returned his greeting; and knowing that the way to the heart lies through the stomach, they at once gave their dusky guest "strong water, biscuit, butter, cheese, and some pudding, with a piece of mallard."†

The heart of the savage was gained; the taciturnity characteristic of his race gave way, and he told his entertainers many things which they had long desired to know.

They ascertained that he was a chief of a tribe of Indians whose hunting-grounds were distant five days' journey; that the country in their vicinity was called Pawtuxet; that some years previous a pesti-

* Bradford, Young, Pilgrims' Journal. † Ibid.

lence had swept off the tribes that inhabited the district, so that none remained to claim the soil.

When asked how he came to speak English, he replied that he had picked up what little he knew from the fishermen who frequented the coast of Maine. In response to inquiries concerning the interior of the country and the tribes inhabiting the inland plateaus, he imparted valuable information.*

The Pilgrims gleaned these facts from his recital: A sagamore named Massasoit was their nearest powerful neighbor. He was disposed to be friendly; but another tribe, called the Nausets, were greatly incensed against the English, and with sufficient cause. It seems that a captain by the name of Hunt, who had been left in charge of a vessel by Captain Smith in 1614, had lured twenty or thirty of their brother red men on board his ship on pretence of trading; then, when they accepted his invitation, he set sail for Spain, where he sold his victims into slavery.†

The whole Nauset tribe panted to avenge the atrocious treachery of "this wretched man, who cared not what mischief he did for his profit;" and it was with them that the Pilgrims had had their skirmish when exploring the coast in the December sleet.‡

The Indian from whose broken English these things were learned was Samoset. He was the first of the aborigines who held friendly and intelligent

* Bradford, Young. † Ibid. Pilgrims' Journal. ‡ Ibid.

intercourse with the forefathers. His frank, hearty "welcome" was the only one the Pilgrims received; and his faithful, life-long attachment to the English interests, which "made him often go, in danger of his life, among his countrymen," won the grateful recognition of the exiles, and deserves the plaudits of posterity.

Samoset was the first Indian whom many of the Pilgrims had ever seen. He was therefore scanned with no little curiosity. He is thus described in the Journal of the Pilgrims: "He was a man free in speech; a tall, straight man; the hair of his head black, long behind, short before, and no beard. He was stark naked, save only a strip of leather about his waist, with a fringe a span long or a little more. He had a bow and two arrows, the one headed, the other not."*

The settlers treated Samoset with great hospitality, as duty and sound policy alike demanded. Nevertheless, when night came they desired him to leave. This he seemed loath to do. They proposed that he should lodge on board the "Mayflower." He assented; but the tide was so low and the wind was so fresh, that the shallop could not gain the vessel's side. Nothing remained but to entertain their guest on shore. He was conducted to the house of Stephen Hopkins,† and was stealthily watched, "as we feared evil," comments the narrator; "which, however, did not come."‡

* Pilgrims' Journal.   † Elliot, vol. 1, p. 71.
‡ Pilgrims' Journal.

On the following morning, Samoset quitted Plymouth, carrying with him a variety of presents, a knife, a bracelet, a ring; and he promised to return soon and bring with him some of Massasoit's Indians, to open a trade in furs with the colonists.* He also said that he would do his utmost towards securing an interview between the English and the Indian sagamore, as preliminary to a lasting treaty and a prosperous peace.†

Samoset, true to his promise, did indeed return within three days, bringing with him five companions. All were cordially welcomed; but as it was Sunday, no business was transacted, the guests being dismissed as early as possible. Samoset remained at Plymouth; his friends affirmed their purpose to come again on the morrow. The morrow came but the Indians did not. Samoset was sent in quest of them. The next day he returned again, this time with four other warriors, each provided with a few skins and dried herrings, which they were anxious to barter.

One of these Indians was named Squanto. His history was somewhat romantic. He belonged to the company kidnapped by Hunt and sold in Spain. There he, with the others, had been liberated through the exertions of the monks of Malaga, and he had made his way to England. He dwelt in Cornhill, London, with an English merchant, for some time; and thence he had finally made his way back to his forest home, to be, as the event

* Bradford, Young. † Ibid. Banvard.

proved, a valuable friend, interpreter, and ally to the whites.*

Samoset and his friends were but the advance guard of a larger host. An hour later, Massasoit himself appeared on a neighboring slope, accompanied by his brother, Quadequina, and a cloud of warriors. At the outset both Englishman and Indian were shy of each other; but at last, after much passing to and fro, they came to parley. Massasoit and Standish saluted each other; after which the soldier conducted the sachem to an unfinished house in the vicinage, where he laid for his guest a green rug and four cushions.†

Presently the Pilgrim governor advanced, in as great state as he could command, with beat of drum and blare of trumpet, and a squad of armed men as a body-guard. Salutations, which consisted of mutual kisses, being over, the governor and the sagamore seated themselves. Meat was then served, and the new friends drank to each other's health and happiness.‡

* Bancroft, Elliot, Banvard.
† Bradford, Pilgrims' Journal.
"On the 22d of March, the first interview took place between the Pilgrims and the Indians, with their great chief Massasoit, Squanto acting as interpreter. This was conducted becomingly on both sides, and according to the manner of the time. After Gov. Carver had drunk some 'strong water'—rum—to the sachem, Massasoit 'drunk a great draught that made him sweat all the while after.' The result of the conference was an alliance, offensive and defensive, between the governor and the chief, applauded by the followers of both, and Massasoit was received as an ally of the dread King James." Elliot, vol. 1, p. 72.
‡ Young's Chronicles, Pilgrims' Journal.

Negotiations ensued; and "a treaty of friendship was soon completed in few and unequivocal terms. The respective parties promised to abstain from mutual injuries, and to deliver up offenders; the colonists were to receive assistance if attacked; to render it, if Massasoit should be assailed unjustly. The treaty included the confederates of the sachem: it is the oldest act of diplomacy recorded in New England; it was concluded in a day, and, being founded on reciprocal interests, was sacredly kept for more than half a century. Massasoit desired the alliance, for the powerful Narragansetts were his enemies; his tribe, moreover, having become habituated to some English luxuries, were willing to establish a traffic; while the emigrants obtained peace, security, and the opportunity of a lucrative commerce."*

Massasoit is thus described by the Pilgrim journalist: "In his person he is a very lusty man, in his best years, an able body, grave of countenance, and spare of speech; in his attire little or nothing differing from the rest of his followers, save only in a great chain of white beads about his neck; behind his neck, attached to the chain, hangs a pouch of tobacco, which he smoked, and gave us to smoke. His face was painted with a seal red, and he was oiled both head and face that he looked greasily."†

The sagamore's favorite haunts were along the northern shores of Narragansett Bay, between

* Bancroft, p. 317.   † Pilgrims' Journal, p. 58.

Taunton and Providence, one of his principal seats being Mount Hope,* that

> ———"throne of royal state, which far
> Outshone the wealth of Ormus or of Ind,
> Or where the gorgeous east, with richest hand,
> Showers on her kings barbaric pomp and gold."

In the latter part of March, 1621, an event occurred which evinced alike the promptitude and the decision of the self-governed Puritan colony. It has been said that "God sifted three kingdoms to get the Pilgrim wheat" of the New England enterprise; yet despite this care the chaff was not all gotten rid of. It seems that one John Billington, a "lewd fellow of the baser sort," had come from London and smuggled himself on board the "Mayflower," for the purpose of stealing a voyage to the new world. He had no sympathy with the religious feelings of the Pilgrims, nor did he share their love of order and civil liberty.† He had frequently given offence, and now he was convicted of "contempt of the captain's lawful command, and of making opprobious speeches."‡ His sentence was peculiar: "he was to have his neck and heels tied together."§ He begged so hard that he was forgiven on this occasion; but he continued to be a profane, ungovernable, vicious knave, and finally came to a bad end.

At about this same time another offence was committed against the civil peace of the colony. Two servants of Stephen Hopkins met and fought

---

* Elliot, p. 73.　　† Bancroft, Pilgrims' Journal.
‡ Ibid.　　§ Ibid.

a duel with sword and dagger. Both combatants were wounded; but they were immediately seized, convicted, and sentenced "to have their head and feet tied together, and so to lie for twenty-four hours without meat or drink."*

The hostile lackeys were bound, in exact accordance with the verdict; but "after lying an hour they begged piteously for mercy; whereon the governor, on the entreaty of their master, released them, they promising to keep the peace in future."†

These sentences convinced the refractory that the colonial government was something more than the shadow of a name; and it held them in awe of provoking its severity.

Through all these months disease was busy among the Pilgrims. But though pain racked many a weakened form, no one spoke of returning to England. As winter faded into spring the mortality became dreadful. Every house was a hospital.

> "There was no hearthstone, howsoe'er defended,
> But had one vacant chair."

"Death," says Elliot, "had reaped a ripe, fat harvest, and of the one hundred scarce fifty remained. Six had died in December; eight in January; seventeen in February; thirteen in March."‡ Yet the Pilgrims kissed the rod; and though "the searching sharpness of that pure climate had crept into the crevices of their crazed bodies, causing death,"§ they said "the Lord gave and the

* Pilgrims' Journal, † Banvard.
‡ Elliot, p. 74. § Bradford's Journal.

Lord hath taken away; blessed be the name of the Lord."

The dead were buried in a bank, at a little distance from Plymouth rock; and lest the Indians should learn the weakened condition of the colony, the graves were levelled, and sown with grass.* Over these the unflinching survivors locked hands, and wiping their eyes, looked up, firm, devout, hopeful as ever.

In April, 1621, Governor Carver died. "Whilst they were busy about their seed, he came out of the field very sick, it being a hot day. He complained greatly of his head, and lay down; within a few hours his senses failed, and he never spoke more. His death was much lamented, and caused great heaviness, as there was cause."† Shortly after, William Bradford, the historian of the colony, was elected governor, "and being not yet recovered from a severe illness, in which he had been near the point of death, Isaac Allerton was chosen to be an assistant unto him."‡

On the very day of Carver's death, the 5th of April, the "Mayflower" sailed for England.§ Not a soul returned in her of that devoted band. It has been well said that the departure of the "Mayflower" surpasses in dignity, though not in desperation, the burning of his ships by Cortez. Through the struggles of the winter she had always been in

---

* Holmes' Annals, Thatcher's Plymouth, p. 37.
† Bradford, Hist. Plymouth Plantation, p. 101.
‡ Ibid.　　　　　　　§ Holmes, Thatcher, Elliot, etc.

sight, a place of refuge and relief in any desperate emergency. While the good ship lay moored in Plymouth harbor, they had a hold upon the outer world. But now, as grouped upon the shore they stood and watched her, as she slowly spread her sails and crept out of the bay and from their sight, they felt inexpressibly dreary and bereaved: when the sun set in the western forest, the "Mayflower" had disappeared in the distant blue.*

> "Can ye scan the woe
> That wrings their bosoms, as this last frail link
> Binding to man and habitable earth
> Is severed.? Can ye tell what pangs were there,
> What keen regrets, what sickness of the heart,
> What yearning o'er their forfeit land of birth;
> Their distant dear ones?"†

But they did not long despair. "The sky was not inky, nor their future desperate," says Elliot; "the sun still shone gloriously; the moon still bathed the earth with light; and the stars kept their ceaseless vigils. Spring here, as of old, followed winter, the murmuring of streams was heard, and the song of the turtle; birds builded their nests, the tender grass sprang up under their feet, and the trees budded and burst forth in wondrous beauty. God was over all—God, their God, their Friend—their protector here as in the older world; nay, more their helper now than ever before,"‡ for they were the orphans of humanity.

* Elliot, p. 75.   † Sigourney.   ‡ Elliot, ut antea.

CHAPTER VIII.

THE FIRST SUMMER IN NEW ENGLAND.

"The spring's gay promise melted into thee,
   Fair summer; and thy gentle reign is here;
Thy emerald robes are on each leafy tree;
   In the blue sky thy voice is rich and clear;
And the free brooks have songs to bless thy reign—
They leap in music 'midst thy bright domain."
Willis G. Clark.

God has transmuted the primal curse into a blessing. Labor is a panacea for many ills; and now the fullness of their new life crowded out homesickness and all fainting of the heart among the Pilgrim exiles. They had no time for dreams. The weighty cares of the present exorcised every fevered phantom of regret and apprehension.

Swiftly and pleasantly in the manifold employments of the field passed the glowing, pregnant spring. The exiles knew that they were set to subdue the wilderness, to marry the continent with roads, to dot the forests with schools and churches and hamlets. Daily and nightly they invoked God's blessing on their infant colony; and with God's kiss upon their brows, they toiled in the full assurance of success—they knew that hope would be changed to full fruition.

Thus far they had experienced no lack of food. The variety afforded by wild fowl, fish, and the native fruits, together with the stores which they had brought with them in the "Mayflower," amply sufficed to supply the cravings of hunger.* For the future the presage was good. The crops promised well. Six acres had been sown with pease and barley. Twenty acres had been planted with the seed-corn which it had been the good fortune of the exiles to dig out of the subterranean Indian store-houses;† this Squanto, the friendly Indian interpreter, had instructed them how to sow and hill and manure with fish.‡

> "Like the swell of some sweet tune,
> Morning rises into noon,
> May glides onward into June;"

and as the season advanced, native grapes and berries were found in endless variety and inexhaustible abundance. The Pilgrim journalist also records that wild-flowers of various hues and "very sweet" fragrance contributed their beauty and incense to the charming summer scene.§

"A visitor to Plymouth, in this first summer of the Puritan settlement, as he landed on the southern side of a high bluff, would have seen, standing between it and a rapid little stream, a rude log-house, twenty feet square, containing the common property of the plantation. Proceeding up a gentle acclivity between two rows of log-cabins, nineteen in number, some of them perhaps vacant since the

---

* Bradford, Young, Thatcher.
† Pilgrims' Journal. Winslow. ‡ Ibid.
§ Pilgrims' Journal.

death of their first tenants, he would have come to a hill, encircled by a plank platform for cannon. And glancing thence over the landscape, he might have counted twenty men at work with hoes in the enclosures about the huts, or fishing in the shallow harbor, or visiting the woods or the beach for game; while six or eight women were busy in household affairs, and some twenty children, from infancy upward, completed the domestic picture."*

The month of June found the colonists so far advanced in the necessary labors of the season, that they gained a little leisure to open the volume of local nature, and to scan its pages more accurately than had been possible in the haste of the initial December days.

Many a lesson was taken by the wondering settlers in New England forestry under the skilful tuition of Squanto or Samoset. "Once," says the quaint old record, "a party of us got belated in the forest, where the night was spent; in the morning, wandering from the track, we were shrewdly puzzled, and lost the way. As we wandered, we came to a tree, where a young sprit was bowed down over a bow, and some acorns strewed underneath; Stephen Hopkins said it had been fixed to catch deer; so as we were looking at it, William Bradford being in the rear, when he came up looked also upon it, and as he went about, it gave a sudden jerk up, so that he was immediately caught fast by the leg. It was a very pretty device, made with a rope of

* Palfrey, Hist. New England, vol. 1, p. 182.

their own making, and having a noose as artificially fixed as any roper in England could make, and as like ours as can be: this we brought away with us."* This was a pleasant jest to the hunters, in which the gravest of them doubtless indulged in a laugh at their too curious governor, thus caught in the Indian deer-trap. The hint, however, was well worth their study; and often afterwards it served them a good turn, ere their ringing axes frightened the timid deer into following the dusky native hunters beyond the encroaching and ever-widening circle of civilization.

To increase the general stock of information, and to relieve the routine *tedium* of the settlement, several expeditions were planned during this first summer; and these looked into the continent a few miles distant in the east, the north, and the west.†

The first of them took the shape of an embassy to Massasoit. As the warm weather brought the Indians to the seashore in search of lobsters and to fish, they proved to be a sad annoyance to the colonists. They were treated with uniform courtesy, and this kindness furnished a motive for frequent visits, so that men, women, and children, were always hanging about the village, clamorous for food and pertinaciously inquisitive. It was partly to abate this nuisance, and "partly," says the old chronicle, "to know where to find our savage allies, if occasion served, as also to see their strength, explore the country, make satisfaction for some inju-

* Pilgrims' Journal.   † Palfrey, vol. 1, p. 182.

ries conceived to have been done on our parts, and to continue the league of peace and friendship between them and us,"* that Stephen Hopkins and Edward Winslow were now delegated to wait upon the friendly sagamore in his forest home.

In July, 1621, these earliest negotiators of New England set out upon their mission, "not with the pomp of modern diplomats, but through the forest and on foot, to be received, not to the luxuries of courts, but to share in the abstinence of savage life." Marks of the devastation caused by the pestilence which had preceded their settlement, of "the arrows that flew by night," were visible wherever the envoys went, and they witnessed the extreme poverty and feebleness of the aborigines.†

On, on pressed the Englishmen through the intricate mazes of the woods, and they never ceased to wonder at the ease and certainty with which Squanto, who accompanied them as guide and interpreter, picked out the right path from the labyrinthine tracks.‡ A walk of fifteen miles brought them to an almost "deserted village," called *Namasket*, in what is now Middleborough, where the few remaining natives received them with the most gracious rites of Indian hospitality, and gave them "a kind of bread," and the spawn of shad boiled with old acorns.§ Here they tarried for an hour in the afternoon. Eight miles farther inland they bivouacked, with the sky for a covering and the trees

* Pilgrims' Journal. † Bancroft, vol. 1, pp. 317, 318.
‡ Chronicles of the Pilgrims. § Ibid., Palfrey.

for blankets. A number of Indians had assembled at this place to fish, but these had erected no shelter. Around them they discerned under the moonlight the evident marks of former extensive cultivation. "Thousands of men had lived there," says Winslow, the historian of the mission, "who died in the great plague not long since."*

In the morning, rising early, they resumed their journey. Their retinue was swollen by six savages who insisted upon bearing them company, and who bore their arms and baggage. At the various fords the friendly red men carried the Englishmen across dry-shod upon their shoulders,† a mark of unprecedented complaisance when coming from the proverbially lazy Indian of the northeast coast.

In due time the envoys reached Pokanoket, the residence of Massasoit. The sachem was not at home. Ere long, however, he returned. The Englishmen received him royally, and saluted him by a discharge of their muskets. Massasoit reciprocated their greeting in true Indian style.‡

The Pilgrims had been careful to provide their envoys with a plentiful supply of those trinkets which the red men so highly prized; and now, ere any business was opened, these presents were delivered. The sagamore was given "a horseman's coat of red cotton, decked with a slight fringe of lace," and a copper chain. When he had put on this scarlet garment, and hung the chain about his

---

* Winslow in Chronicles of the Pilgrims, p. 201.
† Ibid.   ‡ Ibid.

neck, he seemed greatly pleased by his unwonted bravery of attire, while his warriors appeared to be equally gratified by the grand appearance of their king.*

This ceremony completed, all squatted upon the ground, a circle was formed, and amid deep silence the pipe of peace was smoked, each individual taking a whiff and then passing the pipe to his next neighbor. After this—and it should seem that even among the untamed children of the forest there existed a "circumlocution office," where there was red tape to be cut—the envoys explained the object of their visit. The sagamore listened courteously to their recital, and was pleased to grant each and all of their requests.

"To the end that we might know his messengers from others," writes Winslow, "we desired Massasoit, if any one should come from him to us, to send the copper chain, that we might know the savage, and hearken and give credit to his message accordingly."†

The sagamore seemed well content to renew the alliance with the English. He promised to promote the traffic in skins, to furnish a supply of corn for seed, and to ascertain the owners of the underground granaries which the conscientious Pilgrims had rifled in the preceding winter, and for which they were anxious to make restitution.‡ He also

---

* Winslow in Chronicles of the Pilgrims, p. 201. Banvard, Wilson. † Chronicles of the Pilgrims.
‡ Ibid. Palfrey, vol. 1, p. 184.

warned his allies to beware of the Narragansetts, a powerful and warlike tribe, inimical to him, seated on the borders and in the vicinity of Narragansett Bay.* Massasoit said that the Narragansett warriors had not been thinned by the pestilence, and that they carried on an extensive trade with the Dutchmen in the west.†

Having thus by skilful diplomacy reduced the future political intercourse between the nascent New England republic and the Indian sachem to some degree of certainty and mutual confidence, the ambassadors remained to partake of the hospitality of the forest lords.

They did not think very highly of Massasoit's housekeeping. The brave sagamore chanced to be out of provisions, so his guests were obliged to go supperless. When they expressed a wish to sleep, they were conducted into a wigwam, and, as a mark of special honor, allowed to sleep in the same bed with the sachem and his squaw—one end of a hard, rude-looking bed, covered with a coarse, thin mat, and raised three or four inches above the earthern floor, being assigned to them, while their Indian majesties reposed at the other extremity.‡ Like other royal favors, this proved somewhat irksome to the recipients, who had to complain of very straitened accommodation, and record that they "were worse weary of their lodgings than of their journey."§

* Chronicles of the Pilgrims. Mount, Journal, p. 45.
† Ibid. ‡ Wilson, p. 386. § Ibid. Pilgrims' Journal.

The next day the colonial ambassadors had **no** breakfast, but the morning was taken up in receiving visitors—rumors of their presence having collected several subordinate sachems to do them honor and cement a friendship—and in witnessing the Indian games, which had been gotten up for their entertainment.*

About noon, Massasoit, who had gone hunting at dawn, returned, bringing with him two fishes; these were soon boiled and divided among forty persons;† this was the first meal taken by the envoys for a day and two nights.‡

Heartily sick of Indian entertainment, in the gray dawn of the following day they set out for Plymouth. The chief was sorry and ashamed that he had been able to receive them in no better style; but while friendship was in his heart, abundance was not in his cabin.§ After a dismal and stormy jaunt, they reached the welcome settlement on the fifth day of their absence. Hard and uncouth as it was, after their recent experience, it seemed to them an elysium. So severe had been the hardships incident to their mission, so faint and giddy were they from hunger and want of sleep and over-exertion, that several days' repose was required to recruit them back to health and strength.‖

In the course of the excursion just happily

---

* Banvard. Chronicles of the Pilgrims.
† Palfrey, vol. 1, p. 184. Banvard, p. 55. Wilson, p. 386.
‡ Chronicles of the Pilgrims. Mount, Journal, p. 47.
§ Banvard, Plymouth and the Pilgrims, p. 55.
‖ Mount, Journal. Chronicles, etc.

ended, the Pilgrims had acquired considerable knowledge of their Indian neighbors—of their habits, their motives of action, their social forms. They saw that rivalry, and enmity begotten of rivalry, stirred constant feuds among the tribes by whom they were surrounded. The sight of a strange Indian never failed to fill their dusky guides with alarm and watchfulness; among the red men, in the most literal sense, "eternal vigilance" was "the price of liberty."*

The first settlers of Plymouth generally dealt honorably and amicably with their Indian allies, more so than the later colonists of New England, as the treaty with Massasoit, unbroken for fifty years, amply proves. Trade was of course an object with them; but it was not selfishly paramount. This fair dealing begot in its turn corresponding friendship and good feeling among the red men; it put kindliness into their hearts at a time when a revengeful temper might have led them to combine and sweep the feeble handful of usurping interlopers, weakened by disease and decimated by death, into the Atlantic on whose verge they stood.

We can never be sufficiently thankful that God moved both colonists and savages to cement so long and fair a peace. Yet from the very outset the Indian recognized the superiority of the white man; he made a reluctant yet irrepressible obeisance to civilization. Dryden has well expressed this innate consciousness:

* Wilson.

> "Old prophecies foretell our fall at hand,
> When bearded men in floating castles land."

The sagamore, as he gazed on the Plymouth settlement, stood grief-stricken to think that his lease of ages of the forests approached its end. He seemed to see in the recent plague a grant of the land to another race, engrossed by the hand of the Great Spirit himself. That rifled burial-mound of the Wampanoags, in which the Pilgrims found their seed-corn, was typical; it was the new tenant entering upon the estate, taking possession in the name of God, and for the common good. Yet

> " Who shall deem the spot unblessed
> Where Nature's younger children rest,
> Lulled on their sorrowing mother's breast?
> Deem ye that mother loveth less
> These bronzed forms of the wilderness
> She foldeth in her long caress?
> As sweet o'er them her wild-flowers blow,
> As if with fairer hair and brow
> The blue-eyed Saxon slept below."*

* Whittier, Ballads and other Poems.

CHAPTER IX.

IN THE WOODS.

"Actions rare and sudden, do commonly
Proceed from fierce necessity."
              SIR WILLIAM DAVENANT.

Two or three days after the return of Winslow and Hopkins from Massasoit's forest rendezvous, the routine life of the colonists was broken by the sudden disappearance of one of the younger members of the Plymouth commonwealth. John Billington was nowhere to be found. Though he was a vicious lad, the pest of the colony, his absence caused great anxiety. Whither had he gone? Was he drowned? Had he been kidnapped? Had he wandered away and lost his course in the tangled cross-paths of the forest?

Though the season, already declining towards autumn, called for the active labor of the settlers, the supposed peril of the lost boy swallowed up all other considerations, and a squad of ten men was recruited to go in search of him.* The clumsy shallop was rigged, and, led by Standish, all embarked. They had not sailed far ere a sudden squall, accompanied by a severe thunderstorm, peculiar to the season and the latitude, struck them,

---
* Pilgrims' Journal, Palfrey, Bradford.

as it were, with clenched fists. A water-spout, the first they had ever seen, flung up the hissing sea to a sheer height of fifty feet within a stone's toss of the shallop, already half capsized.* Drenched and weary, they landed in Cummaquid, now Barnstable harbor, where they bivouacked.† Here an Indian runner, despatched by Massasoit, met them, and said that the lad they sought might be found at Nauset, some miles farther down the coast. In the morning, as they were about to embark, they espied two Indians, strangers, whom they hailed. Squanto and another friendly sachem named Tokamahamon were with the scouting party, and they now acted as interpreters. These natives corroborated Massasoit's report of the whereabouts of young Billington; and at their invitation, six of the Englishmen accompanied them to an interview with their chief, Iyanough, who lurked in the vicinity. When they met the sagamore, they found him to be a handsome man, in the May of youth, courteous in his manners, and unlike an Indian save in his costume.‡ The entertainment to which he invited his pale-face guests was in harmony with his decorous appearance, being various and abundant.§

While they were feasting, they saw an old, withered squaw, who seemed bowed down beneath the weight of a hundred years, hobbling eagerly tow-

---

* Banvard, p. 56. Prince; Mount in Young, pp. 214–218.
† Mount in Young. Banvard.   ‡ Bradford, p. 103.
§ Banvard, p. 56. Mount.

ards the spot of green sward where they reclined. She had never seen an Englishman, and was naturally curious to gaze upon the pale-face strangers. On reaching their vicinage she became intensely excited, and commenced to howl and rave and weep, pausing between each sob to curse her chieftain's guests. The Pilgrims were astonished. They asked why the old squaw cried and cursed, and were told that Hunt had kidnapped three of her sons, at the same time that he had carried Squanto into Spanish servitude. They told the old squaw, through an interpreter, that Hunt was a bad man, condemned by all good Englishmen; said that they would not do so wicked an act for all the skins in New England; and to convince her of their sincerity, gave her some trinkets, which served to placate her exuberant wrath.*

Taking a friendly leave of Iyanough, the Pilgrims returned to the shallop, and at once set sail for Nauset, the Indian name of what is now the pleasant village of Eastham. On their arrival, the shallop was surrounded by a swarm of natives, who greatly annoyed them by their officious offers of assistance.† Standish was impelled to keep on the alert by the remembrance that this tribe was the one which had assailed the English coasting party in December, 1620.‡ Among these savages the Pilgrims found the long-sought owner of the corn which they had taken from the burial-mound; he

---

* Mount in Young.   Banvard.   † Ibid.
‡ Bradford, p. 103.

was invited to visit Plymouth, where he was **promised** ample payment.*

Towards evening, a sagamore named Aspiret came to them, bringing with him the lost lad. He had wandered over the hills and through the woods for five days, living upon the berries and wild fruit of the season. Finally he reached an Indian village at Menomet, where Sandwich is now located; and here the Indians had sent him to the Nausets, among whom he was now found.†

The boy was decked out in the tawdry Indian style when Aspinet delivered him to the settlers, and several pounds of beads hung suspended from his neck.‡

Standish rewarded the sachem for his care of the boy; he also distributed some presents among his tribe. Here a rumor of war between the Narragansetts and Massasoit reached them; and Aspinet also said that the great sagamore had been captured by his vengeful foemen.§ Apprehensive for the welfare of the colony, and conscious that they ought to render Massasoit assistance in case he had been unjustly attacked, the Englishmen bade Aspiret a hasty but cordial farewell, and instantly reëmbarked.‖

Plymouth was regained without further adventure. Their return was welcome, for these ten constituted half the martial force of the commonwealth; and in their absence the remaining settlers

* Banvard, p. 58.   † Mount in Young. Banvard.
‡ Ibid.   § Ibid. Prince, vol. 1, p. 107.   ‖ Ibid.

had learned of dangerous intrigues against their peace, stirred by a sachem called Corbitant, an ally of Massasoit's, but never a friend to the Pilgrims.*

> "The flying rumors gathered as they rolled;
> Scarce any tale was sooner heard than told;
> And all who told it added something new,
> And all who heard it made enlargement too;
> In every ear it spread, on every tongue it grew."†

At first this startling intelligence was flung into the ears of the settlers: "The Narragansetts have invaded Massasoit's territory; the sagamore is either a prisoner or has fled; an attack upon Plymouth may immediately be expected."‡

Squanto, Tokamahamon, and a warrior named Habbamak, who had come to live among the colonists, "a proper, lusty man, of great account for his valor and parts among the Indians,"§ were at once despatched to reconnoitre. Hardly had they disappeared in the skirting forests ere word was brought that Massasoit was safe, that the Narragansetts were not near, but that Corbitant was using every wile to detach the sagamore from the English alliance, while he threatened death to Squanto, Takamahamon, and Habbamak, the counsellors of the sachem who were so actively friendly to the Pilgrims.‖

Events hustled each other; for scarcely had the settlers time to breathe freer after this recital, ere "Habbamak came running in all sweating," and

---

* Palfrey, vol. 1, p. 185. Bradford, p. 103. † Pope.
‡ Palfrey, Banvard, Bradford, Pilgrims' Journal.
§ Bradford, p. 103, ‖ Palfrey, vol. 1, p. 185.

informed the clustering colonists that he and his two friends had been surprised and overpowered at Namasket by Corbitant; that he had managed to escape, but that he feared Squanto and Tokamahamon were dead, as he saw Corbitant press a knife to their breasts, and say, "If Squanto were dead, these English would lose their tongue."*

The Pilgrims never appear to greater advantage than in moments of trial; they are always equal to the occasion;

> "Like a ball that bounds
> According to the force with which 't was thrown;
> So in affliction's violence, he that's wise,
> The more he's cast down, will the higher rise."†

'T was so with the Pilgrims. Danger seemed powerless to abash them. They "walked softly before the Lord," but they "feared no evil." They were profoundly penetrated with John Marston's maxim: "Through danger safety comes; through trouble rest."

So now in this strait, they wasted no time in technical deliberation. Justice to themselves, to Squanto, to Massasoit, demanded action, prompt, efficient. Impunity was a bounty on offence. They were too weak to dare let an insult go unpunished. Besides, it was remembered that "if they should suffer their friends and messengers to be thus wronged, they would have none to cleave unto them, or bring them intelligence, or do them any good service afterwards, while next their foes would

* Banvard, p. 62. † Nabb's Microcosmos.

fall upon themselves. Whereupon it was resolved to send Standish and fourteen men well armed, and to go and fall upon the Indian village at Namasket at night; and if they found that Squanto was killed, to cut off Corbitant's head, but not to hurt any not concerned in the murder. Habbamak was asked if he would go and be their guide. He said he would, and bring them to the very spot, and point out Corbitant. So they set out on the evening of August 14th, 1621."*

The night was dark and tempestuous. Habbamak himself was often puzzled to find the path, and at times groped blindly. Towards midnight the little army halted and made a supper in the dark. As they were now near Namasket, the final preparations for the assault were made. Knapsacks were thrown aside, and each man received his specific directions. The plan was to surround the wigwam of Corbitant and seize him ere he could escape. None were to be injured unless an attempt to escape was made.†

The march was now resumed. Cautiously and silently they trod in the footsteps of their dusky guide, casting furtive glances into the enveloping gloom, and pausing momentarily to listen and to watch. At length the Indian village was reached. There it lay, calm and oblivious of danger, the eyes of its inmates sealed in sleep. Softly but swiftly the assailants stole like spectres half round the

* Bradford, pp. 103, 104.
† Mount in Young; Banvard, Bradford.

drowsy town, and instructed by Habbamak, the wigwam of the hostile sachem was surrounded. Then came another brief pause, and each man's heart seemed throbbing in his throat, so new and so exciting was the situation. The signal followed; the hut was entered; its inmates, still half asleep, were deprived of speech by fright and drowsiness. Soon, however, they regained their senses, and great commotion ensued. Standish asked if Corbitant was there. Unable or unwilling to reply, several of the aroused Indians essayed to pass the guard. Then the guns of the invaders increased the hubbub, and flashed angrily in the pitchy darkness. The women, rushing to Habbamak, called him "Friend, friend!" The boys, noticing that no injury was attempted against the squaws, shouted, "I am a girl, I am a girl!"*

After a time silence was regained. Standish, speaking through the lips of Habbamak, explained the object of the assault, and again demanded to know the whereabouts of Corbitant. Reassured, the Indians said that the wily sachem, fearing some revengeful action, had decamped; that Squanto and Tokamahamon had not yet been murdered, but were held as captives in a neighboring wigwam.†

The friendly sachems were speedily released, and while their deliverers heartily rejoiced over their escape, they regretted that of Corbitant.‡ The whole party breakfasted with Squanto; after which the Namasket Indians were assembled, and

* Banvard, p. 64. † Mount in Young. ‡ Ibid.

IN THE WOODS. 129

Standish informed them of his determination to hunt Corbitant, and to punish all who should plot evil against the colony, or who should presume to contend against the authority of Massasoit. He also regretted that any had been wounded in the night attack, and invited those who pleased to accompany him back to Plymouth, where an English physician would heal their hurts. Three, two men and a squaw, accepted this invitation, and tarrying until their wounds were dressed, medicined, and cured, they were then dismissed in peace.*

This expedition, so successful and so bloodless, had a prodigious effect. By some system of primitive telegraphing, the news of it, and of the awful fire-weapons of the pale-faces, spread throughout the forests. The red men did not want such "medicine men" for their foes. Nine sachems, representing jurisdictions which extended from Charles River to Buzzard's Bay, came to Plymouth and made their submission.† The Indians of an island which the settlers had never seen, sent to sue for their friendship;‡ and Corbitant himself, though too shy to come near Plymouth in person, used the mediation of Massasoit to make his peace.§

The result was, broader amity and firmer peace. But the Pilgrims conquered as much by their moderation and self-command as by their energetic

---

* Bradford, Mount, etc.
† Bradford, p. 104. Felt, Hist. of New England, vol. 1, pp. 64, 65. Palfrey, vol. 1, p. 183.   ‡ Bradford, ut antea.
§ Ibid., Felt, Palfrey.

6*

heroism. The anxious care with which they treated the injured warriors of their midnight raid, and the candor of their speech, placated resentment and inspired respect. Still the basis of this feeling was a knowledge that the white men would not suffer insult; and it has been finely said, that if we justly estimate it, there was more of sound policy and gallant daring in the midnight raid of this handful of strangers, than has marked many a deed of arms which historians have delighted to record, and to which nations still look back with exultant pride.*

Just as autumn began to smile, the Pilgrims made another expedition. This had a twofold purpose: to explore the country, and to cement a peace with the northeastern tribes.†

Entering the shallop at midnight, Standish and nine others, with three Indians to interpret, of whom Squanto was one, embarked with the ebb-tide.‡ They sailed along the coast to the bay on which Boston now stands, called in the contemporaneous record, *Massachusetts Bay*.§ "On the second morning after leaving Plymouth, they landed upon a beach under a cliff, and received the submission of a chief on promising to be 'a safeguard from his enemies.' They surveyed the 'fifty islands' of Boston harbor; and passing the night on

---

* Wilson. † Bradford, p. 104. Palfrey, Banvard.
‡ Palfrey, vol. 1, p. 186.
§ The word *Massachusetts* signifies an arrow-shaped hill. It is supposed to have been given to the surrounding country from the Blue Hills of Milton, which were formerly called Massachusetts Mount. See Banvard, p. 65.

board their boat, went on shore again the following day and walked a few miles into the country. They observed land which had been cultivated, two forts in decay, untenanted huts, and other tokens of recent depopulation. They noted 'the fair entrance' of the river Charles, and 'harbors for shipping' than which 'better could not be.' They conciliated the few natives whom they met, and traded with them for some skins. They learned that the principal personage in the neighborhood was the female chief, or 'squaw sachem' of the Massachusetts; that this tribe had suffered from the hostile incursions of the Tarratines, and that its people owed a certain allegiance to Massasoit. The third evening, by 'a light moon,' the party set sail for home, which they reached before the following noon. The accounts they brought of the seat of their explorations naturally led their friends to 'wish they had been seated there;'[*] but "the Lord, who assigns to all men the bounds of their habitations," remarks Bradford, "had appointed it for another use."[†] The party "found the Lord to be with them in all their ways, and to bless their outgoings and incomings, for which let his holy name have the praise for ever to all posterity."[‡]

Standish and his friends had returned on the 22d of September. Their services were needed; the nodding crops were to be reaped, and all "be-

---

[*] Palfrey, vol. 1, p. 186. For a fuller account of this expedition, see Mount in Young, pp. 224-229.

[†] Bradford, p. 105.   [‡] Ibid.

gan now to gather in the small harvest they had."* The husbandry of the year proved a prosperous beginning. The rivers supplied manure in abundance, and the weather had been not unfavorable.† "All the summer there was no want." While "some were thus employed in affairs abroad, others were exercised" in domestic avocations, in "fishing for cod and bass and other fish, of which they took great store, giving every family its portion."‡

When the fields were gleaned, the pease turned out "not worth the gathering, the sun having parched them in the blossom;" the barley was "indifferent good;" and there was "a good increase of Indian corn." "They had about a peck of meal a week to a person; or now, since harvest, Indian corn to that proportion."§

Seven substantial dwelling-houses had been built, "and four for the use of the plantation," while others were being constructed. Fowl were so abundant in the autumn, that "four men in one day killed as much as, with a little help besides, served the community almost a week." "There was great store of wild turkeys, of which they took many, besides venison." The fowlers had been sent out by the governor, "that so they might, after a special manner, rejoice together, since they had gathered the fruit of their labors;" this was the origin and the first celebration of the national fes-

* Bradford, p. 105.   † Palfrey.   ‡ Bradford.
§ Palfrey, vol. 1, pp. 186, 187.

tival of New England, the autumnal THANKSGIVING. On that occasion of hilarity they "exercised their arms," and for three days "entertained and feasted" Massasoit and some ninety of his people, who made a contribution of five deer to the festivity. Health was restored; household fires were blazing brightly; and in good heart and hope the lonely but thankful settlers disposed themselves to meet the rigor of another winter.*

"Here was free range; the hunter's instincts could bourgeon and grow; the deer that browsed, the fish that swam, the fowl that flew, were free to all—might be captives to each man's bow and spear. Here were 'herring, cod, and ling,' 'salt upon salt,' 'beavers, otters, furs of price,' 'mines of gold and silver,' 'woods of all sorts,' 'eagles, gripes, whales, grampus, moose, deer,' 'bears, and wolves,' 'all in *season*, mind you, for you cannot gather cherries at Christmas in Kent.' Who then would live at home in degradation, only to eat, and drink, and sleep and to die?"†

* Winslow in Mount, etc., cited in Palfrey, vol. 1, p. 187.
† Smith's Description of New England, cited in Elliot, vol. 1, p. 77.

CHAPTER X.

REINFORCEMENT.

"A golden treasure is the tried friend;
But who may gold from counterfeits defend?
Trust not too soon, nor yet too soon mistrust;
Who twines betwixt, and steers the golden mean,
Nor rashly loveth, nor mistrusts in vain."
MIRROR FOR MAGISTRATES.

ON the morning of the 9th of November, 1621, after morning prayer—for the Pilgrims commenced each fresh day by the solemn invocation of God's blessing on its labors, and at evening sealed the record by devout thanksgiving—when the thrifty settlers had separated each to his respective task, an Indian runner came breathless into the settlement, and announced that a vessel might be seen off Cape Cod, apparently crowding sail for Plymouth harbor.*

As no friends were expected at that season, this intelligence caused great excitement. A rush for the neighboring heights was made. There, indeed, spotting the dim horizon, a strange ship might be discerned. Endless were the speculations as to her character and objects. Was she manned by the inimical Frenchman? Was she a buccaneer, bent on murderous pillage? Could she be a friend? The Pilgrims were cautious and provident men. In the

* Russell's Pilgrims' Memorial, p. 131. Young's Chronicles, p. 232.

wilderness the common law maxim was reversed—all were necessarily held to be guilty until proved innocent. So now preparation was made to repel intruders, should they come with hostile intent. The governor ordered a cannon to be fired to summon the scattered pioneers home. All were armed; then, in painful suspense, the colonists waited the approach of the stranger craft. Nearer she drew and yet nearer. Intently was her every motion viewed. Her architecture was studied; her rigging was observed; and all eyes were directed towards the peak where should flap her flag: it was not there. But, suddenly, it was run up, and, lo, it was the English jack!

The colonists were delirious with joy, for that flag meant friends at hand and news from "home;" so their welcoming shouts went echoing across the water to their incoming reinforcers.

Soon the ship anchored; then the boats passing to and fro bore the friends to each other's arms; and amid kindly greetings and warm welcomings the news was asked and told.

It was the "Fortune" which had just arrived. She brought Cushman and thirty-five others to reinforce the infant colony.* Among this company were several who had embarked in the "Speedwell," balked of a passage then, but now safely arrived.† The meeting was not untinged with sadness. "Death had been busy; Carver was gone, and more than

---

* Mount, in Young, pp. 224-229. Russell's Pilgrim's Manual, p. 153. † Bradford, Elliot, Banvard.

half of those to whom Cushman had bidden God-speed in the "Mayflower" rested under the sod, the grass growing on their levelled graves."*

But as was their wont, the Pilgrims looked on the bright side of the picture; and all thanked God that some remained to welcome the new-comers.

When the home budget was opened it was found to contain several items of moment to the colony. The patent of the London company under which the emigrants had expected to possess their American homes, was made to cover Virginia alone, and this was rendered nugatory by the debarkation in New England.†

The London company was now under a cloud. The active prominence of its chiefs as popular leaders of the Parliamentary reformers against the royal prerogative, had provoked the pique of James; and his hostility was increased by the cunning of the Spanish court, with which he was then on friendly terms, and which desired to repel English neighbors from the Spanish settlement in Florida.‡

James exhibited his resentment by favoring the interests of a rival company of which Gorges, and Sheffield, and Hamilton, were the leaders. To them a new incorporation was granted, and assuming the title of the "Plymouth Company," they were empowered "to order and govern New England in America."§

---

* Elliot, vol. 1, p. 79.   † Palfrey, vol. 1, p. 190.
‡ Ibid. Peckham's Life of Nicholas Ferrar. London, 1852.
§ Gorge's Brief Narrative, chap. 16.

Upon the domain of the new corporation the Pilgrims had settled without leave; they were therefore liable to a summary ejectment.* The company of Merchant-adventurers, under whose auspices they had sailed, informed of their position by the return of the "Mayflower," immediately applied to the Plymouth company for a patent which should cover the soil now colonized.† It was granted "to John Pierce and his associates," and was in trust for the benefit of the colony.‡

Thomas Weston, the agent of the Merchant-adventurers, sent a copy of this charter to the Plymouth colonists, accompanying it with a letter in which, after complaining of the long detention of the "Mayflower" in America, and of her return without a cargo, he said that "the future life of the business depended on the lading of the 'Fortune,'" which being done, he promised never to desert the Pilgrims, even if all the other merchants should do so;§ adding, "I pray you write instantly for Mr. Robinson to come to you; and send us a fair engrossment of the contract betwixt yourselves and us, subscribed with the names of the principal planters."‖

While the "Fortune" lay moored in Plymouth harbor, Bradford penned a weighty and dignified

* Palfrey, vol. 1, p. 193. † Ibid.
‡ "It was dated June 1, 1621, and is interesting, as being the first grant made by the great Plymouth company. 'Twas first printed in 1854, in 4th Mass. Hist. Coll., vol, 11. The original is now at Plymouth. 'Tis probably the oldest document in Massachusetts officially connected with her history," Bradford, Ed. note, pp. 107, 108.
§ Bradford, p. 107, Russell, Morton, Young. ‖ Ibid.

reply to Weston's animadversions. After reciting the incidents which had checkered the twelvemonth of their settlement, including the death of Carver, to whom the agent of the Merchant-adventurers had directed his missive, he said, with an unconscious touch of pathos, "If the company has suffered, on the side of the settlers there have been disappointments far more serious. The loss of many honest and industrious men's lives cannot be valued at any price. It pleased God to visit us with death daily, and with so general a disease that the living were scarce able to bury the dead, and the well not in any measure sufficient to tend the sick. And now to be so greatly blamed for not freighting the ship, doth indeed go near us, and much discourage us."*

Preëminently conscientious, and earnestly desirous to give the Merchant-adventurers no just cause of complaint, the Pilgrim colonists made every effort to secure a speedy and profitable cargo for the "Fortune's" homeward voyage. The ship was a small one of but fifty-five tons burden;† but she was at once "laden with good clapboards, as full as she could stow, two hogsheads of beaver and other skins, with a few other trifling commodities," in all to the value of five hundred pounds.‡ Barely fourteen days elapsed between her arrival and her readiness to depart.§

* Bradford, pp. 108, 109.
† Elliot, Felt, Banvard, Mount in Young.
‡ Bradford, p. 108. About twenty-five hundred dollars.
§ Ibid.

Just before the "Fortune" sailed, the colonists were busy in preparing epistles for their friends in England and for the dear Leyden congregation. These were intrusted to Robert Cushman, who was to return to London and make a report of the situation of the Plymouth colony.* He himself, just on the eve of his return, delivered a memorial discourse in the block citadel on Fort-hill—which was at once church and castle—in which he recited vividly the cause of the emigration, the incidents attending it, the spirit of the actors, and the auguries of the future; and this was printed at London in 1622.†

In the dedicatory epistle to this sermon—whose object was to draw the attention of Puritans at home to the advantages of the Plymouth settlement as a residence where the virtues of religion might be more than ordinarily exemplified, as is proved by the fact that it was so speedily published in England—Cushman says: "If there be any who are content to lay out their estates, spend their time, labor, and endeavors for the benefit of those who shall come after, and who desire to further the gospel among the poor heathen, quietly contenting themselves with such hardships as by God's providence shall fall upon them, such men I should advise and encourage to go to New England, for in that wilderness their ends cannot fail them. And whoso rightly considereth what manner of entrance,

---

* Palfrey, vol. 1, p. 197. Bradford.
† Dr. Young has reprinted it in his Chronicles, p. 262, et seq.

abiding, and proceeding we have had among the savages since we came, will easily think that God hath some great work in store for us. By reason of one Squanto, who lives amongst us, who can speak English, we can have daily commerce with the Indian kings; and acquaint them with our causes and purposes, both human and religious."*

Three things, according to Winslow, are the bane and overthrow of plantations: The vain expectation of instantaneous profit, without work; ambition; and the lawlessness of settlers.† These rocks long wrecked the prosperity of the American colonies outside of New England. Cushman bade emigrants beware of entertaining the too common error of supposing that the wilderness was an actual Eldorado, as the Spanish had taught, and as the Virginia colonists had imagined.‡ "No," he said, "neither is there any land or possession now like unto that which the Jews had in Canaan, being legally holy, and appropriated unto holy people, the seed of Abraham, in which they dwelt securely, and had their days prolonged, it being by an immediate voice said, that the Lord gave it to them as a land of rest after their weary travels, and as a type of eternal rest in heaven. But now there is no land of that sanctity, no land so appropriated, none typi-

* Cushman, cited in Felt, vol. 1, p. 67.
† Winslow's Good News, London, 1624.
‡ "Captain Smith describes the Virginia settlers as made up of forty-eight needy 'gentlemen' to four carpenters, who were come to do nothing else 'but dig gold, make gold, refine gold, and load gold.'" Elliot, vol. 1, p. 79, note.

cal, much less any that can be said to be given of God to any one people, as Canaan was, which they and theirs must dwell in till God sendeth upon them sword and captivity. Now we are all, in all places, strangers and pilgrims, travellers and sojourners. Having no dwelling but in this earthly tabernacle, no residence but a wandering, no abiding but a fleeting,"* where work makes a home, and labor keeps it.

In a private letter addressed by Edward Winslow to a friend in London, and which helped to swell the budget which went out by the "Fortune," that stout old worthy says: "We have found the Indians very faithful to their covenant of peace with us, very loving and ready to pleasure us. We often go to them, and they come to us. Some of us have been fifty miles by land into the interior with them, the occasions and relation whereof you shall understand by our general and more full declaration of such things as are worth noting. Yea, it hath pleased God so to possess the Indians with fear of us, and love unto us, that not only the greatest king amongst them, called Massasoit, but also all the princes and tribes round about us have sent their messengers to us to make suit for peace, so that there is now great peace amongst the Indians themselves, which was not formerly, neither would have been but for us; and we, for our part, walk as peaceably and safely in the wood as in the highways in England. We entertain them pleasantly and famil-

* Cited in Elliot, vol. 1, pp. 79, 80.

iarly in our cabins, and they as friendly bestow their venison on us. They are a people without any religion, yet trusty, quick of apprehension, ripe—withal just."*

By this same opportunity William Hilton, who had come out in the "Fortune," thus sums up an account to his "loving cousin" of the natural wealth and prospects of the country on whose soil he had recently set foot: "Better grain cannot be than the Indian corn, if we will plant it upon as good ground as a man may desire. We are all freeholders; the rent-day doth not trouble us; and of all the blessings we have, which and what we list we may take in season. Our company are, for the most part, very honest, religious people. The word of God is sincerely taught us every Sabbath; so that I know not any thing a contented, earnest mind can here want. I desire your friendly care to send my wife and children to me when occasion serves, where I wish all the friends I have in England."†

Winslow gives us some significant hints of the social life and wants of the colony by describing to his friends the stores most needful to send out for their use; and we get no little insight into the hardships and very homely accommodations of the forefathers through the glass of his request that the next ship may "bring paper and linseed oil for the windows, with cotton yarn for the lamps."‡

* Winslow, in Young's Chronicles.
† Wilson, p. 389. Felt, vol. 1, p. 67.
‡ Smith, New England's Trials. Prince, vol. 1, p. 115.

And now, on the 14th of December, 1621, all being ready and leave-taking said, the little "Fortune," crammed with the "first fruits" of the Pilgrim enterprise, set sail for England. But alas, just as she had almost reached the English coast, she was clutched by a French privateer, robbed of her precious freight, and sent into the Thames an empty hull, to the bitter chagrin of the company of Merchant-adventurers, and the sad disappointment of the Plymouth colonists, when, at a later day, they learned of the misfortune.*

* Bradford. Young.

CHAPTER XI.

THE MORALE OF THE COLONY.

"Good name in man and woman, dear my lord,
Is the immediate jewel of their souls."
SHAKSPEARE, *Othello.*

ON the return of the settlers from the shore where they had said good-by to the "Fortune," it was arranged that the new-comers should for the present, in the absence of other accommodations, be received into the families already provided with cabins.* Unhappily, the "Fortune" had brought out no store; indeed, she was obliged to rely on the colonists for provisions for her larder on the home voyage. The emigrants whom she landed were absolutely destitute, having "not so much as biscuit-cake or any other victuals set aside for present want. Neither had they any bedding, nor pot nor pan to dress meat in, nor over-many clothes."†

Though the plantation rejoiced at this increase of strength, yet they would have been better pleased had many of the emigrants come better provided and in fitter condition to winter in the wilderness.‡

With the provident promptness which is so omnipresent a trait in their character, the Pilgrims at once "took an exact account of all their provisions

---

* Bradford, Mount in Young, Russell.
† Ibid. Prince, vol. 1. ‡ Bradford, p. 106.

in store, and proportioning these to the number of persons, found that, owing to the arrival of so many unexpected and necessitous guests, they would not hold out above six months, or till the spring, on half-allowance; and they could not well give less this winter-time, till fish came in again. But all were presently put on half-allowance, which began to be hard, but it was borne patiently."*

Indeed, the Pilgrims bore this hardship with something better than mere patience. "I take notice of it as a great favor of God," wrote one of the sufferers, "that he has not only preserved my life, but given me *contentedness* in our straits; insomuch that I do not remember ever to have wished in my heart that I had never come into this country, or that I might be again in my father's house."† It was said of Brewster, that "with the most submissive patience he bore the novel and trying hardships to which his old age was subjected, lived abstemiously, and after having been in his youth the companion of ministers of state, the representative of his sovereign, familiar with the magnificence of courts, and the possessor of a fortune sufficient not only for the comforts, but the elegances of life, this humble, devoted Puritan labored steadily with his own hands in the 'histic stibble-fields' of the unkempt wilderness for daily subsistence; while on the Sabbath, as elder of the church, and in the absence of an ordained minister, he broke the bread of life for the Pilgrim flock. Now, destitute of meat, of

* Bradford, p. 110.   † White's Incidents, etc.

fish, and of bread, over his simple meal of clams he would return thanks to the Lord that he could suck of the abundance of the sea and of treasures hid in the sand."*

An eminent historian bids us beware of the error of supposing that the community planted at Plymouth was of a strictly homogeneous character. "The devoted men who, at Leyden, had debated the question of emigration, did not constitute the whole company even of the 'Mayflower.' They had been joined in England by several strangers who, like themselves, had come under engagement to the Merchant-adventurers of London. That partnership had business objects, and was by no means solely swayed by religious sympathy with the Leyden Pilgrims."†

Of the twenty men of the "Mayflower's" company who survived the first winter, several are unfavorably known, as Billington, the foul-mouthed contemner of Standish's authority, and Dotey and Lister, the lackey duelists of Hopkins' quiet household.‡

So of the reinforcement by the "Fortune." Some were old and devout friends of the colonists, as Simonson and De la Noye, members of the Leyden church; John Winslow, Edward's brother; Thomas Prince, afterwards governor; Cushman's son, and a son of Brewster.§ Others were turbu-

---

* White's Incidents, etc.
† Palfrey, vol. 1, pp. 187–189.   ‡ Chap. 7, p. 106.
§ Winslow in Brief Narration, in Hypocrisie Unmasked, p. 393. Also, Palfrey, vol. 1, p. 189, note.

lent and restless rovers, impatient of control, careless in religion, and burning for adventure; in Bradford's phrase, "lusty young men, and many of them wild enough, who little considered whither or about what they went."* Happily for the peace of the little commonwealth and for posterity, "the advantage of numbers and the authority of superior character determined that events should proceed at Plymouth according to the policy of Bradford, Brewster, and their godly friends. Still internal tendencies to disturbance are not to be left out of view in a consideration of the embarrassments with which the forefathers had to contend."†

Under Bradford's government, the laws were few and mild, but firm; and neither the lazy nor the godless received countenance, though tender consciences were never pinched. Take this incident as an illustration: "On the day called Christmas day, the governor called the settlers out to work, as was usual; but the most part of the new-comers excused themselves, and said it went against their consciences to work on Christmas. So the governor told them if they made it a matter of conscience, he would spare them till they were better informed. On this, he led away the rest, and left them; but when the laborers came home from work at noon, they found the scrupulous new-comers in the street at play openly; some pitching the bar, some at foot-ball, and others at kindred sports. Immediately the governor went to them, and took

* Bradford, p. 106. † Palfrey, vol. 1, p. 189.

away their implements, and told them that it was against his conscience that they should play while others worked. If they made the keeping of Christmas matter of devotion, let them keep their houses; but there should be no gaming or revelling in the streets; since which time nothing hath been attempted that way, at least openly."*

In this and kindred ways, the commonwealth was controlled and moulded into higher courses. Practical consistency was gained, and the elements out of which homogeneity might grow were planted at every hearth-stone.

> "In companions
> That did converse and spend their time together,
> Whose souls did bear an equal yoke of love,
> There needs should be a like proportion
> Of lineaments, of manners, and of spirit."

* Bradford, p. 112.

CHAPTER XII.

THE PILGRIM GOVERNMENT.

"A free republic, where, beneath the sway
Of mild and equal laws, framed by themselves,
One people dwell, and own no lord save God."
    Mrs. HALE's *Ormond Grosvenor*.

JUST here it is perhaps fit that the salient features of the unique government under which the forefathers lived and prospered should be briefly sketched; and in order that this exposition may be clear, claiming the privilege of a chronicler, we shall command the clock of this narration to stand still, while we peer at times into the then future, in tracing some law to its result, or in depicting the change of front of an exploded policy.

At the outset, the arrangements of the Pilgrims were extremely simple, and grew naturally from their needs, from their crude ideas of liberty, and their imperfect conception of a model state. Nominally, the sovereignty of Britain was recognized; in fact, all through these opening decades of American history, the colonists were despised by the home government, and left free to plant the most radical principles of a "proper democracy." It was only when the greed of gain squeezed her heart, not repentance nor love, that England recognized the legitimacy of the neglected child whom she had pronounced a bastard, and left to freeze in the winter wilderness. When God wrote success upon the frontlet of the colony, the Shylocks on the Rialtos of the world were eager to invest in the enterprise, while England, with motherly pride, patted New England upon the head and said, "I rocked your cradle; but, bless me, how you are grown, and how like me you are. You may pay me your earnings, and I'll send you a governor."

But through the bitter months of the incipient settlement Shylock could see nothing in New England but a barren coast, while Britain could not discern Plymouth Rock across the water; nor if she had would any craving governor have itched to set up his chair of state in a cheerless Eldorado of ice and snow.

So the Pilgrims were left to shift for themselves until, strengthened by incessant tussles with a rugged climate and the savage foe, they expanded into robust manhood. In these first months, the Plymouth colonists regarded themselves as one family, at whose head stood the governor, *in loco parentis.** But as business increased, the whole burden of government was felt to be too onerous for the single shoulders of the governor to bear; and when Bradford stepped into the gubernatorial chair left vacant by the death of Carver, he was voted an assistant.† In 1624, he was given five assistants. Afterwards, in 1633, the number was increased to seven; and

* Allen's Biog. Dict.. Thatcher's Plymouth, p. 77.
† Chap, 7, p. 108.

these, called "the Governor's Council,"* governed the commonwealth in conjunction with their primitive executive. The vote of each councillor counted one, and the vote of the chief magistrate was but double—the only check he had over the action of the Council.†

The governor was chosen annually, by general suffrage,‡ as were also the councillors.§ The name of the man who was disposed to shirk his civil duty we do not know; "but a curious law was passed in in 1632, that whoever should refuse the office of governor, being chosen thereto, should pay twenty pounds; and that of magistrate, ten pounds. Very singular, certainly; and we may suppose that that race has run out even in Massachusetts."‖

The legislative body was at first composed of the whole company of voters.¶ Then, when their numbers grew, church-membership was made the test of citizenship**—a test which endured till 1665, when it was reluctantly yielded at the requisition of the king's commissioners.†† It was not until 1669 that the increase of population warranted the establishment of a House of Representatives.‡‡

"Narrow as the restriction of citizenship to church-members was, it is easy to explain it by remembering that toleration, in any large sense,

---

* Morton's Memorial, Prince's Annals, Hall's Plymouth Records.   † Ibid.   ‡ Ibid. Elliot, vol. 1, p. 109.
§ Hall, Prince, Thatcher.   ‖ Elliott, vol. 1, p. 110.
¶ Graham, vol. 1. Massachusetts Historical Records. Hazard, vol. 1.   ** Ibid.
†† Thatcher's Plymouth.   ‡‡ Graham, vol. 1, p. 230.

was hardly entertained by the most liberal religionists in that twilight age, and that the one idea which inspired this emigration and nerved these men for the bitterest sacrifices was, that they and their children might be free from an ecclesiastical tyranny which, if it followed, would endanger them. It should also be borne in mind that the history they studied, and the guide they felt bound to follow, was the Jewish theocracy, ordained by God, as they doubted not, to be a model in church and state for all time; and that, under that dispensation, death was the punishment for smaller errors than dissent. These facts explain and palliate the religious precision and severity afterwards practised in New England. But the free idea with which they started gradually grew broader, overcame the evil customs of the time, and strangled the prejudices of the Pilgrims themselves."*

So early as the 17th of December, 1623, it was decreed that "all criminal facts, and all manner of trespass and debt betwixt man and man, should be tried by the verdict of twelve honest men."† Thus the jury trial, the distinctive badge of Saxon civilization, a right which a long line of able lawyers, from Coke and Hale to Mansfield and Erskine, have united in styling the palladium of civil liberty, was planted in America.

Previous to the year 1632, the laws of Plymouth colony were little more than the customs of the

* Elliot, vol. 1, pp. 112, 113.
† Plymouth Records. Hazard, vol. 1.

people.* In 1636 these were digested, and prefaced with a declaration of rights; and, with various alterations and additions, the whole manuscript collection was printed in 1671.† Let us open the ponderous old folio, and cull from the mass a few specimen and characteristic samples. Early provision was made for the education of youth. Many of the Pilgrims were men of liberal culture, as Winslow and Brewster,‡ and all recognized its value and necessity; so, in order that knowledge and civil liberty might clasp hands, it was enacted, "that twelve pounds should be raised for the salary of a teacher, and that children should be forced to attend school."§

Decreed: "For ordering of persons and distributing the lands, That freemen shall be twenty-one years of age; sober and peaceable; orthodox in the fundamentals of religion. That drunkards shall be subject to fines, to the stocks, and be posted; and sellers be forbidden to sell them liquors.

"Horse-racing is forbidden; so also walking about late o' nights.

"The minister's salary shall be paid by rate levied on all the citizens. Sabbath work and travelling is forbidden; also all visiting on that day.

"Profane swearing punishable by 'placing in the stocks; lying, by the stocks or by fine.'

"Fowling, fishing, and hunting, shall be free.

"Every wolf's head shall be worth, to an In-

* Plymouth Records. Hazard, vol. 1. Elliot. † Elliot.
‡ Thatcher's Plymouth, Morton's Memorials, etc.
§ Book of Laws of New Plymouth, 1671.

dian, twelve shillings or 'a coat of duffels;' to a white man, twenty shillings.

"Haunters of ale-houses shall be disciplined by the church.

"A motion of marriage to any man's daughter, if made without obtaining leave, shall be punished by fine or corporal punishment, at the discretion of the court, so it extend not to the endangering of life or limb.

"Women shall not wear short sleeves; nor shall their sleeves be more than twenty-two inches wide:"* an enactment the object of which was, to prevent indecent extremes and extravagance in dress.

So runs this "quaint old volume of forgotten lore." If some of these laws seem severe, as we scan them through the vista of two centuries, and in an age when sumptuary laws are perhaps too little known, it may be said in their defence, that they were quite upon a level with the kindred legislation of Europe, even in their most obnoxious features, while their progressive and liberal tone is as new and unique as the colony which gave them birth, and whose ideas they mirror.

In May, 1621, the first marriage in New England was celebrated.† Edward Winslow espoused the widow of William White, and the mother of Peregrine White, whose infant lullaby was the first ever sung by Saxon voice in New England.‡ "Ac-

---

* Laws of New Plymouth, cited in Elliot, vol. 1, p. 111.
† Prince, Annals, vol. 1, pp. 76, 98, 103, 105. Bradford, p. 101.
‡ Ibid.

cording to the laudable custom of the Low Countries," says Bradford, "the ceremony was thought most requisite to be performed by the magistrate, as being a civil contract upon which many questions of inheritance do depend, with other things most proper for their cognizance, and most consonant to the Scriptures,* it being nowhere found in the gospel to be layed on ministers as a necessary part of their office. This practice continued, not only among them, but it was followed by all the famous churches of Christ in those parts to the year 1646."†

* Ruth, chap. 4.   † Bradford, p. 101.

CHAPTER XIII.

THE COLONIAL ROUTINE.

"Still to ourselves in every place consigned,
Our own felicity we make or find;
With silent course, which no loud storms annoy,
Glides the smooth current of domestic joy."
GOLDSMITH'S *Traveller*.

Now, as their second wilderness winter began to benumb the fingers and chill the blood of the Pilgrim colonists, they were necessarily shut out from many of the employments of the spring, the summer, and the autumn. They were busied chiefly in fishing, hunting, the collection of fuel, hewing timber, and exploring expeditions, varying this routine by occasional traffic with Indian trappers.*

Devoutly thankful were the forefathers for God's mercy and protection in the past, and with tranquil faith they set their faces towards the future. So full was their devotion, that it constantly cropped out, even setting its impress upon the seal of the commonwealth, which represented four men in the midst of a wilderness, each resting on one knee, and raising his clasped hands towards heaven in the attitude of prayer.†

---

* Palfrey, vol. 1, p. 196.
† This seal was dated 1620, and circumscribed with the words, "Sigillum Societatis Plymouth, Nov. Anglia."

With the Pilgrims, faith was the spur of labor; and this active enterprise eased and conquered all obstacles. Still, causes for solicitude and trials infinite constantly arose. The lean condition of their larder was a care urgent for the passing time and weighty in the future; and to this a new source of anxiety was added. In the depth of winter, a report was bruited that active hostilities might momentarily be looked for, fomented by the restless enmity of the Narragansetts.*

That the Narragansetts were inimical they soon learned. One day one of the warriors of that tribe entered Plymouth, and announced himself to be a messenger from his renowned sagamore Canonicus. He asked for Squanto, but seemed pleased when told that he was absent. He said he had a package for Squanto. This consisted of a bundle of new arrows, wrapped in a rattlesnake's skin. It was enigmatical to the English; but, suspicious that it could not be the Indian olive-branch, and might mean mischief, Standish detained the messenger as he was about to quit the settlement, and determined to hold him until Squanto's return should solve the riddle.†

At first the savage was frightened; but after a little, seeing that his captors meant him no harm, he became quite friendly, and began to chat. The Pilgrims learned from him, that an envoy whom they had despatched to negotiate a peace with the Narragansetts, in the preceding summer, had played

* Winslow's Good News from New England.   † Ibid.

Judas, and betrayed his trust. Withholding from Canonicus the presents which the colonists had sent him as tokens of amity, he had used his influence to kindle a war. The imprisoned runner said Canonicus would not have uttered sinister threats, had he thought the English friendly to him. When he returned, and informed the Narragansetts of the real sentiments of the pale faces, firm peace would come.*

Somewhat affected by these representations, Bradford concluded to release the Indian; previous to which, however, he bade the envoy inform Canonicus that the pale faces had heard of his threats, and were offended; that they desired to live in amity with their red brothers; yet if any warlike demonstrations were made, they would be prepared to meet them.†

Then the governor urged the savage to take some food; but he was too anxious to quit the dangerous vicinage to remain a moment after his liberation; so, after expressing his gratitude, he immediately set out, in the midst of a driving storm, to find his way through the white, shivering December woods to his wigwam and his people.‡

When Squanto came in, the settlers at once crowded about him, and showing him the sphynx-like Indian package, asked him to spell the riddle. With a laugh and a shrug, he explained that it expressed enmity, and was the red man's declaration

---

* Winslow's Good News from New England. Banvard, p. 70.
† Winslow in Young.   ‡ Ibid. Banvard.

of war. The settlers were startled; all adjourned to the fort; and here, after deliberation, it was resolved to meet menace by menace. They thought, rightly, that a determined attitude would in their case be safest; and though Bradford had no anxiety to pit his fifty-odd men against the five thousand warriors whom Canonicus could muster, he was bold and defiant in appearance.*

The governor filled the rattlesnake-skin with powder and bullets, and despatched it to the Narragansetts by a special messenger, with this word: "If we were supplied with ships, we would save the Narragansett sagamore the trouble of coming so far to meet us by sailing to him in his own dominions. As it is, if he will come to the colony, he will find us ready to receive him."†

When Canonicus heard this message, he was profoundly impressed with the courage of his paleface neighbors; and when the skin was tendered him, he refused to receive it; but the Pilgrim envoy would not take it back; so it was passed from hand to hand among the Narragansetts, till finally, pushed from the forest by superstitious fear, it reached the Plymouth settlement *unopened*.‡

Though this prompt action cowed the Narragansetts for a time, the rumor of intended hostilities continued to vex the colonists through the winter. "This made them the more careful to look to themselves; so they agreed to enclose their dwell-

---

* Winslow in Young, Banvard, Bradford.
† Winslow in Young, Banvard. ‡ Ibid., Bradford.

ings with a strong pale, with flankers in convenient spots, and gates to shut, which were every night locked, and a watch kept; when need required, there was also warding through the day. The company, by the advice of Standish and the governor, was divided into four squadrons; and every man had his position assigned him, to which he was to repair in case of sudden alarm. If there should be a cry of fire, a squad was appointed for a guard, with muskets, whilst others quenched the flames. All this was accomplished very cheerfully; and to prevent Indian treachery, the whole town was impaled round by the beginning of March, while every family had a pretty garden-spot secured."*

The Pilgrims were regularly drilled by Standish, who had learned the science of war in Flanders. On these occasions, part of the exercises consisted in a general rush, each man to his station, and a simultaneous discharge of musketry. After this, the men escorted their officers to their cabins, fired a salute in their honor, and then dispersed. This may be considered "the first general muster in New England." It was the germ of the present militia system of thirty-six states.†

This diligent training ere long moulded the Pilgrims into a finely disciplined company; and they were quite proud of their proficiency in arms. Thus

"Spake, in the pride of his heart, Miles Standish, the captain of Plymouth:
  'Look at these arms,' he said, 'the warlike weapons that hang here,

* Bradford, pp. 111, 112. † Banvard, p. 72.

Burnished, and bright, and clean, as if for parade or inspection.
This is the sword of Damascus I fought with in Flanders. This breastplate—
Well I remember the day—once saved my life in a skirmish.
There in front you can see the very dint of the bullet
Fired point-blank at my heart by a Spanish Arcabucero.
Had it not been of shear-steel, the forgotten bones of Miles Standish
Would at this moment be mould in their grave in the Flemish morasses.
Look! you can see from this window my brazen howitzer, planted
High on the roof of the church—a preacher who speaks to the purpose,
Steady, straight forward, and strong, with irresistible logic;
Orthodox, flashing conviction right into the hearts of the heathen.
Now we are ready, I think, for an assault of the Indians.
Let them come, if they like, and the sooner they try it the better.
Let them come, if they like, be it sagamore, sachem, or powwow,
Aspinet, Samoset, Corbitant, Squanto, or Tokamahamon.'"*

When, in the preceding summer, the Pilgrims had visited Massachusetts bay, they had promised the tribes in that vicinity to come again in the next spring and renew a trade with them. Now, in the latter part of March, Standish and his friends commenced preparations for this voyage. Rumors, constantly renewed, still foreboded an outbreak against the peace and safety of the little commonwealth; and though the winter had been spent without the yell of the war-whoop, Bradford's fast friend, Habbamak, strongly advised against the expedition of Standish, since he feared that the northeastern

* Longfellow's Miles Standish's Courtship, pp. 9-12.

tribes were in close league with the Narragansetts, and anxious to precipitate a war.*

Finally the colonists concluded to undertake the expedition, but to do so with extreme caution.† Accordingly, Standish embarked. He had not sailed far, ere he was becalmed. Suddenly he heard a cannon-shot, the signal of danger. Instantly putting about, he bade his men row with their utmost strength and skill. Soon Plymouth was reached, and Standish learned that, just as he had sailed, an Indian, one of Squanto's family, had brought word that the Narragansetts, with Corbitant and Massasoit, were marching on the settlement.‡ Habbamak was confident that, even if this tale were true, Massasoit was not on the war-path; so confident, that he sent his squaw, under pretence of some message, to spy out the facts in the great sagamore's village.§

Meantime watch was kept through the night, and the whole settlement rested on its arms.‖

Nothing came of it all; not an Indian appeared; and when Habbamak's wife returned, she said that she found Massasoit at home and quiet.¶ "After this," says Bradford, "the traders proceeded on their voyage, and had a good traffic; returning in safety, blessed by God."**

From various circumstances, the settlers began

---

* Winslow in Young. Bradford. † Ibid.
‡ Bradford, p. 113. § Ibid. Winslow.
‖ Ibid. Young's Chronicles. Thatcher's Plymouth.
¶ Ibid. ** Prince.

to suspect that Squanto "sought his own ends and played his own game" in his relations with them. He was the most travelled and learned of the Indians, and with the spirit of braggadocio and the love of great stories common to his race, and also to his white prototypes, he was fond of working on the fears of his more ignorant and credulous brothers of the wood, by boasting of his influence with the pale faces, by reciting wild and terror-striking stories of the magical power of the English, and by offering to insure the peace and security of all who bought his services.*

In this way Squanto drove quite a trade, the patent for his truth being his knowledge and singular European adventures.

"These English," he would say to a wondering and superstitious group of Indians, "are a wise and powerful people. Diseases are at their command. They have now buried under their storehouse the plague. They can send it forth to any place or upon any people they please, and sweep them all away, though they went not a step from home."† "Ugh! ugh!" would be the responses of the gaping believers. Many was the skin, many the piece of wampum, given Squanto to purchase his powerful intercession on their behalf, to lay the plague of the pale-face magicians.

Once Squanto, being sent for by the governor, entered the house accompanied by Habbamak and several other Indians. A hole had been dug in the

* Bradford, p. 113. † Banvard, pp. 76, 77.

floor for the purpose of concealing certain articles, and the ground was left in a broken state. Habbamak, glancing at it, asked Squanto,

"What does that mean?"

"That," retorted the wily sachem, "is the place where the plague is buried that I told you about."

Habbamak, to satisfy himself of the truth or falsity of this statement, asked one of the settlers, shortly after, if this was so.

"No," said the stern, truthful Puritan; "we have not the plague at our command; but the God whom we worship has, and he can send it forth to the destruction both of his enemies and ours."*

Having learned these things, the Pilgrims spared no pains to contradict Squanto's misstatements; and so angered were the neighboring tribes, all of whom he had repeatedly swindled and misled, that Massasoit and Habbamak both strenuously insisted upon putting him to death; for the American Indian forgave any thing sooner than an attempt to cheat him; in which he was unlike civilized communities, which often admire in proportion as they are cozened, and frown on and resent nothing but a *clumsy* cheat.

But Squanto, with all his faults, was too useful to the Pilgrims to be surrendered to the cruel vengeance of his foes; so he was saved from death, though not without difficulty, and at the risk of estranging Massasoit.†

This made the rescued sachem "walk more

* Banvard, pp. 76, 77. † Winslow in Young. Banvard.

squarely, and cleave unto the English till he died." There was great jealousy between Squanto and Habbamak. Both were competitors for the goodwill of the Pilgrims; and of this emulation good use was made. The governor seemed to countenance the one, and the captain the other, by which *ruse* the colonists got better intelligence, and kept the two scouts more diligent.*

Towards the latter part of May, 1622, the scanty provisions of the Pilgrims quite gave out. Actual hunger began to pinch. The wild fowl, so plenty in the preceding season, were now grown shy of Plymouth, and could not be found. Their hooks and seines for fishing were worn out. It was yet hardly time to plant, as the frost still clutched the soil in its icy hand; and even if it were, weary weeks must elapse ere a crop could be reaped. The future looked black, yet even in this strait they trusted in God, "knowing that he would not desert his own."†

While the Pilgrims were thus perplexed to know where their next mouthful was to come from, they espied one day a shallop off their harbor. It proved to be a boat from a ship sent by Thomas Weston to fish off the coast of Maine. It contained six or seven passengers and a parcel of home letters.‡

These emigrants, like those who came in the "Fortune," were destitute of provisions, and the colonists were requested by Weston to provide for their necessities. Despite their own wants, "they

* Bradford, p. 114.   † Ibid., p. 124.   ‡ Ibid., 114.

took compassion on the needy new-comers, and in this famine gave them as good as any of their own."*

The Pilgrims got cold comfort from their letter-bag. "Some of the adventurers," wrote Weston, "have sent you herewith some directions for your furtherance in the common good. It seems to me that they are like those St. James speaks of, that bade their brother eat and warm himself, but gave him nothing; so they bid you make salt and uphold the plantation, but send you no means wherewithal to do it. Soon I purpose to send more people on my own account."†

It seemed from other letters, that the company of Merchant-adventurers was exhausting its energy in internal bickerings. Nothing was said about forwarding the remainder of the congregation at Leyden; nothing was promised for the future; a simple command was sent, that the colonists should assent to the breakage of the joint-stock contract, and despatch to them a paper to that effect, ratified and certified.‡

"All this," says Bradford, "was cold comfort to fill their empty bellies; and on the part of Mr. Weston, but a slender performance of his late promise never to forsake the colony;§ and as little did it fill and warm cold and hungry men, as those the

---

* Bradford, p. 114. † Cited in Bradford, pp. 115, 116.
‡ Bradford, p. 116. By the third article of the agreement, this was permitted to be done by general consent. See Bradford, p. 46.
§ Chap. 10, p. 137.

apostle James spoke of, by Weston before mentioned. Well might it remind the settlers of what the psalmist saith, 'It is better to trust in the Lord than to have confidence in man.'* And again, 'Put not your trust in princes'—much less in merchants—'nor in the son of man; for there is no help in them.'† 'Blessed is he that hath the God of Jacob for his help, whose hope is in the Lord his God.'‡

"These things seemed strange to the settlers. Seeing this inconsistency and shuffling, it made them think there was some mystery at bottom. Therefore the governor, fearing lest, in their straits, this news should tend to disband and scatter the colony, concealed these letters from the public, and only imparting them to some trusty friends for advice, concluded for the present to keep all quiet, and await the development of events."§

* Psalm 118:8. † Ibid. 146:3. ‡ Ibid. verse 5.
§ Bradford, pp. 116, 117.

CHAPTER XIV.

THE RIVAL COLONIES

"Look here, upon this picture, and on this."
SHAKSPEARE, *Hamlet.*

It was towards the close of May, 1622, that the seven pioneers from Weston's fishing smack had landed at Plymouth. About a month later, in the end of June or beginning of July, a new colony arrived. Two vessels, the "Charity" and the "Swan," rounded Cape Cod and anchored off the Pilgrim settlement.* They brought out a fresh batch of home letters, which Bradford and his coadjutors eagerly opened, hoping to discover the hidden meaning of these strange movements.

Weston's missive was first searched. It was to this effect: "The 'Fortune' is arrived, whose good news touching your estate and proceedings I am very glad to hear. And howsoever she was robbed on the way by the Frenchmen, I hope your loss will not be great, for the conceit of a vast return doth animate the merchants. As for myself, I have sold my adventure and debts unto them, so I am quit of you and you of me. Now, though I have nothing to pretend as an adventurer among you, yet I will advise you a little for your good, if you can apprehend it. I perceive and know as well as any one

* Smith's General History, folio ed., p. 236. Winslow in Young, p. 296.

the disposition of the Merchant-adventurers, whom the hope of gain hath drawn on to this they have done; yet that hope will not draw them much farther. Besides, most of them are against the sending of the Leyden congregation, for whose cause this business was first begun; and some of the most religious of the company except against them for their creed."*

This presaged disaster, and Weston's desertion after his volunteer promises, made the Pilgrims profoundly sad. Next a letter from two of the Merchant-adventurers was read. This warned the colonists to beware of Weston, as one who sought his own single end, and " whom the company had bought out and were glad to be quit of."†

Then a letter from their old friend Cushman was opened. "Weston," he said, "hath quite broken off from our company, and hath now sent two small ships on his own venture for a new plantation. The people which they carry are no men for us, wherefore I pray you, entertain them not. If they offer to buy any thing of you, let it be such as you can spare, and make them give the worth of it. 'Tis like they will plant to the south of the cape. I fear these people will deal harshly with the savages. I pray you signify to Squanto that they are a distinct body from us, and that we have nothing to do with them, neither must be blamed for their faults, nor can warrant their fidelity."‡

* Cited *in extenso* in Bradford, pp. 118, 119.
† Ibid., pp. 119, 120. ‡ Ibid., 122, 123.

Weston had overhauled these letters, and so become familiar with their contents. After criticising them severely, he added: "Now if you be of the mind of these writers, deal plainly with us, and we will seek our residence elsewhere. If you are friendly, as we have thought you to be, give us the entertainment of friends. I shall leave in the country a little ship—if God send her safe thither—with mariners and fishermen, who shall coast and trade with the savages and the old plantation. It may be that we shall be as helpful to you as you to us. I think I shall see you in person next spring."*

The Pilgrims were in a quandary. They stood on the verge of starvation. The recent comers had brought out no stock of provisions, but were dumped destitute upon the charity of those whom they had come to supplant. "As for the harsh censures and suspicions intimated in these letters," remarks Bradford, "they desired to judge as charitably and wisely of them as they could, weighing them in the balance of love and reason; and though the epistles of warning came from godly and loving friends, yet they conceived that many things might arise from over-deep jealousy and fear, together with unmeet provocation; though they well saw that Weston pursued his own ends, and was embittered in spirit. All these things they pondered and well considered, yet concluded to give his men friendly entertainment; partly in regard to that gentleman's past kindness, and partly in compassion to the people who were now

---

* Cited *in extenso* in Bradford. ut antea.

come into the wilderness—as themselves were—and were by their ships to be presently put ashore; for they were to carry other passengers into Virginia;* and they were altogether unacquainted, and knew not what to do. So, as they had received Weston's former company of seven men, and victualed them as their own, now they also received these, being about sixty lusty men, and gave housing for themselves and their goods; and many, being sick, had the best the place could afford them."†

Of course, so great and unexpected an accession of numbers added vastly to the embarrassment of the Pilgrims, and "amidst these straits, and the desertion of those from whom they had expected a supply, when famine began to pinch them sore they knew not what course to take." But God stood behind the cloud, "keeping watch above his own." One day a boat came into Plymouth, and brought word of a massacre in Virginia,‡ and gave a warning to the New England colonists. The kind sender of this message was captain of a fishing-smack then fishing off the Maine coast.§

When this boat returned, "the governor sent back a thankful answer, as was meet, and also despatched the shallop of the colony in its company, in which was Edward Winslow, whose object was to

* The vessels were gone most of the summer.
† Bradford, pp. 123, 124.
‡ This massacre occurred on the 22d of March, 1622. Smith says that three hundred and fifty settlers were slain. General Hist., pp. 144–149.
§ Bradford.

secure what provisions he could from the fishermen. He was kindly received by the mentor captain, who not only spared what he could of his own stock, but wrote others to do the same. By these means Winslow got some good quantity, and returned in safety; whereby the plantation had a double benefit; first, a refreshing by the food brought; and secondly, they knew the way to those parts for their benefit hereafter. Still, what was got and this small boat brought, being divided among so many, came but to little, yet, by God's blessing, it upheld them till harvest."* The daily allowance was a quarter of a pound of bread to each person; and this the governor doled out, for had it not been in his custody, it would have been eaten up and all had starved; but thus, with what eels they could catch, they "made pretty shift till corn was ripe."†

The Pilgrims soon perceived the truth of Cushman's estimate of the character of Weston's colonists, and found, indeed, that "they were not the men for them." In the lump they were a rude, profane, improvident, thievish set, and peculiarly unfit to be the founders of a state.‡ They ate of the bounty of their entertainers, wasted their corn, brought riot and profanity into the quiet, devout homes of the Pilgrims, and repaid kindness by backbiting and reviling.§ Their coming was purely a business affair. It was a speculation. It was en-

* Bradford, p. 125. † Ibid. Winslow in Young.
‡ Thatcher's Plymouth, Prince's Annals, Banvard.
§ Banvard, p. 82.

tirely destitute of every religious element, though it abounded with irreligious ones. Fearing neither God nor man, they hated the Puritans, and ought never to be confounded with the Forefathers.* They were, in fact,

> "A lazy, lolling sort,
> Unseen at church, at senate, or at court,
> Of ever-listless loiterers, that attend
> No cause, no trust, no duty, and no friend."†

These godless drones remained at Plymouth most of the summer, until their ships came back from Virginia.‡ Then, under Weston's direction, or that of some one whom he had set in authority over them, these pests removed into Massachusetts Bay, and selecting a spot called by the Indians Wessagusset, now Weymouth, they essayed to plant a settlement.§ "Yet they left all their sickly folks with us, to be nursed and cared for," says Bradford, "till they were settled and housed. But of their stores they gave us nothing, though we did greatly want, nor any thing else in recompense of our courtesy; neither did we desire it, for 'twas seen that they were an unruly company, having no good government,—sure soon to fall into want by disorder."‖

Such a colony "was not, nor could it come to good." Mismanagement and lazy improvidence invited penury. Ere long they ran foul of the Indians; already the bane of the Pilgrims, they speedily became a pest among the savages, whom they robbed

* Banvard, p. 82.   † Pope.   ‡ Bradford.
§ Weston in Young, Thatcher, Prince.   ‖ Bradford.

and swindled without conscience. In this way they exasperated the Indians, and by their bad courses were nigh bringing ruin on their neighbors as well as on themselves.* On one occasion they stood provisionless. They could expect no succor from the natives, and they had despoiled every Indian cornfield in their vicinity. In this extremity, Sanders, their chief man, sent to inform Bradford of his intention to get some corn from the Indians by force. The Pilgrims sent back a strong protest against the pillage; advised the new planters to make shift to live, as they did, on ground-nuts, clams, and muscles; and from their own well-nigh exhausted storehouse sent their disorderly and wasteful rivals a supply of corn.†

This stock was soon gone; then the Westonians desired the Pilgrims to unite with them in an expedition to the Indian settlements on the coast line, in search of corn, beans, and other kindred commodities. They, not unwilling to assist the needy planters in all honest ways, assented, and terms of agreement were signed designating the division of the articles obtained.‡ Detachments from both colonies embarked in the "Swan," the smaller of Weston's vessels, and the shallop was also taken. Squanto accompanied the forage as interpreter.§ The Indians were very shy and could hardly be approached. But finally the kindness and tact of

---

* Cotton Mather, Magnalia, vol. 1, p. 58.
† Palfrey, vol. 1, p. 200. Prince, Thatcher.
‡ Banvard. § Ibid.

Bradford and Standish thawed their icy reserve, so that the enterprise was crowned with success. Twenty-seven hogsheads of corn and beans were bought.* Owing to the stranding of the shallop, the Plymouth governor was compelled to foot it home, some fifty miles; but he "received all the respect that could be from the Indians on the journey."†

The "Swan" returned, a day or two later, with the provisions, and, after their distribution, Weston's men sailed from Plymouth in her to their plantation.‡

This was destined to be Squanto's last service. A violent fever, which struck him on the expedition, soon laid him low. "Pray for me," said the dying Indian to Governor Bradford, "pray for me, that I may go to the white man's God in heaven." Shortly after, he distributed various trinkets among his English friends as memorials, and expired.§ Despite his pranks and vanity, Squanto was a true friend to the Pilgrims, and his loss was a severe blow to the colonial interests.‖

Immediately on recovering from the fatigue incident to the late voyage, the Pilgrims went out into their fields to reap the harvest. The crop was slender, owing partly to the ignorance of the planters of the culture of Indian corn; partly to their many other employments; but chiefly to their inability

---

* Thatcher, Winslow in Young.   † Ibid.
‡ Banvard.   § Banvard, Bradford.
‖ Thatcher, Winslow in Young.

properly to attend it, caused by weakness from want of food.*

It was apparent that famine must be entailed upon the next year also, unless some other source of supply should be opened. This seemed impossible. There were no markets; and they were out of trinkets for their Indian traffic. "Behold now another providence of God," says Bradford; "a ship sent out by English merchants to discover all the harbors betwixt Virginia and the shoals of Cape Cod, and to trade along the coast where it could, entered our bay. She had on board a store of beads—which were then good trade—and some knives, but the crew would sell nothing save in the bunch and at high prices. However, we bought of them, and by this means were fitted again to trade for beaver and for corn with the red men."†

In this same summer a new fort was built, "both strong and comely, which was a sure defence." Isaac De Rasieres, who visited Plymouth at a somewhat later day, has left this description of the block citadel: "Upon the hill they have a large square house, with a flat roof, made of thick-sawn planks, stayed with oak-beams. On the top are ranged six cannon, which shoot iron-balls of four or five pounds, and command the surrounding country. The lower part they use for their church, where preaching is had on Sundays and the usual holidays. The settlers assemble by beat of drum, each with his musket or firelock, in front of the

* Bradford. † Ibid.

captain's door; they have their cloaks on, and place themselves in order, three abreast, and are led by a sergeant without beat of drum. Behind comes the governor, in a long robe; beside him on the right hand walks the preacher, and on the left hand the captain, with his side arms and cloak on, and with a small cane in his hand. So they march in good order, and on reaching the fort each sets his arms down near him and within easy grasp."*

An open Bible in one hand, a shotted musket in the other—such was the manner in which the Pilgrim fathers went to church.

* Cited in Russell's Guide to Plymouth, p. 143.

CHAPTER XV.

THE EXPLOIT OF MILES STANDISH.

"And when they talk of him, they shake their heads,
And whisper one another in the ear;
And he that speaks doth gripe the hearer's wrist;
Whilst he that hears makes fearful action
With wrinkled brows, with nods, and rolling eyes."
SHAKSPEARE.

ONE short twelvemonth witnessed the birth and the death of Weston's colony. Its cradle was its grave. The Westonians, by their own wickedness and folly, beckoned ruin and blood to be their guests. The ears of the Pilgrims ached with listening to the Indians' complaints of their injustice and robberies. Not a day passed which did not witness some woful scene of outrage.* Bradford and his coadjutors talked themselves hoarse in denunciation; messengers ran themselves footsore in carrying protests of warning, of expostulation, of appeal.†

"Once," says Cotton Mather, "in preaching to a congregation there, one of the Pilgrims urged these settlers to approve themselves a *religious* community, as otherwise they would contradict the main end of planting this wilderness; whereupon a well-known individual, then in the assembly, cried

---
* Winslow in Young. Thatcher, Bradford.
† Prince, Hubbard, Banvard.

out, 'Sir, you are mistaken; you think you are preaching to the people at Plymouth bay: our *main end* was *to catch fish.*'"*

The scoffers were soon to learn, under the bitter tuition of experience, that fish are a slippery foundation for a colony to build on--not so firm and sure as open Bibles and common schools.

The loose morality and vicious courses of their mischievous neighbor-colonists caused the Pilgrims infinite trouble and unfeigned grief. And now, in the midst of their anxiety on this account, a report gave voice to the dangerous sickness of Massasoit;† it was said that the great sagamore, who had been their faithful friend, could not survive.‡ The Plymouth settlers were profoundly sad; they were also somewhat alarmed, for Corbitant, their former open foe, would, so they were told, clutch Massasoit's sceptre and wear his mantle on the chieftain's death.§ The Pilgrims at once decided to send ambassadors to visit Massasoit, see if haply something might not be done for him, and, in case of his decease, to negotiate a new peace with the succeeding sachem.‖

For this service Winslow and Habbamak were selected; and a gentleman who had wintered in Plymouth, and who was desirous of seeing the Indians in their wigwam-homes, Mr. John Hampden,¶

* Cotton Mather, Magnalia, vol. 1, p. 66.
† Winslow in Young. Bradford, p. 131.   ‡ Ibid.
§ Ibid. Banvard, p. 95.
‖ Banvard, Winslow's Good News, etc.
¶ "Mr. Baylies, in his Memoirs of Plymouth, assumes that

was, at his urgent solicitation, permitted to bear them company.*

They set out at once, but had not gone very deep into the forest ere some Indians, whom they met at a river-ford, told them that Massasoit was dead. The envoys were shocked; and Habbamak began to wail forth his chief's death-song: "Oh, great sachem, Oh, great heart, with many have I been acquainted, but none ever equalled thee." Then turning to his pale-face friend, he said, "Oh, Master Winslow, his like you will never see again. He was not like other Indians, false and bloody and implacable; but kind, easily appeased when angry, and reasonable in his requirements. He was a wise sachem, not ashamed to ask advice, governing better with mild, than other chiefs did with severe measures. I fear you have not now one faithful friend left in the wigwams of the red men."† He would then break forth again in loud lamentations, "enough," says Winslow, "to have made the hardest heart sob and wail."‡

But time pressed, and Winslow, bidding Habbamak "leave wringing of his hands," trudged on over the patches of snow, through the naked forests shivering in the gusty winds of March, under the sullen sky. Corbitant's lodge was near; here it was hoped that fuller intelligence might be gain-

---

this was the great Hampden, vol. 1, p. 410. I find no facts sufficient to sustain that opinion." Elliot, vol. 1, p. 93, note.

* Elliot, Banvard, Winslow. † Winslow's Good News.
‡ Ibid.

ed. Corbitant was not at home, but his squaw informed them that Massasoit was not yet dead, though he could scarcely live long enough to permit his visitors to close his eyes.*

Reinvigorated by this news, and persuaded that while there was life there was hope, the envoys again pressed forward with eager footsteps. Soon Massasoit's wigwam was reached. A cordon of visitors surrounded it; and so great was the crowd, that it was with difficulty that the Pilgrims pushed through and gained an entrance. "When they succeeded, they beheld a scene so repulsive and so annoying as to be quite sufficient to banish whatever vitality the sick sagamore might still possess. Not only was the lodge crammed with filthy Indians, whose number effectually excluded all fresh air, but the pow-wows were busied in yelling their magical incantations, now rubbing the sick sachem, now wailing, now making frantic gestures; so that, had the disease possessed intelligence and been cognizant of what was taking place, it would have been effectually frightened away. Six or eight 'medicine-men' were manipulating him at once, and his ears were dinned with yells, when he should have been perfectly quiet."†

When the pow-wows had concluded their superstitious spells and exorcisms, they told Massasoit that Winslow had come to visit him. The sick Indian, turning on his skin couch, greeted the Englishman kindly. Disease had almost choked him,

---

* Winslow's Good News. † Banvard, pp. 95, 96.

and quite robbed him of sight; he was indeed near death. Winslow at once conveyed the assurance of the deep grief of the colonists at his sickness, informed him that the pale-faces had sent physic for his restoration to health, and offered himself to undertake the cure. These words, being translated by Habbamak, the Indian at once and cordially thanked Winslow, and accepted his good offices.*

The skilful Englishman, with a "confection of many comfortable conserves," soon worked a cure. The convalescent sagamore said, "Now I know that the English are indeed my friends, and love me; while I live I will never forget this kindness."† Nobly did he keep his word; for, after requesting "the pale-face medicine" to exercise his skill upon others of his tribe, who were down with the same disease which had laid him low, his gratitude was so warm that he disclosed to the pale-face leech the fact that a wide-spread and well-matured conspiracy was afoot to exterminate Weston's colony, in revenge for injuries heaped upon the Indians; that all the northeastern tribes were in the league; and that the massacre was to cover the Pilgrims also, lest they should avenge the fall of their neighbors. "A chief was here at the setting of the sun," added Massasoit, "and he told me that the pale-faces did not love me, else they would visit me in my pain, and he urged me to join the war party. But I said, No. Now if you take the chiefs of the league, and

* Winslow's Good News. † Ibid.

kill them, it will end the war-trail in the blood of those who made it, and save the settlements."*

Thankful to Massasoit for this disclosure, and profoundly impressed with its importance, the envoys speedily bade the sagamore good-by, and started for Plymouth. Reaching Corbitant's lodge towards evening, they decided to sleep with him. "We found him," says Winslow, "a notable politician, yet full of merry jests and squibs, and never better pleased than when the like are turned again on him."†

"If I were sick, as Massasoit has been," asked he, "would Mr. Governor send me medicine?"

"Yes," said Winslow.

"Would you bring it?" queried Corbitant.

"Certainly," was the reply.

At this the sachem was delighted. He resumed his questions.

"How did you dare to go so far into our hunting-grounds, with only one pale-face and Habbamak?"

"Because," said Winslow, "where there is true love, there can be no fear; my heart is so upright towards the Indians, that I have no cause to fear to go among them."

"If you love us so much," retorted the shrewd chief, "why is it that, when we go to Plymouth, you stand on guard, and present the mouths of your big guns at us?"

"Oh," was the reply, "that's the most honor-

---

* Winslow's Good News. ‡ Ibid.

able reception we could give you. 'Tis the English way of saluting distinguished guests."

"Ugh," said Corbitant, with the peculiar Indian grunt and shrug, "perhaps; but I do n't like such ways of shaking hands."*

Having noticed that before and after each meal his guests offered thanks, Corbitant asked them why they did it. " This led to a long conversation upon the character and works of the great Father; on the relations which his creatures sustain to him as their preserver and constant benefactor, and the duties which all owe to him as such, with which the chief seemed pleased. When the ten commandments were recited, he approved of all save the seventh; he saw many objections to tying a man to one woman."†

"This," says Banvard, "is a specimen of the manner in which the Pilgrims endeavored to communicate religious truths to the minds of their ignorant Indian neighbors. When among them, they observed religious exercises at their meals; continued the practice of morning and evening services; strictly regarded the Sabbath; and thus provoked inquiries. Then, when opportunity was given, they imparted, in a homely, familiar way, the elementary truths of the Bible."‡

After passing a pleasant night in Corbitant's wigwam, the Pilgrims resumed their journey, and after twenty-four hours' walk reached Plymouth.

They immediately imparted what they knew of

* Banvard, pp, 101, 102. † Ibid. ‡ Banvard. p. 102.

the Indian plot to the governor. Bradford summoned the settlers to deliberate. Upon examination other evidence was found which corroborated Massasoit's disclosure; and even in the midst of this consideration, one of Weston's pioneers came in, like Bunyan's Pilgrim, "with a pack on his back;" and "though he knew not a foot of the way, yet he got safe to Plymouth by losing his way," as he was pursued by the Indians, and would have been caught had he travelled by the accustomed track.*

"He told us," says Bradford, "how affairs stood at Wessagusset; how miserable all were; and that he dare not tarry there longer, as, by what he had observed, he apprehended those settlers would shortly be all knocked in the head."†

Startled by the imminence of the peril, Bradford at once despatched Standish with a small squad of men to warn and succor the menaced colonists. On reaching Wessagusset Standish boarded the "Swan," which lay moored in the harbor. Not a soul was on her. Surprised, the Pilgrim captain fired his musket. Several colonists then ran down to the shore. "How dare you leave your ship unguarded, and live in so much security?" asked he. "Why," was the reply of the colonists, who were insensible of their peril, "we have no fear of the Indians, but live with them, and suffer them to lodge with us, without ever having a gun or sword, or ever needing one."

* Winslow's Good News. † Bradford, p. 131.

"Well, well," cried Standish, "if you have no occasion for vigilance, so much the better." He then went ashore. Pitiful was the situation of the pioneers; four words paint the picture; filth, hunger, disease, nakedness. "After they began to come into want," remarks the old Pilgrim chronicler, "many sold their clothes and bed-coverings; others—so base were they—became servants to the Indians, and would cut wood and fetch water for them, for a cup of corn; some fell to stealing, and when they found the hiding-places where the natives stored their corn, they despoiled them, and this night and day, while the savages complained grievously. Now they were come to such misery that some starved and some died of cold. One, in gathering shell-fish, was so weak from hunger that he stuck fast in the mud, and not being able to pull clear, he was drowned by the incoming tide. Most had left their cabins and were scattered up and down through the woods and by the water-side, here six and there ten, grubbing for nuts and clams. By this carriage they were contemned and scorned by the Indians as 'paleface squaws,' and they insulted over them right insolently; insomuch that many times, as they lay thus scattered abroad, and had set a pot over a fire and filled it with ground-nuts or shell-fish, when it was ready the natives would come and, pushing them aside, eat it up; and at night the Indians, to revenge their thefts, stole their blankets and left them to lie all night in the cold. Yea, in the end, they were fain to hang one of their own men, whom they could not reclaim from stealing, at the dictation of the savages."*

Standish at once assembled the leading colonists, and opened to them his budget of news. The proposed massacre, the actors, all was laid bare. As frightened now as they were blinded before, all besought him to save them, and placed themselves in his hands. All stragglers were called in and supplied from his stores, a pint of corn a day for each man. This done, Standish began to dissemble; he wished to lure the chiefs of the conspiracy into his clutches, and so fight guile with guile.†

Though suspecting that their plot had been discovered, the Indians so greatly despised the colonists that they came daily into Wessagusset, uttering gibes and menaces loud and deep. They even ventured to taunt Standish. One of the braves, Pecksuot, a bold fellow, but a braggadocio, "went to Habbamak, who was with Standish as his interpreter, and told him that he had been informed that the captain had come to 'kill him and his friends.' 'Tell him,' he said, 'we know it, but we neither fear him nor will we shun him; let him attack us when he pleases, he will not surprise us.' "‡

At other times the Indians would enter the plantation, and, in the presence of the captain, sharpen their knives, feel their points, and jeer. One of their chiefs, Witawamat, often boasted of the fine qualities of his knife, on the handle of which was cut a

* Bradford, pp. 130, 131.
† Winslow's Good News. ‡ Banvard.

woman's face; "but," said he, "I have another at home with which I have killed both French and English, and that hath a man's face on it; by-and-by these two must marry."* Not long after, he said again, holding up his knife, "By-and-by this shall see and eat, but not speak," in allusion to the muskets of the English, which always reported their doings.†

Pecksuot was an Indian of immense muscular size and strength; Standish was a small man. Once the brave said to the captain: "You are a great officer, but a little man; and I am not a sachem, yet I possess great strength and courage."‡

Standish quietly pocketed these insults, and awaited his chance. It soon came. Pecksuot, Wetawamat, and two others, chiefs of the conspiracy, were finally all entrapped in one cabin. Standish with three comrades and Habbamak were also present. The door was secured and a terrific death-grapple at once ensued. There were no shrieks, no cries, no war-whoops. Nothing was heard save the fierce panting of the combatants and the dull thud of the blows given and returned. Habbamak stood quietly by, and meddled not. Soon the Englishmen were successful; each slew his opponent, and Standish himself closing with Pecksuot, snatched from the braggadocio's neck his vaunted knife, and plunged it into his foeman's heart. One blow did not kill him; frenzied and glaring, he leaped on Standish and tugged wildly at his throat. The struggle was brief but awful,

* Banvard, p. 116. † Ibid. ‡ Ibid.

and Standish called his whole skill into requisition to complete his victory. At length the death-blow was dealt:

> "See, his face is black and full of blood;
> His eye-balls farther out than when he lived;
> Staring full ghastly, like a strangled man;
> His hair upreared, his nostrils stretched with struggling;
> His hands abroad displayed, as one that grasped
> And tugged for life, and was by strength subdued."*

After the tragedy was over, Habbamak said to Standish, while a smile played over his swarthy features: "Yesterday, Pecksuot, bragging of his strength and stature, said you were a great captain, but a little man; but to-day I see that you are big enough to lay him on the ground."†

Standish did not pause for congratulation, nor did he care much for it; knowing the value of promptitude, he at once headed a foray on the neighboring Indian villages. Several skirmishes ensued; the savages, beaten and terrified, retreated from morass to morass. The conspiracy was buried with its originators; and many of the sachems who had joined the league, Conacum, Aspinet, Iyanough, died from diseases contracted in their headlong flight.‡

This was considered the "capital exploit" of Miles Standish. It struck such wholesome terror into the hearts of the surrounding tribes, that, in connection with the uniform justice and kindliness of the Pilgrims, it secured peace for half a century.§

---

* Shakspeare.   † Winslow, cited in Banvard, p. 120.
‡ Winslow, Elliot, Palfrey.   § Ibid.

The Westonians, discouraged and disgusted, resolved to break their ranks and give up their settlement. Standish "offered to escort them to Plymouth, and give them entertainment till Weston or some supply should come," says Bradford; "or if they liked any other course better, he promised to help them all he could. They thanked him, but most of them desired him to grant them some corn, then they would go with their ship to the eastward, where, haply, they might hear of Weston, or of some supply from him. That failing, since it was the time of year for ships to frequent the fishing waters, they could work among the fishermen till they could get passage into England. So they shipped what they had of any value, and the captain gave them all the corn he could—scarcely leaving himself sufficient to take him home—and saw the colonists well out of the bay; then he himself sailed back to Plymouth in triumph."*

There the head of Wetawamat was impaled, and set up prominently in the fort; and an Indian who had been sent in pursuit of that pioneer who had first brought word to the Pilgrims of the condition of his fellow-settlers, and had been himself captured, recognized it. The Pilgrim Fathers were not revengeful; they did not love to shed blood; so when Habbamak vouched for the friendship of this captive, he was liberated, and sent home to tell his tribe that the colonists loved peace, but that they could fight in case of need. Ere long the offending

* Winslow, Bradford, Thatcher.

red men sent peace-offerings into Plymouth, and sued for and obtained amity.*

Bradford, Winslow, and the rest, kept their friends in England and Holland as fully informed as possible of the daily history of the colony; and of course so memorable an event as this conspiracy and its suppression, received a profuse recital. When Robinson heard of the rencontre, he wrote back these words, finely illustrative of his character: "Oh, how happy a thing had it been, that you had converted some before you killed any."†

As for Weston's colony, this was the last of it. Some of the better of the pioneers went to Plymouth; others finally found their way back to England. They had landed under far better auspices than the Pilgrims. They were welcomed by fellow-countrymen, and sheltered throughout the winter. They commenced their settlement in the summer, when nature laughed, and the hillsides were gay with flowers, and the air sweet with the songs of birds. They possessed a ship. They had had been left competently provided in the wilderness. Yet they were no sooner *settled* than they were *unsettled*. Bankrupt and starving, they sought safety in flight. This was the fate of a colony whose "main end was to fish," which was founded on no higher law than the greed of gain.

"'Certainly the best works, and of greatest merit for the public,' observed the childless Lord Bacon,

---

* Winslow, Bradford, Thatcher.
† Morton, Young's Chronicles.

with complacent self-love, 'have proceeded from the unmarried or childless men.' Weston's company, after having boasted of their strength as far superior to Plymouth, which was enfeebled, they said, by the presence of women and children, yet owed their deliverance to the colony that had many women, children, and weak ones, with them."*

Thus it should seem that weakness is sometimes strength. Ethics are better buoys than numbers. Devout weakness is always stronger than self-complacent and impious strength. Justice and a helpful hand—these are the palladiums.

> "Too happy were men, if they understood
> There is no safety but in doing good."†

---

* Bancroft, Hist. United States, vol. 1, p. 319.
† Fountain's Rewards of Virtue.

CHAPTER XVI.

A CHECKERED RECORD.

"Naught shall prevail against us, or disturb
Our cheerful faith, that all which we behold
Is full of blessings."
WORDSWORTH.

A FEW weeks after the final abandonment of Wessagusset by Weston's colonists, a fishing-smack dropped anchor off Plymouth. A boat was lowered, and in a trice an Englishman, in the guise of a blacksmith, was landed. He seemed anxious to learn the condition and prospects of Weston's settlement, and was evidently ignorant of its untoward fate. On being informed of the conspiracy, massacre, and abandonment of the project, he seemed to be profoundly agitated. This stranger was Weston himself, once a prosperous London merchant, now alone in the wilderness, a ruined man. "A strange alteration there was in him to those who had known him in his former flourishing condition," moralizes the old Plymouth governor; "so uncertain are the mutable things of this unstable world. And yet men set their hearts upon them, though they daily see the vanity thereof."*

Weston was anxious to know the worst. He

---

* Bradford, p. 133.

also hoped that something might yet be saved. He sailed in a shallop for the seat of his downfallen venture. But misfortune dogged him. He was shipwrecked, and cast ashore with nothing but the clothes upon his person. Soon after, being discovered by the Indians, he was stripped even of these, and left to find his way nude to the coast of Maine. This he did; and borrowing a suit of clothes from the fishermen, he returned to Plymouth in a pitiable plight, and begged the loan of some beaver-skins as a stock in trade to commence life anew.*

The Pilgrims were themselves in a sad strait, "but they pitied his case, and remembered former courtesies. They told him he saw their want, and that they knew not when they should have a supply; also how the case stood betwixt the Merchant-adventurers and themselves, which he well knew. They said they had not much beaver, and if they should let him have it, it might create a mutiny, since the colony had no other means of procuring food and clothes, both which they sadly needed. Yet they told him they would help him, considering his necessity, but must do it secretly; so they let him have one hundred beaver-skins. Thus they helped him when all the world failed him, and he was enabled to go again to the ships, buy provisions, and equip himself. But he requited his benefactors ill, for he proved afterwards a bitter enemy on all occasions, and repaid his debt in nothing but reproaches and evil words. Yea, he divulged it to

* Winslow in Young. Banvard.

some that were none of their best friends, while he yet had the beaver in his boat, and boasted that he could now set them all by the ears, because they had done more than they could answer in letting him have the skins. But his malice could not prevail."*

Strangled by this episode, Weston was now dead to the Pilgrims, and he disappears from the after-history of Plymouth.†

Through all these months, hunger continued to gnaw the vitals of the Pilgrim colony. To secure a plentiful future, they decided to plant a large grain-crop this spring. But the labor of the settlers was hampered by an abnormal social arrangement. Plymouth fretted under an agreement which robbed work of its spur and its crown. Up to the month of April, 1623, a community of interest was strictly maintained. This did not arise from any peculiar fantastic notions among the colonists, but was required by a clause—reluctantly assented to—of their engagement with the Merchant-adventurers in England.‡ The contract tied the Pilgrims to the communal plan for a specified season.§ Land was not to be owned by individuals; it was common; each man cultivated what he pleased, and threw the product of his labor into the general store.

* Bradford, pp. 133, 134.
† In the latter part of 1623, Weston went to Virginia; thence he returned to England, where he disappears from history. Palfrey, vol. 1, p. 207.
‡ Judge Davis, note on Morton's Memorial.
§ Winslow in Young, p. 346. Palfrey, Thatcher, etc.

From the stock thus gained overseers supplied the settlers in equal quantities.*

Infinite were the vexations, multitudinous were the trials, which resulted. Now a general meeting was called, and this question was anxiously discussed. Finally it was decided, though only for reasons of the sternest necessity, to deviate somewhat from the form of the contract.

As the communal idea has, in our day, won wide favor with theorists and ideal dreamers, we subjoin and commend the weighty words of Bradford, who had experienced the evils of that vicious system, to the Fourierite philosophers:

"At length, after much debate, the governor, with the advice of the chiefest among the Pilgrims, gave way that each man should set corn for his individual benefit, and in that respect trust to himself; though, remembering the contract, all other things were to go on in the communal way till time freed them. So to every family a parcel of land was assigned, but only for present use, no division for inheritance being made, and all boys and youth were ranged under some family. This had good success, for it made all hands very industrious; so that much more corn was planted than otherwise would have been by any means the governor could have brought to bear. He was saved a deal of trouble, and the division gave great content. Even the women went into the field, taking with them their little ones, who before would allege weakness

* Winslow in Young, p. 346. Palfrey, Thatcher, Banvard, etc.

and inability, and whom to have compelled would have been thought grievously tyrannical.

"The experience which was had in this common interest and condition, tried sundry years, and that among godly and sober men, may well evince the vanity of that conceit of Plato and of other ancients, applauded by some of later times, that the abolition of individual property, and the introduction of a community of wealth, would make men happy and flourishing. This community, so far as it went at Plymouth, was found to breed much confusion and discontent, and to retard labor. The young men, that were most able and fit for service, did repine that they should spend their time and strength in working for the families of others, without other recompense than a bare subsistence. The strong man and the man of parts had no greater share than he that was weak, and not able to do a quarter the other could. This was thought injustice. The aged and graver sort—ranked and equalized with the meaner and younger men in the division of labor and provisions—esteemed it some indignity and disrespect unto their gray heads. And for men's wives to be bidden to do service for others, as dressing meat and washing clothes, they deemed it a kind of slavery which many husbands could not well brook. So if this arrangement did not cut off those relations which God hath set amongst men, yet it did at least much diminish and take off the mutual respect that should be preserved amongst them, and destroyed individuality. And things would have been worse, had the Pilgrims been more of a different condition. Let none object that this is man's corruption, and nothing to the philosophy *per se*. Yes; but since all men have this corruption in them, God in his wisdom saw another course fitter for them."*

When the Pilgrims had finished planting, they knew that many weary weeks must elapse ere they could reap what they had sown. Meantime " all their victuals were spent, and they rested on God's providence alone, many times not knowing at night where to get a bit of any thing the next day; so that, as has been well said, they, above all people in the world, had occasion to pray God to give them their daily bread."†

As the colonists had " but one boat left, and she not over-well fitted, they were divided into gangs of six or seven each, and so went out with a net they had bought, to take bass and such like fish by course, each company knowing its turn. No sooner was the boat discharged of what she had brought than the next gang took her. Nor did they return till they had caught something, though it were five or six days before; for they knew there was nothing at home, and to return empty-handed would be a great discouragement to the rest. Yea, they strove which should do best. If the boat was gone over-long or got little, then all went to the shore to seek shell-fish, which at low water they dug from the sand. They also got now and then a deer, one

---

* Bradford, pp. 135, 136. † Ibid., p. 136.

or two of the fittest being appointed to range the woods; and the meat thus gotten was fairly divided. All these wants were borne with great patience and alacrity of spirit."* God was thanked for what he gave, and for the rest all hoped.

The unusually large corn-crop just planted led the Pilgrims to believe that the approaching harvest would definitively stop the hungry mouth of their necessities; but, alas, this expectation seemed about to be blasted. A severe drought met them in the opening months of the summer. From the middle of May to the middle of July there was no rain. All nature seemed to pant with thirst. The streams dwindled, and ceased to laugh. The summer foliage seemed in the "sear and yellow leaf" of autumn. The flowers held out their parched and shrivelled tongues. The sprouting corn began to wither in the blade. Famine seemed inevitable. In this emergency, the devout Pilgrims resorted to the "mercy-seat," and besought Him who had so often appeared to succor them to aid them now. A special day of fasting and prayer was appointed; and we may still

> "hear the Pilgrims' peaceful prayer
> Swelling along the silent air,
> Amid the forest wild."

It has been well said, that answers to prayer do not generally come with *observation*. They are often sent in a way which is hid from most persons, and frequently even from those who receive them.

* Bradford, p. 136.

There are, however, instances in which these answers are so striking as to be visible to all. Some instances of this kind may be found in the early history of New England.*

On this occasion the day, which was kept with marked earnestness and solemnity, opened with a cloudless sky, while the sun poured its clear, scorching rays full upon the shrinking plains; but lo, says Winslow in his recital, ere the close of the services, " the sky was overcast, the clouds gathered on all sides, and on the next morning distilled such soft, sweet, and moderate showers of rain, continuing some fourteen days, and mixed with such seasonable weather, as it was hard to say whether our withered corn or our drooping affections were most quickened and revived, such was the bounty and goodness of our God."†

Habbamak, who was in Plymouth at this time, exclaimed as the rain began to fall, "Now I see that the Englishman's God is a good God, for he has heard you, and sent you rain, and that without storms and tempests, which we usually have with our rain, and which beat down our corn; but yours stands whole and erect still; surely your God is a good God."‡

But while these timely and gentle showers saved their crop and secured the future, the pinching want of the passing days was not stayed. Indeed, so bitter grew the famine, that on one occasion the colony

---

* White's Incidents, p. 41. † Winslow in Young.
‡ White's Incidents, p. 42.

was reduced to a single pint of corn; which, when divided among the Pilgrims, gave each five kernels.*

During the height of this suffering, a package of home-letters was received. From these the settlers gleaned some news which was of interest to them. It seems that Mr. John Pierce, in whose name their patent had been taken,† had grown covetous, and attempted to play both the Pilgrims and the Merchant-adventurers false. When he saw "how hopefully the Plymouth colony was seated," the trustee grew desirous of becoming lord-proprietary, and holding them as his tenants, "to sue in his courts as lord."‡ So he surreptitiously sued out a new patent, of much larger extent, in his own name, and then fitted out an expedition headed by himself, to go and take possession of his usurped domain.§ But "God marvellously crossed him." "Having sailed no farther than the Downs," says Cotton Mather, "his ship sprang aleak; and besides this disaster, which alone was enough to have stopped the voyage, one strand of the cable was accidentally cut, by which means it broke in a stress of wind, and all were in extreme danger of being wrecked upon the sands. Having with much cost recruited this loss, and increased the number of emigrants, Pierce again put to sea; but in mid-

* Banvard, Thatcher, Morton's Memorial.
† Chap. 10, p. 137.
‡ Bancroft, vol. 1, p. 320.   Bradford, p. 138.
§ Morton's Memorial, pp. 95-97.   Palfrey, vol. 1, pp. 210, 211,

ocean one of the saddest and longest storms known since the days of the apostle Paul drove the ship home to England once more, the vessel well-nigh torn to pieces, and the emigrants, though all saved, weary and affrighted. Pierce, by all his tumbling backward and forward, was by this time grown so sick of his patent that he vomited it up. He assigned it over to the home company;* but they afterwards obtained another, under the umbrage whereof they could more effectually carry on the affairs of their colony."†

The letter from the Merchant-adventurers, which recited these facts, closed with a cheering promise: "We have agreed with two merchants for a ship of a hundred and forty tons, called the 'Anne,' which is to be ready the last of this month of April, to bring sixty passengers and sixty tons of goods to you."‡

While the Pilgrims, enlivened by this news, were living on hope and five kernels of corn, they received a visitor. Captain Francis West, admiral of New England, who sailed under a commission to prevent all trading and fishing on the coast-line without a license from the Home Council, called at Plymouth. Of him the necessitous Pilgrims purchased a few edibles at high prices.§ The old sailor's mission failed; the fishermen were too strong and independent to be repressed. Ere long,

---

* Pierce sold his patent for five hundred pounds; he gave fifty for it." Banvard, p. 133. See Palfrey, ut antea, on this point.

† Cotton Mather's Magnalia, vol. 1, p. 60.

‡ Cited in extenso in Bradford, pp. 139, 140.

§ Bradford, p. 141. Winslow in Young.

on their petition, Parliament decreed that fishing should be free.*

Two weeks after the departure of West, the promised reinforcements arrived; the "Anne" landed her recruits, and a goodly store of provisions besides.†

So low was the colonial larder, that "the best dish they could present their friends with was a lobster or a piece of fish, without bread, or any thing else but a cup of fair spring water."‡

The "Anne" was shortly followed by the "Little James," a vessel of forty-four tons burden, "built to stay in the country."§

"Among the pioneers just arrived," says Cotton Mather, "were divers worthy and useful men, who were come to seek the welfare of this little Israel; though at their coming they were as differently affected as the rebuilders of the temple at Jerusalem; some were grieved when they saw how bad the condition of their friends was, and others were glad that it was no worse."‖

Among the arrivals at this time "were, Cuthbertson, a member of the Leyden church, the wives of Fuller and Coake, and two daughters of Brewster. There were at least twelve ladies. One of these became the wife of Bradford; Standish married another. Alice Southworth, Bradford's second

---

* Banvard, p. 134.
† Morton's Memorial, Thatcher, Palfrey.
‡ Bradford, p. 146.   § Palfrey, vol. 1, pp. 211, 212.
‖ Mather's Magnalia, vol. 1. p. 60.

wife, is said to have been his first love. Both being widowed, a correspondence took place, in the sequel of which she came out from England, and married her some-time lover at Plymouth."*

"Some of your old friends go to you with these lines," wrote Cushman; "they come dropping to you, and by degrees I hope ere long you shall enjoy them all."†

Now also this commercial partnership beheld a vision of the immortal renown to which its humble agents were destined. "Let it not be grievous to you," wrote the prescient scribe of the Home Company, "that you have been instruments to break the ice for others who came after you with less difficulty; the honor shall be yours to the world's end. We bear you always in our hearts, and our cordial affection is toward you all, as are the hearts of hundreds more who never saw your faces, but who pray for your safety as for their own, that the same God who hath so marvellously preserved you from seas, foes, famine, will still preserve you from all future dangers, and make you honorable among men and glorious in bliss at the last day."‡

* Palfrey, vol. 1, p. 212, note.
† Bradford, p. 145. ‡ Ibid., pp. 145, 146.

CHAPTER XVII.

WOLVES IN THE SHEEPFOLD.

"I, under fair pretence of friendly ends,
With well-placed words of glozing courtesy,
Baited with reason not unplausible,
Wind me into the easy-hearted man,
And hug him into snares."
MILTON's *Comus.*

THE Plymouth colonists were men of active enterprise. They were miserly of time, and hoarded their hours. They were also anxious to please the Merchant-adventurers. So now, as quickly as might be, the "Anne" was laden with clapboards, beaver skins, and divers furs; letters whose every line was a loving pulsation, were indited to the lingering absentees at Leyden and to home circles in England; and on the 10th of September, 1623, the vessel sailed, carrying with her Edward Winslow, who was sent over to report progress, and to procure such necessities as were demanded by the imperious wants of the expanding colony.*

After watching the "Anne" until she dipped below the horizon, the pilgrims returned from the shore and prepared to go into the harvest field. This season "God gave them plenty, and the face of things was changed, to the grateful rejoicing of all hearts." The granaries were filled. Some of

* Prince, Morton's Memorial, Bradford, Thatcher's Plymouth.

the abler and more industrious had to spare, and the perturbed ghost of famine, which had so long haunted Plymouth, was definitively laid.*

Many attributed this plenteous harvest to the partial abandonment of the communal plan, and in consequence the desire for complete emancipation from its thraldom became more general and earnest.†

Some of the late comers had sailed not under articles of agreement with the company of Merchant-adventurers, but on their individual account; so they landed free from those conditions which shackled the elder settlers. Under these circumstances it was thought fit, ere these outsiders were received and permitted to settle and build in Plymouth, to exact of them certain specified conditions precedent. So reasonable a requisition won ready assent, and an agreement was signed to this effect: The colony on its part, the outsiders on theirs, covenanted to show each the other all reasonable courtesies; all were to be alike subject to such laws and orders as were already made, or might thereafter be made, for the public good; the outsiders were freed and exempted from the general employments which the communal condition required of its participants, except for purposes of defence and such work as tended to the lasting welfare of the colony; they were taxed for the maintenance of the government, and debarred from traffic with the Indians for their individual profit, until the expiration of

* Bradford, p. 147. † Ibid.

the seven years which tied the colonists to the communality.*

Towards the middle of September, while the Pilgrims were in the midst of their harvest labors, Robert Gorges, a son of Sir Ferdinand Gorges, famous as a *voyageur* and discoverer, sailed into Plymouth bay.† He had recently returned from the Venetian wars, and now came armed with a commission from the New England council as governor-general of the territory from Acadia to Narragansett Bay.‡ With him were families of emigrants equipped to commence a settlement, and a learned and worthy clergyman of the English church, William Morrel, an important item of whose mission was to "exercise superintendence over the New England churches."§

Gorges tarried at Plymouth about a fortnight, receiving friendly and cordial entertainment.‖ He had been advised to select Admiral West, Christopher Levett, and the existing governor of Plymouth, as his advisers. This he did; and in this body was vested the full authority to administer justice in all cases, "capital, criminal, and civil," throughout the province of New England.¶ This arranged, Gorges sailed for Wessagusset, the site of Weston's discomfiture, and, landing his colonists, essayed to plant on that inauspicious coast a permanent settlement.**

This colony, like its predecessor, was fated.

* Bradford, p. 148.
† Felt, Hist. New England, Prince, Bradford.
‡ Felt, Bradford, Morton's Memorial, etc.
§ Felt, vol. 1, p. 77. ‖ Bradford, p. 149.
¶ Ibid. Morton's Memorial. ** Ibid.

Hardly surviving its birth, it lingered through a twelvemonth, and then dissolved. Sir Ferdinand Gorges and his company, discouraged by the opposition of the Parliament to their New England schemes, would adventure nothing.* In the spring of 1624 he summoned his son home; and a little later Morrel, who had made no effort to exercise his superintendency, followed him, and this gave the second settlement at Wessagusset its *coup de grâce*.†

Morrel was not spoiled by his disappointment. "I shall always be desirous for the advancement of those colonies," he said.‡ And in a Latin poem addressed to the New England Council, he wrote:

> "If these poor lines may win that country love,
> Or kind compassion in the English move,
> Or painful men to a good land invite,
> Whose holy works the natives may enlight,—
> If Heaven grant this, to see there built I trust,
> An English kingdom from the Indian dust."§

But while "unmerciful disaster followed thick and followed faster" this enterprise of Gorges and several kindred ones,‖ smiting them into early graves, Plymouth, clasping hands with God, strengthened daily, and walked forward to assured success. Early in 1624, the annual election occurred. Governor Bradford, anxious to retire, pleaded hard for "rotation in office," and alleged that that was the "end

---

* Felt. † Ibid. Bradford, Morton's Memorial.
‡ Felt, vol. 1, p. 78. § Cited in Felt, ut antea.
‖ "There were also this year some scattering beginnings made in other places, as at Piscataway, by Mr. David Thompson, who was sent over by Mason and Gorges, at Monhegin, and some other places by sundry others." Bradford, p. 154.

of annual elections." But the Pilgrims rightly regarded him as a pivotal-man, and with rare good sense they reëlected him unanimously.* When the election was over the "Little James" was well victualed and despatched to the eastward on a fishing expedition. On reaching Damarin's cove " there arose such a violent and extraordinary storm that the seas broke over such places in the harbor as were deemed absolutely secure, and drove the vessel against great rocks, which beat a hole in her hulk that a horse and cart might have gone through, and afterwards drove her into deep water, where she sank. The master was drowned; the rest of the men, except one, saved their lives with much ado; and all the provisions, salt, tackle, and what else was in her, was lost."† Saddened by this mishap, but undismayed, the Pilgrims now commenced their preparations for planting. "A great part of liberty," says Seneca, "is a well-governed belly, and to be patient in all wants."‡ And Corbett, borrowing the same idea, put it into homely English by affirming that "the stomach is the cause of civilization." He meant that hunger begets labor to satisfy its cravings. "Wants awaken intellect. To gratify them disciplines the mind. The keener the want, the lustier the growth."§

The famine of the past had revealed to the Pilgrims the weakness and inefficiency of the com-

---

* Prince, Bradford, Pilgrims' Journal.
† Bradford, pp. 156, 157.   ‡ Seneca's Epis. 123.
§ Phillips' Letters and Speeches, p. 372.

munal plan. It educated them; for on an individual basis they reaped plenty. They overcame hunger by patience. They flanked famine by a skilful social arrangement. Now, as before, each man broke ground for himself.* There was no longer an Elysium for sluggards; each reaped as he had sown.

In March, 1624, Winslow returned to Plymouth, after an absence of eight months.† He brought with him three heifers and a bull—the first neat cattle that came into New England.‡ The exiles could no longer say, "We are without cattle, and we have no Egypt to go to for corn."§ Cattle they now had, and they created an Egypt.

Winslow also brought some "clothing and other necessaries; a carpenter, who died soon, but not until he had rendered himself very useful;" a "saltman," who proved "an ignorant, foolish, self-willed fellow," and only made trouble and waste; and "a preacher, though none of the most eminent and rare"—to whose transportation Cushman wrote that he and Winslow had consented only "to give content to some in London."‖ Winslow informed his coadjutors of a sad "report that there was among the Merchant-adventurers a strong faction hostile to Plymouth, and especially set against the coming of the rest from Leyden"¶—which explains

---

° Prince, Bradford. † Morton's Memorial.
‡ Thatcher's Plymouth, p. 111.
§ Morton's Memorial, p. 103. ‖ Palfrey, vol. 1, p. 215.
¶ Bradford, pp. 159, 160, 167.

the long tarry of Robinson and his flock in Holland.

"It will be remembered," remarks Palfrey, "that the London adventurers were engaged in a commercial speculation. Several of them sympathized more or less in religious sentiment with the Pilgrims; but even with most of these considerations of pecuniary interest were paramount, and they were, besides, a minority when opposed to the aggregate of those adventurers who had no mind to interest themselves in religious dissensions to the damage of their prospect of gain. Under such circumstances, the policy of the English partners would naturally be to keep in favor with the court and with the council for New England, of which Sir Ferdinand Gorges and other churchmen were leaders. This it was that occasioned the thwarting embarrassments which were persistently interposed to frustrate Robinson's wish to collect his scattered flock in America. Neither the Virginia Company, nor the Merchant-adventurers as a body, would have preferred to employ Separatists in founding American colonies, and giving value to their land. But the option was not theirs. At the moment, no others were disposed to confront the anticipated hardships, and none could be relied upon like these to carry the business through. This was well understood on both sides to be the motive for the engagement that was made.

"If Separatists were per force to undertake the enterprise, it was desirable that they should be persons not individually conspicuous, or obnoxious to displeasure in high quarters; and when Brewster, and not Robinson, accompanied the first settlers to New England, it was a result, if not due to the intrigues of the Adventurers, certainly well according with their policy. Brewster was forgotten in England; nor had he ever been known as a literary champion of his sect. The able and learned Robinson was the recognized head of the *Independents*, a rising and militant power. He had an English, if indeed it may not be called a European reputation. No name could have been uttered in courtly circles with worse omen to the new settlement. The case was still stronger when, having lost their way, and in consequence come to need another patent, the colony was made a dependency of the Council for New England, instead of the Virginia Company. In the Virginia Company, laboring under the displeasure of the king, and having Sandys and Wriothesley for its leaders, there was a leaven of popular sentiment. The element of absolutism and prelacy was more controlling in the councils of the rival corporation.

"From these circumstances the quick instinct of trade took its lesson. To the favor of the Council for New England, with Sir Ferdinand Gorges at its head, and the king taking its part against Sir Edward Coke and the House of Commons, the Merchant-adventurers were looking for benefits which some of them had no mind to hazard by encouraging their colony to exhale any offensive odor of schism. This gives us an insight into the policy of that action to which Robinson referred when, in a letter to Brewster, now brought by Winslow, he wrote: 'I persuade myself that for me, they of all others are unwilling I should be transported, especially such of them as have an eye that way themselves, as thinking if I come there their market will be marred. And for these Adventurers, if they have but half the wit to their malice, they will stop my course when they see it intended.'

"In these circumstances, also, we find an explanation of the selection of a minister 'not the most eminent and rare,' and such as Cushman and Winslow could agree to take only 'to give content to some in London.' To send a clergyman avowedly of the state church was a course not to be thought of. The colonists could not be expected to receive him. The best method for their purpose was, to employ some one of a character and position suited to get possession of their confidence, and then use it to tone down their religious strictness, and, if circumstances should favor, to disturb the ecclesiastical constitution which they had set up.

"As the financial prospects of the colony faded, the more anxious were the unsympathizing London partners to relieve it and themselves from the stigma of religious schism. The taunt that their colonists were Brownists depressed the value of their stock. It was for their interest to introduce settlers of a different religious character, and to take the local power, if possible, out of the hands of those who represented the obnoxious tenets. To this end it was their policy to encourage such internal disaffection as already existed, and to strengthen it by the infusion of new elements of discord. A part even of the 'Mayflower' emigrants, without religious sympathy with their superiors, and jealous of the needful exercise of authority, were fit subjects for an influence adverse to the existing organization. The miscellaneous importation in the 'Fortune' followed; and the whole tenor of the discourse of Cushman, who came out and returned in her, shows that there were 'idle drones' and 'unreasonable men' mixed with the nobler associates of the infant settlement. The 'Anne' and her partner, the last vessels despatched by the Adventurers, brought new fuel for dissension in those of that company who came 'on their particular' account. Nor does it seem hazardous to infer, alike from the circumstances of the case and from developments which speedily followed, that some of these persons, in concert with the 'strong faction among the Adventurers,' came over on the errand of subverting the existing government and order."*

The clergyman now sent over, and mentioned in the home-letters, was John Lyford. He was the seed of many and sad disturbances. "When he first came ashore," says Bradford, "he saluted the colonists with such reverence and humility as is seldom seen, and indeed made them ashamed, he so bowed and cringed unto them; he would have kissed their hands, if they had suffered it. Yet all

* Palfrey, vol. 1, pp. 216-219.

the while, if we may judge by his after-carriage, he was but like him mentioned by the psalmist,* that croucheth and boweth that heaps of poor may fall by his might. Or like that dissembling Ishmael† who, when he had slain Gedeliah, went out weeping, and met them that were coming to offer incense in the house of the Lord, saying, 'Come to Gedeliah,' when he meant to slay them."‡

The Pilgrims received Lyford cordially, giving him the warmest of welcomes and the heartiest. A larger allowance out of the general store was allotted him than any other had; and as the governor was wont, "in all weighty affairs, to consult with Elder Brewster as well as with his special assistants, so now, from courtesy, he called Lyford also to advise in all important crises."§

Ere long he professed to desire to unite with the Pilgrim church. He was accordingly received, and "made a large confession of his faith, and an acknowledgment of his former disorderly walking and entanglement with many corruptions, which had been a burden to his conscience; so that he blessed God for this opportunity of liberty to enjoy the ordinances of God in purity among His people."‖

For a time all things went comfortably and smoothly; but in this calm, Lyford contracted an intimacy with one John Oldham, who had come out in the "Anne" on his own account, and had been a

---

* Psalm 10 : 10.   † Jeremiah 41 : 6.
‡ Bradford, p. 171.   § Ibid.   ‖ Ibid., p. 172.

factious bawler from the outset.* From so congenial an association, evil could not but be begotten. The bully and the hypocrite soon nursed it and set it afoot. Both Oldham and Lyford grew very perverse—though just before Oldham also had been received as a member of the Plymouth church, "whether from hypocrisy or out of some sudden pang of conviction God only knows"—and "showed a spirit of great malignancy, drawing as many into faction as they could influence. The most idle and profane they nourished, and backed in all their lawlessness, so they would but cleave to them and revile the Pilgrim church. Private meetings and back-stair whisperings were incessant among them, they feeding themselves and others with what they should bring to pass in England by the faction of their friends among the Adventurers, which brought both themselves and their dupes into a fools' paradise. Outwardly they set a fair face on things, yet they could not carry things so closely but much both of their sayings and doings was discovered."†

Finally, when the vessel in which Winslow had returned was laden, and ready to hoist anchor and spread sail for home, it was observed that Lyford and his coadjutors "were long in writing and sent many letters, and communicated to each other such things as made them laugh in their sleeves, thinking they had done their errand efficiently."‡

---

* Bradford, p. 172.   Morton's Memorial, p. 112.   † Ibid.
‡ Bradford, p. 173.

Scenting mischief, Bradford watched them closely; and when the ship left the harbor, he followed her in the shallop, and demanded Lyford's letter-bag. The captain, who was friendly to the colonial government, and cognizant of the plot afoot, both in Britain and at Plymouth, to overreach the Pilgrims, at once acceded. Above twenty letters, many of them long, and pregnant with slanders, false accusations, and malicious innuendoes, tending not only to the prejudice, but the ruin and utter subversion of the settlement, were found. Most of these Bradford let pass, contenting himself with abstracts. But of the most material true copies were taken, and then forwarded, the originals being detained, lest their writer should deny his work, in which case he would now be compelled to eat his own penmanship.*

The ship had sailed towards evening; in the night the governor returned. Lyford and his faction "looked blank when they saw Bradford land; but after some weeks, as nothing came of it, they were as brisk as ever, thinking that all was unknown and was gone current, and that the shallop went but to despatch some well-nigh forgotten or belated letters. The reason why Bradford and the rest concealed their knowledge was, to let affairs drift to a natural development, and ripen, that they might the better discover the intentions of the malcontents, and see who were their adherents. And they did this the rather, because they had learned

* Bradford, p. 173.

from a letter written by one of the confederates, that Oldham and Lyford intended an immediate reformation of the church and commonwealth, and proposed at once, on the departure of the ship, to unite their forces, and set up a worship on the English model."*

The Pilgrims had not long to wait. Oldham, with the natural instinct of a bully, picked constant quarrels, refused to mount guard, and pelted Standish with vile epithets. Lyford, a more cautious knave, had no heart for fisticuffs, but he set up another worship on the Sabbath, and openly celebrated sacraments† which were to the Pilgrims instinct with vicious tyranny and idolatrous significance; and to escape from which, they had crossed the channel into Holland, and plunged across the Atlantic into the winter wilderness.

The colonists at once acted. Oldham was tamed. "After being clapped up awhile, he came to himself." Lyford was formally impeached. A court was convened, and the settlers at large were summoned to attend. Bradford himself conducted the prosecution in this primitive trial. He said that, "being greatly oppressed in Britain, the Pilgrims had come to America, here to enjoy liberty of conscience; and for that they had passed through frightful hardships, and planted this settlement on the sterile rocks. The danger and the charge of the beginning were theirs. Lyford had been sent over at the general expense, and both himself and

* Bradford, p. 175. † Ibid.

his large family* had been maintained from the common store. He had joined their church, and become one of themselves; and for him to plot the ruin of his entertainers was most unjust and perfidious. As for Oldham and his crew, who came at their own charge and for their particular benefit, seeing they were received in courtesy by the plantation, when they came only to seek shelter and protection under its wings, not being able to stand alone, they were like the fable of the hedgehog whom the cony, in a stormy day, from pity welcomed into her burrow; but who, not content to take part with her, in the end, with her sharp pricks forced the poor cony to forsake her own burrow, as these do now attempt to do with us."†

Here Lyford denied that he had been guilty of any wrong. Bradford at once "put in" his intercepted letters as evidence. The unmasked hypocrite was dumb. But Oldham, mad with rage, attempted to rouse an *émeute* on the spot.‡ No hand was uplifted at his appeal, and Bradford caused the whole parcel of letters to be read; after which, resuming his speech, he reminded Lyford of his humble confession on being received into the church, of his solemn promise not to attempt to perform the functions of a clergyman until he had another call to that sacred office; in open violation of which, he had assumed the clerical garb, in virtue of his

---

* He had a wife and four children. Bradford, p. 175, editor's note.
† Ibid, pp. 175, 176.   ‡ Ibid.

ordination, drawn aside a small clique, and by attempting to officiate at the Lord's table on the Sabbath, broken his solemn pledge and disturbed the public peace.*

The proof was so patent, the falsehoods which impregnated the insolent letters were so bold, that the factionists were absolutely dumb. No voice was raised in extenuation of the roguery. Conviction was speedy. Oldham and Lyford were both sentenced to banishment.†

Oldham at once left Plymouth, and repaired to Nantasket, where the Pilgrims had a station to accommodate the Indian trade.‡ But Lyford, as weak as he was vicious, burst into tears, and "confessed that he feared he was a reprobate, with sins too heavy for God to pardon;" and he promised amendment with such emphasis, and pleaded so piteously for forgiveness, that the kind and merciful settlers consented to keep him on probation for six months.§

But he was an ingrained knave, and amendment was not in him. Not long after this scene, he wrote a second letter to the Merchant-adventurers, in which he justified all his former charges, and elaborated them. Unhappily for him, the messenger to whom he intrusted this precious missive surrendered it into the hands of Bradford, who simply filed it for the present, and let his just wrath accumulate.‖

---

* Bradford, pp. 175, 176. † Ibid., p. 182.
‡ Palfrey, vol. 1, p. 221, note. Morton's Memorial, p. 117, note. § Ibid. ‖ Bradford.

In the mean time the ship, with Lyford's batch of letters aboard, dropped anchor in the Thames. The lies of their masquerading agent were eagerly conned by the London partners. A conclave was held. The inimical adventurers pointed triumphantly to Lyford's testimony. But, fortunately for the Pilgrims, Winslow, who had returned to London, had become acquainted with certain disreputable and damning facts in Lyford's home-career, both in England and in Ireland, where he had officiated as pastor, which proved him to be a lecher and a swindler, who soiled the surplice and the cope. With these facts, and followed by grave and unimpeachable witnesses, Winslow hurried into the room where the merchants were assembled, and made his *exposé*, which "struck Lyford's friends with sudden dumbness, and made them shame greatly."*

But these reports, together with their disappointment in not harvesting an immediate fortune, impelled two thirds of the original members of the London Company to withdraw from the venture; "and as there had been a faction and siding amongst them for two years, so now there was an utter breach and sequestration."†

Some of the partners, however, remained friendly; and these, assuming the debt of the colony—amounting to some fourteen hundred pounds sterling—fitted out a ship for another voyage, wrote in terms of comfort and cheer, and sent out cattle,

* Palfrey, vol. 1, p. 221.
† Winslow, quoted in Palfrey, ut antea.

tools and clothing, which they sold to the planters, despite their friendly professions, at an exorbitant advance on the market value.*

In the spring of 1625, Winslow came back with this ship thus freighted; and he brought with him besides, the news of the disaffection among the Merchant-adventurers. On landing, he was the surprised witness of a strange ceremony. In the village street was drawn up a guard of musketeers in two files, between which a man was running. As he passed, each soldier gave him a thump behind with the but of his musket.† This was called "running the gauntlet," and was a custom borrowed from the Indians. So engrossed were the settlers in this odd sport, and so convulsed were the soberest of them with laughter at the victim's odd grimaces on being struck and bidden "mend his manners," that Winslow advanced quite up to the crowd ere he was discovered and recognized. He then learned that the sufferer of this singular punishment was Oldham, who, despite his banishment, had ventured to return to Plymouth and revile his judges.‡

Winslow at once informed the clustering colonists of the effect of Lyford's letters in England, and repeated his *exposé* of that bad man's abhorrent private character.§ The Pilgrims were not surprised. Lyford's own wife, "a grave matron of good carriage," had herself, in the sorrow of her

* Thatcher, Prince, Palfrey, Bradford. † Bradford, p. 190.
‡ Ibid., p. 192. Morton's Memorial, p. 120. § Ibid.

heart, disclosed some secrets and uncloaked some crimes which led them to believe Lyford capable of perpetrating any villany.*

Now, since his probationary time had expired, and he was a more dangerous rascal than before, he was ordered to quit the colony. This he did, joining Oldham at Nantucket; whence, a little later, he wandered into Virginia, dying there very miserably.†

Eventually Oldham repented of his evil conduct, and became reconciled to the Pilgrims; "so that he had liberty to come and go, and converse with them at pleasure," until, some years later, the Indians, in a petty quarrel, knocked his brains out with a tomahawk.‡

Thus ended the "Lyford troubles." Led by God, the Plymouth colonists safely surmounted one more obstacle, the insidious assault of masqueraders who "stole the livery of heaven to serve the devil in."

The winter of 1624–5 had passed without any special occurrence save this Lyford affair; and here see one strange thing: "Many who before stood something off from the church," says Bradford, "now, seeing Lyford's unrighteous dealing and malignity against it, came forward and tendered themselves as members, professing that it was not out of any dislike of any thing that they had stood so long aloof, but from a desire to fit

* Bradford, p. 192. Morton's Memorial, p. 120. † Ibid.
‡ Chiever's Journal, p. 327. Morton's Memorial.

themselves better for such a connection, and that now they saw that the Lord called for their help. So that Lyford's crusade had quite a contrary effect from that hoped; which was looked at as a great work of God, who drew men on by unlikely means, and by occurrences which might rather have set them farther off."*

Lyford had complained to the Merchant-adventurers that the Pilgrims had no regularly ordained minister. To this charge Bradford made a fine retort: "We answer, the more is our wrong, that our pastor is kept from us by these men's means, who then reproach *us* for it. Yet have we not been wholly destitute of the means of salvation, as this man would have the world believe; for our reverend elder, Mr. Brewster, hath labored diligently in dispensing the word of God unto us; and, be it spoken without ostentation, he is not inferior to Mr. Lyford—and some of his betters—either in gifts or learning, though he would never be persuaded to take higher office upon himself."†

Brewster taught twice every Sabbath powerfully and profitably, and without stipend, which he steadily declined, working for his bread with his own hands, and earning it in the sweat of his brows, thus approximating to the early Christian practice. "He did more in one year," asserts old John Cotton, "than many who have their hundreds per annum do in all their lives." So it seems that there is one brilliant exception to the Indian maxim,

* Bradford, p. 189. † Ibid., p. 188.

"Poor pay poor preach." The good elder had a singular gift in prayer, "yet was seldom wordy or prolix." Without the afflatus of ordination, he was so much better than most ministers with it, that, though destitute of "consecrated ministrations," the colonists did not suffer much, and mainly regretted the absence of sacraments, which Brewster, unordained, was not competent to celebrate.*

Prince gives a summary of the religious tenets of the Plymouth church:

I. "It held that nothing is to be accounted true religion but what is taught in the Holy Scriptures."

II. "It held that every man has the right of private judgment, of testing his belief by the sacred writ, and of worshipping God in his own way as that text directed."†

On this doctrine the Pilgrims thrived. "Brown bread and the gospel is good fare," they said to one another.‡ Indeed it was; and there on the desolate coast, where wheat froze and the bitter winter congealed six months of the twelve, men grew. "At last," says Elliott, "in the beginning of the seventeenth century, we see a church with no priest, with no hierarchy, with no forms; none like it since that at Corinth; none so entirely free to work out its ideas into life and action. It was a religious democracy. Its doctrines and practices were the outcome

---

* Elliot, vol. 1, pp. 119, 120.
† Ibid., p. 116. Prince's Chronology. Thatcher's Plymouth.
‡ A Brief Review of the Rise and Progress of New England. London, 1774.

of the time, and were decided on by the votes of the members as men. In theory, the majority ruled in the Plymouth church. 'T is a noticeable thing in human history, and it has had its influence in both church and state. The day had come when a few brave men could take this step in advance towards freedom, and not be swallowed up and lost. The day had come when democracy was possible in the church, foretelling its speedy coming in the state."[*]

[*] Elliot, vol. 1, p. 135.

CHAPTER XVIII.

SAD NEWS FROM ENGLAND.

"Thou know'st 'tis common; all that live must die.
Passing through nature to eternity."
Shakspeare's Hamlet.

The Pilgrims were fretted by the unsatisfactory and clogging conditions of their compact with the London partners. Their prosperity was perpetually menaced by the factions and the chicanery of a herd of merchants whose only god was mammon, and who cared nothing for justice and sober living and their plighted word, if only they might make their heaps high and massy.

Early in 1625, the colonists determined to initiate measures which should look to their disenthralment, and whose result should be to give them in fee simple those lands which their patient skill had wrung from the sturdy hand of unwilling and churlish nature. Standish was commissioned to go to England, and open negotiations with the Merchant-adventurers.*

Two ships, which had come out on a trading voyage, were now about to sail for home. In the larger of these the redoubtable captain embarked. "Being both well laden, they went joyfully home

---

* Morton, Prince, Hazard, Bradford, Thatcher, Banvard.

together, the greater towing the lesser at her stern all the way over. And they had such fair weather, that they never once cast off till both were shot deep into the English channel. Yet there the little vessel was unhappily seized by a Turkish rover, and carried into Sallee, where master and crew were made slaves; and her cargo of beaver-skins was sold at sixpence a piece. Thus were their hopes dashed, and the joyful news they meant to carry home was turned to heavy tidings."*

Fortunately for Standish, the Turk was satisfied with the morsel he had already gotten into his capacious maw, and did not pursue the bigger ship; so that he escaped a life of Eastern servitude, and safely reached the English soil. Wasting no time, he hastened to meet the London partners; and so skilful was his diplomacy, that he made arrangements for the gradual absorption of the Plymouth debt by the settlers, "taking up a hundred and fifty pounds of it on the spot, though at fifty per cent. interest, which he bestowed in trading and in the purchase of such commodities as he knew to be requisite for colonial use."†

In the spring of 1626, he returned to Plymouth,‡ bringing with him the mournful intelligence of the death of Cushman in England and of Robinson in Leyden,§ a double bereavement to the Pilgrim pioneers.

The loss of no other two men could have dealt

* Bradford, pp. 202, 203. † Palfrey, vol. 1, p. 224.
‡ Hazard, Bradford, Palfrey. § Ibid.

so stunning a blow to the infant settlement. Plymouth was almost buffeted from its feet. The loss seemed irreparable to human eyes; but God, who uses his servants, delights to show the world that they are not indispensable to him. Cushman had been "as their right hand to the Pilgrims, and for divers years had done and agitated all their business with the Adventurers, to the great advantage of his friends."*

But Robinson was mourned with a peculiar sorrow. Attached to their great teacher by the tenderest personal ties, by many favors rendered and received, by marriage vows plighted at his altar, by mutual perils undergone for a common faith, by expectation of his arrival and reunion on the bleak New England strand, is it strange that Plymouth at large wept sore for him, and plucked its beard?

"Robinson's powerful ascendency over the minds of his associates, acquired by eminent talents and virtues, had been used disinterestedly and wisely for the common good. With great courage and fortitude, he had equal gentleness and liberality; and his intellectual accomplishments and the generosity of his affections inspired mingled love and admiration. Though he passed his life in the midst of controversy, it was so far from narrowing his mind, that his charity towards dissenters distinguished him among the divines of his day as much as his abilities and learning, while his broad and

* Bradford, p. 207.

tolerant views continued to ripen and expand as he grew towards age,"* and bloomed into the grave.

In especial he won the benediction of the seventh beatitude; for he was famous as a peacemaker, and there are many instances of reconciliation between those at variance effected by his fine Christian tact.†

"He fell sick Saturday morning, February 22, 1625. Next day he taught twice; but in the week, grew feebler every day, and quit this life on the 1st of March. All his friends came freely to him; and if prayers, tears, or means, could have saved his life, he had not gone hence."‡

He died in his fifty-first year, " even as fruit falleth before it is ripe, when neither length of days nor infirmity of body did seem to call for his end."§ The discarded flesh-tabernacle was laid to rest in the chancel of one of the churches at Leyden,‖ allotted by the Dutch for the use of the English exiles; and the magistrates, ministers, professors, and students, followed him to the grave.¶

Robinson was the Moses of the Pilgrims, and like his prototype, he looked into the promised land from the top of Pisgah, but he did not enter it. Intrigue balked him of that felicity, and "hope de-

---

* Palfrey, vol. 1, p. 225. † Banvard, p. 151.
‡ Elliot's Biog. Dict. § Young's Chronicles, p. 481.
‖ "It is not certain where he lies buried; George Sumner thinks in St. Peter's church, Leyden." Elliot, Hist. New Eng., vol. 1, p. 125, note.
¶ Stoughton, Heroes of Puritan Times, p. 102.

ferred made his heart sick." But ideas cannot be barred out. His entered the wilderness, and germinated democracy and the representative system. "His truth, planted at Plymouth, has blossomed on the rocky shores, in the sheltered valleys, and on the breezy hills of New England, and borne a grand harvest."

CHAPTER XIX.

PROGRESS.

"And when our children turn the page
To ask what triumphs marked our age—
What we achieved to challenge praise,
Through the long line of future days—
This let them read, and hence instruction draw:
 'Here were the many blest,
 Here found the virtues rest,
Faith linked with Love, and Liberty with Law.'"
Sprague's *Centennial Ode.*

The progress of population at Plymouth was slow for a decade. The lands in the vicinity were not fertile. Still the plantation had struck deep root and was bound to spring up and bear a hundred fold.* If the colonial prosperity was not imposing, it was thriving. A little earlier than this Smith learned in Virginia that there were on this New England slope "about a hundred and eighty persons; some cattle and goats; many swine and a good store of poultry; and thirty-two dwelling-houses; forming a town which was impaled about half a mile's compass, with a fort built of wood, loam, and stone; also a fair watch-tower; and able to freight a ship of a hundred and eighty tons burden."†

Fifty ships were on the coast engaged in fishing, every one of which was an enlargement of their

---

* Bancroft, vol. 1, p. 321. † Smith's General History, p. 247.

market for the sale and purchase of essential commodities.*

"It pleased the Lord," says Bradford, "to give the plantation peace, and health, and contented minds, and so bless the labors of the colonists that they had provisions in plenty, and to spare; and this without receiving any food from home at any time, except what they brought out in the Mayflower."†

Owing to the competition in the fishing-waters, the Pilgrims esteemed it wiser now to forego that pursuit and to turn their whole attention to "trading and planting." "To every person," says Bradford, "was given an acre of land, and only an acre to them and theirs, as near the town as might be, and they had no more till the contract with the London partners was bought up. The reason was, that all might be kept close together both for better safety and defence, and the better improvement of the common employments. This condition of theirs did make me think of what I once read in Pliny‡ of the Romans and their beginnings in Romulus' time, when every man contented himself with two acres of land and had no more assigned him; how it was thought a great reward to receive a pint of corn at the hands of the Roman people; how, long after, the greatest present given to a captain who had gotten them a victory over their enemies, was as much ground as he could till in one day; he being counted not a good but a dangerous man, who could not content him-

* Palfrey, vol. 1, pp. 221, 222. † Bradford, p. 204.
‡ Pliny, lib. 18, chap. 2.

self with seven acres of land; as also how they did pound their corn in mortars, as these colonists did many years before they could get a mill."*

In turning from fishing to agriculture the settlers were decided gainers, and "ere the close of the year 1626 they had nearly extricated themselves from debt, including the obligation lately incurred for them by Standish, and had besides stored 'some clothing for the people and some commodities beforehand.' "†

The winter of 1626-7 was given to trading, and purchases were made of merchandise from some Englishmen stationed at Monhegan, and from a French ship wrecked off their coast. For several months they had the society of the passengers and crew of a vessel bound to Virginia, but which, losing her reckoning, and falling short of provisions, had moored under Cape Cod and sent to them for succor.‡

Just before winter closed in the Pilgrims had despatched one of their number, Mr. Allerton, to England with authority to continue the negotiations for a transfer of title opened by Standish with the Merchant-adventurers.§ Allerton found the plague —which had somewhat retarded the movements of Standish, and carried off some of the most efficient supporters of the colony‖—quite abated. He also learned that James I., the pedantic bigot who had threatened to "harry" the Puritans out of England,

---

* Bradford, p. 168. † Palfrey, vol. 1, p. 225.
‡ Ibid. § Bradford, Morton's Memorial.
‖ Felt, Hist. New England, vol. 1, p. 91.

was dead, and that he had been succeeded by his son Charles I., the fated prince who afterwards fell under Cromwell's axe on the Whitehall scaffold.

The Plymouth agent was successful, though "the curse of usury, which always falls so heavily upon new settlements, did not spare" the Pilgrims, since they were compelled to borrow money at an exorbitant interest. Allerton had carried out nine bonds, each for two hundred pounds—eighteen hundred pounds being the price at which the partnership held their mortgage. These bonds were given by eight of the most prominent Pilgrims,* and were made payable in nine equal annual instalments, commencing in 1627.† Thus it was that a bevy of patriotic colonists purchased the rights and assumed the responsibilities of the "Company of Merchant-adventurers." They were known in the phrase of that day as "The Undertakers," and they emancipated Plymouth from its harassing thraldom to a greedy horde of money-changers.

The Pilgrims were much gratified by this success, though they knew that their undertaking was not without grave hazard. "They knew not well," remarks Bradford, "how to raise this yearly payment, besides discharging their other engagements and supplying their annual wants, especially since they were forced by necessity to take up money at such high interest. Yet they undertook it."‡

---

* These were Bradford, Brewster, Standish, Allerton, Fuller, Jeremy, Alden, Howland. Prince, Bradford, Hazard, etc.
† Bradford, pp. 212, 213.   Palfrey.   ‡ Ibid., p. 214.

Of course, this purchase of the right of the home company necessitated a new organization, and a redistribution of property at Plymouth. After mature deliberation, it was decided to erect a commonwealth, in which each settler should own a share, but under an agreement that trade should be managed as before until the total discharge of the debt incurred for liberty.*

The division was at once made of the stock and land heretofore the joint estate of the adventurers and their partners in the soil. Every man had a share; and "every father of a family was allowed to purchase one share for his wife and one for each child living with him."† One cow and two goats were assigned by lot to every six shareholders, "and swine, though more in number, yet by the same rule." In addition to the land which each already held, "every person had twenty acres allotted him; but no meadows were to be laid out; nor were they for many years after, because they were straitened for meadow land. Every season each was given a certain spot to mow in proportion to the cattle owned."‡ The houses became the private property of their respective tenants by an equitable assignment,§ and henceforward there were to be New England freeholders. The vassalage to foreign merchants was ended.‖

It should not be forgotten that in the allotment of land, there was a grant to the Indian Habbamak.

---

* Bradford, p. 214. † Ibid., p. 214. Morton's Memorial.
‡ Ibid. § Ibid. ‖ Palfrey, vol. 1, p. 229.

He held by the Pilgrims and by their God, spite of enticements and obstacles, and died "leaving some good hopes in the settlers' hearts that his soul had gone to rest."*

"The first coveted luxury of the emancipated plantation was a reunion with their long-detained comrades in Holland. Hitherto the pleasure of others might decide who should join them. That embarrassment was now happily withdrawn. Their tender mutual recollections had naturally been refreshed by the common moaning for their 'loving and faithful pastor;'" so now "the Plymouth governor and some of his chiefest friends had serious consideration, not only how they might discharge the engagements which lay so heavily upon them, but also how they might —if possibly they could— devise means to help their friends at Leyden over to them, these desiring to come as heartily as they to have them. To effect this they resolved to run a high course and of great venture, not knowing otherwise how to compass it; which was, to hire the trade of the colony for six years, and in that time to undertake the liquidation of the whole impending debt, so that when the specified time was ended the plantation should be set free, with freedom of trade to the generality."†

Allerton was again sent to England with full power "under the hand and seal" of *the Undertakers*, to close the old bargain and to negotiate "with some of the special friends of the colony to join with

* Elliot, vol. 1, p. 85. † Bradford, p. 226.

them* in this trade."† The mission was promptly completed. In the spring of 1628, Allerton returned, "bringing a reasonable supply of goods." He "reported that he had paid the first instalment to the Adventurers, delivered the bonds for the residue of the debt, and obtained the due conveyance and release; also that he had engaged a quartette of friends‡ to accept an interest in the six years' hire of the colonial trade, in return for which they had agreed to charge themselves with the transportation of the Leyden congregation. Lastly, he had obtained from the New England Council a patent for land on the Kennebec, which was at once turned to account by the erection of a block-house "in that river, in the most convenient place for Indian trade" and a traffic with the Maine fishermen.§

At this same time Allerton brought out with him a young minister named Rogers, the first, save Lyford, if we may dignify him by that name, possessed by the Plymouth Pilgrims.‖ But he proved only a vexation and an expense; for, being "crazed in the brain," he was sent back to Britain ere a twelve-

---

* The names of the formers of the trade were: Bradford, Brewster, Standish, Prince, Alden, Howland, and Allerton. Prince had come out in the "Fortune," all the rest in the "Mayflower." Palfrey.

† Hazard, Prince, Cheever's Journal, Thatcher.

‡ These were James Shirley—who became their English agent—John Beauchamp, Richard Andrews, and T. Hathaway—"the glue of the old company." Mass. Hist. Coll., vol. 3, p. 34.

§ Palfrey, vol. 1, p. 230.

‖ Thatcher, Prince, Morton's Memorial.

month had elapsed, and the plantation had recourse once more to stout old Brewster.*

By this time the charge of *Brownism* and bigoted exclusiveness, so often levelled at the Pilgrims, was well nigh laid in England. Hard-fisted facts had smitten that slander so often in the face that it lost its hardihood. Indeed, remembering the character of that age, the Plymouth church was singularly catholic. Winslow cites many instances of the admission to its communion of communicants of the French, the Dutch, and the Scotch churches, merely by virtue of their being so.† He says: "We ever placed a wide difference betwixt those who grounded their practice on the word of God, though differing from us in their exposition and understanding of it, and those who hate reformers and reformation, running into anti-Christian opposition and persecution of the truth." He adds: "'Tis true, we profess and desire to practise *separation* from the world; and as the churches of Christ are all saints by calling, so we desire to see the grace of God shining forth—at least *seemingly*, leaving secret things to God—in all whom we admit to church-fellowship, and to keep off such as openly wallow in the mire of their sins, that neither the holy things of God, nor the communion of saints, may be leavened or polluted thereby. And if any joining us, either formerly at Leyden, or since our New England residence, have with the manifestation of faith and the profession

---

* Cheever's Journal. Bradford, p. 243.
† Mather's Magnalia, vol. 1, p. 62.

of holiness, held forth therewith separation from the church of England, I have divers times, both in the one place and in the other, heard either Mr. Robinson, our pastor, or Mr. Brewster, our elder, stop them forthwith, showing them that we required no such thing at their hands; but only to hold forth Christ Jesus, holiness in the fear of God, and a submission to the Scripture ordinances and appointments."*

Such were the simple tenets of the Plymouth church under the instructions of Brewster—change of heart and a life regulated by the sacred writ the only tests.

And now the Pilgrim enterprise began to take a wide range; they had already acquired rights on Cape Ann, as well as an extensive domain on the Kennebec, now covered by patent; and they were the first to plant an English settlement on the banks of the silvery Connecticut.† All around them the lusty shouts of the pioneers were heard. They no longer stood alone on the verge of the unbroken and primeval forest. Civilization, pushing restlessly towards the setting sun, began to supplement this nucleus colony. English planters were already seated at Saco and at Sagadahoc, in Maine.‡ The red men who haunted the coast line of Massachusetts Bay, were pushed from their marshy hunting-grounds by the Puritan colonists who followed En-

---

* Cited in Mather's Magnalia, vol. 1, pp. 62, 63.
† Bancroft, vol. 1, p. 321.
‡ Felt's Hist. of New England, vol. 1, p. 95.

dicott into the wilderness. And in the west, the patient, phlegmatic Dutch, "without haste, without rest," had founded New Amsterdam on the island of Manhattan, a town which bathed its feet in the waters of old Hendrick Hudson's majestic river, and which has since expanded to be the metropolis of North America.*

No occasion, now, to complain of a lack of company. With all the settlements amicable and cordial relations were cemented by the Pilgrim Fathers of Plymouth. With the Dutch planters, especially, a correspondence was had, by means of which mutually kind wishes and commercial offices were interchanged.† In 1627, Isaac de Rasières, "a chief merchant at New Amsterdam, and second to the Dutch governor of the New Netherlands," visited Plymouth, where he tarried "some days," and received friendly entertainment.‡ A neighborly business intercourse was commenced, and it was at this time that the Pilgrims became acquainted with the value and the uses of *wampum*.§ This was the Indian coin—the dollars and cents of barbarism. It

---

* "The Dutch had trading in those southern parts divers years before the English came, but they began no plantation until after the Pilgrims came and were here seated." Morton's Memorial, p. 133, note.

† Davis' New Amsterdam, Booth's History of New York City, Bradford. ‡ Bradford, p. 222, et seq.

§ In Roger Williams' Key, wampum is considered as Indian money, and is described in the twenty-fourth chapter of that interesting tract. Their *white* money they called *wampum*, which signifies *white;* their *black*, *suckauhack*, sucki signifying *black*. Hist. Col., vol. 3, p. 231.

was made of small pieces of shell, white sometimes, but often purple, and ground, polished, drilled, and strung or beaded.*

"Neither the English of this plantation nor of any other in these parts," remarks Bradford, "had knowledge of wampum till now. But the settlers bought fifty pounds' worth of it from De Rasières, who told them how vendable it was at their Indian stations, and did persuade them that they would find it so at Kennebec; and so it came to pass, for though at first it stuck, and they were two years in working off a small quantity, yet afterwards, when the inland tribes knew of it, the traders could scarce ever get enough to supply the demand, for many years together."†

De Rasières was a close and shrewd observer, and nothing escaped his keen eyes at Plymouth. On his return he wrote a letter in which he described at length the salient characteristics of the Pilgrim colony. Let us take a peep into the quaint old manuscript, and see how New England in its Pilgrim babyhood looked in his eyes:

"New Plymouth lies on the slope of a hill stretching east towards the seashore. It has a broad street about a cannot-shot of eight hundred feet long, looking down the slope, with a street crossing this in the middle, and running northward

---

* Mr. Gookin says: "Wampum is made chiefly by the Narragansett Block Island Indians. Upon the sandy flats and shores of those coasts the wilk shell are found." Hist. Col., vol. 1, p. 152.

† Bradford, p. 234.

to a rivulet, very rapid but shallow, which there empties into the sea, and southward to the land. The houses are built of hewn planks, with gardens, also enclosed behind and at the sides by hewn planks, so that their gardens, court-yards, and houses are arranged in very good order, with a stockade against a sudden attack. At the ends of the streets there are three wooden gates. Their government is after the English form. The governor is annually elected. In inheritance they place all children in one degree, only the eldest has an acknowledgment of seniority. They have made stringent laws on the subject of adultery and fornication, and these ordinances they enforce very strictly, even among the savage tribes which live amongst them.

"Their farms are not so good as ours at New Amsterdam, because they are more stony, and consequently not so fit for the plough. They have their freedom without rendering an account to any one; only, if their king should choose to send them a governor, they would be obliged to recognize him as sovereign chief. The maize-seed which they do not require for their own use they deliver over to the governor, at three guilders the bushel, who, in his turn, sends it in sloops to the north for the traffic in skins amongst the savages. They reckon one bushel of maize against one pound of beaver-skins. They have better means of living than ourselves, since fish swim in abundance before their very doors. There are also many birds, such as geese, herons, and cranes, and other small-legged birds, which are seen in flocks here in the winter.

"The tribes in this neighborhood have the same customs as with us, only they are better conducted than ours, because the English treat them fairly, and give them the example of better ordinances and a better life; and also, to a certain degree, give them laws, by means of the respect they have from the very first established amongst them."*

In 1629, the bulk of the long lingering Leyden exiles—among the rest the wife and two sons of John Robinson†—at length landed at Plymouth.‡ The reunited flock, now sadly thinned by death, greeted each other with mutual tears and caresses; and tightly-clasped hands and wet eyes told what the voice was too choked to say. But in the midst of sadness they were joyous, for

> "Hope was changed to glad fruition;
> Faith to sight, and prayer to praise."

The expense of transporting these friends was very heavy, amounting in the aggregate to six hundred pounds, as we learn by opening Allerton's

---

* Mr. Brodhead, who obtained this valuable letter, only summarized in the text, from the archives at the Hague, gives it in full in the New York Hist. Col., sec. series, vol. 2, p. 343, et seq.

† Prince, vol. 1, p. 160. Deane's Scituate, p. 332. "Mrs. Robinson, widow of Rev. John Robinson, came over with the latter company, with her son Isaac, and perhaps with another son." Editorial note in Bradford, p. 247. "There was an Abraham Robinson early at Gloucester, who is surmised to have been a son of the Leyden minister." Ibid. It has been thought that Mrs. Robinson did not remain in Plymouth, but went to Salem, "where was a Mrs. Robinson very early." MS. Letters of J. J. Babson, Esq., of Gloucester, Mass. ‡ Bradford, pp. 247, 248.

charge roll.* Nor was this all; destitute and homeless, they had to be maintained the better part of fifteen months before they were able to stand on their own feet, and pay their way. They had no harvest of their own to reap. Land was given them and block-houses were run up for their shelter. Then they planted " against the coming of another season."† The Pilgrims, though already overloaded with debt, did not grudge this large addition to the budget of expense, but showed herein "a rare example of brotherly love and Christian care;" for Bradford says that "even thus they were, for the most part, both welcome and useful, as they feared God and were sober livers."‡

But if the devout colonists of the Plymouth slope were "sober livers," all their neighbors were not. It seems that some years before this time, perhaps in 1625, perhaps a twelvemonth earlier, an English Captain Wollaston, inoculated with the general rage for planting settlements, had attempted to drop one on that rocky height near Boston bay which still bears his name.§ Like the foolish architect in the Bible, he built on a sandy foundation, though his colony was bottomed on a rock—so strange are the paradoxes of this mortal life. "Not finding things to answer his expectations," he did not tarry long in his eyry, but pressed on into Virginia with a portion of his emigrants, intending

---

* Bradford, pp. 247, 248.   † Ibid., p. 249.
‡ Bradford's Letter-Book, in Mass. Hist. Col., vol. 3, pp. 69, 70.   § Palfrey, vol. 1, p. 233.

soon to return for the rest.* So much for the intention. But in his absence one of his followers, Thomas Morton, "who had been a kind of pettifogger, of Fernival's Inn," London, and was now broken down into an uneasy bloat, ripe for mischief, obtained an ascendency over the waiting colonists, and thereby assumed control. "Then," says the old recitor, "they fell into great licentiousness of life, in all profaneness, Morton becoming lord of misrule, and maintaining, as it were, a school of atheism. Having gotten some goods into their hands by much trading with the Indians, they spent all vainly in quaffing both wine and stronger liquors in great excess—as some have reported, as much as ten pounds' worth of a morning. They also set up a May-pole, and danced and drank around it, frisking about like so many fairies, or *furies* rather: and worse practices they had, as if they sought anew to revive and celebrate the obscene feast of the Roman goddess Flora, or the beastly practices of the mad Bacchanalians. Morton pretended withal to be a poet, and composing sundry rhymes and loose verses, some tending to lasciviousness and others to detraction and scandal, he affixed these to his idle, or *idol*, May-pole. The name of the height was changed; it was called 'Merry-Mount,' as if this jollity would have been perpetual.

"Now to maintain this riotous prodigality and profuse expenditure, Morton, esteeming himself lawless, and hearing what gain the fishermen made by

* Bradford, p. 236.

trading muskets, powder, and shot amongst themselves, decided, as head of this consortship, to begin the practice in these parts among the Indians, teaching them how to use, charge, and fire their pieces, and the kind of shot fitted to be used for different purposes, as hunting and war. Infinite was the mischief which came by this wicked man's greed; in that, despite all laws for the restraint of selling ammunition and weapons to the natives, base covetousness so far prevailed, that the Indians became amply provided with guns, powder, shot, rapiers, and pistols, also well skilled in their use, and in the repair of defective arms."*

These things, together with the debauchery of Indian women and the incitement of his flaunting and unwhipped crimes, which drew the dissolute from all directions to swell his rabble rout, filled the surrounding colonists with mingled grief and alarm. At the outset expostulation was essayed. "In a friendly and neighborly way, Morton was admonished to forbear these courses." A peculiar characteristic reveals the man—*Ex pede Herculem*. The anarch refused to desist.

"Obtaining false rules prankt in reason's garb,"

he denied the jurisdiction of Plymouth, and answered the remonstrance with an affront. A second appeal was equally futile. Then, with their accustomed stern decision, the Pilgrims acted. Standish was sent to curb this bold blasphemer. "Morton fortified his comrades with drink, barricaded his

* Morton's Memorial, pp. 137, 138.

house, and defied assault." But happily no blood was spilled. The reckless, graceless rake succumbed without a fight. He was taken first to Plymouth, and thence conveyed to England for trial. And so ended this experiment of immorality.*

This episode, with others, is convincing proof that the Pilgrims had not wandered into Utopia; nor did they seek that fabled bourne. They expected trouble, and they serenely accepted toil, thanking God just as joyfully for a little as for much. And, indeed, they felt that they walked on mercies. They "found all things working together for their good." They had already planted a stable government, which had been severely tested by open outbreak and by insidious assault. Their friends had found their way to them across the sea; and since they had

> "Informed their unacquainted feet
> In the blind mazes of this tangled wood,"

their infant state had been emancipated from the mercantile dictation of unfriendly men. The bitterness was past; the night was nearly spent. Jocund day stood a-tip-toe on the misty mountain's top. They rested on God's heart. Surely, they had occasion to

> ———"shake the depths of the desert gloom
> With their hymns of lofty cheer."

They might fitly chant pæans, and sing till

> ———"the stars heard and the sea!
> And the sounding isles of the dim woods rang
> To the anthem of the free."

* Bradford, Morton's Memorial, etc.

CHAPTER XX.

EBENEZER.

"Behold, they come, those sainted forms,
 Unshaken through the strife of storms;
 Heaven's darkest cloud hangs coldly down,
 And earth puts on its rudest frown;
 But colder, ruder was the hand,
 That drove them from their own dear land."
SPRAGUE.

"These are the living lights,
  That from our bold, green heights,
    Shall shine afar,
  Till they who name the name
  Of freedom, towards the flame
  Come, as the Magi came
    Towards Bethlehem's star."
PIERPONT.

WHILE the Plymouth Pilgrims, through these initial years, were engaged in a stern tussle with unkempt nature, in a wrestling-match with froward men, and in an essay to survive the "thousand natural ills that flesh is heir to" in new settlements, writing *victoria sine clade* on every page of the struggle, the Scripture party in England was floundering in a "slough of despond." Charles I. was that most strange and baleful of anomalies, a treacherous moralist. He was the painting of a virtue. Outwardly he was Cato; inwardly he was Iago. "This prince," says Bolingbroke, "had sucked in with his mother's milk those absurd principles which his father was so industrious, and, unhappily, so successful in propagating."* Back of him stood a powerful faction, omnipotent in the church, regnant in the state, as wedded as himself to the tenets of absolutism, and eager to cry Amen to his most doubtful acts—often, indeed, instigating them.

Both the king and his backers were enamoured of that formal Phariseeism which made broad its phylactery, and wrote "holier than thou" upon its forehead. Of course, then, they could not but hate those godly Puritans, both inside and outside of the national Establishment, who, like a reproving Nathan, constantly inveighed against self-righteous ceremonialism, and sought to inaugurate a purer and more spiritual ecclesiasticism. The Conformists had the power, as they had the will. Elizabeth had commenced this crusade against the "Gospellers;" James I. had continued the "harry;" but Charles I. outdid Termagant, and he did out-Herod Herod. Puritanism was girt with a penal code; and now, choked almost purple, it gazed with an agony of interest across the water to America, to see if haply it might here find an asylum. The chances of a successful colonization of these Western wilds were ardently canvassed. The progress of the Pilgrim settlement was closely watched, and the spirits of the English Puritans were at high or ebb tide in proportion as that test enterprise seemed to oscillate towards success or eclipse. As yet only

---

* Vide Harris' Life of Charles I., p. 278.

the low premonitory moanings of the revolution of 1641 were heard. Throughout the island, godly men began to think of seeking safety and freedom of conscience in exile; and in this they were encouraged by the *experimentum crucis* of Plymouth. "I pray you," wrote Shirley, the English agent of the Pilgrims, "subordinate all temporal things to success, that you may disappoint the hopes of our foes, and keep open an asylum into which we may all soon crowd, unless things mend in this now stricken island."*

But "things did not mend," and multitudes began to prepare for emigration. And here mark a singular fact. We have seen how disastrously those enterprises failed which bottomed colonization simply on the greed of gain. The victor's bays were only for the brow of moral pioneers. It was as though God had said, "No; I will not plant men in New England who count religion only twelve and the world thirteen." The only successful colonists of the northeastern coast-line of the Atlantic were men whose motive for emigration was religion, and who based their action on an idea—faith.

It happened, in 1624, that Roger Conant, "a most religious, prudent, worthy gentleman," and a Puritan, but not a Separatist, somewhat dissatisfied with the rigid rule of Bradford, left Plymouth in the crisis of the Lyford muddle,† and entering his pin-

* Bradford's Letter-book.
† "'T is not known when Conant came over. Nothing appears in any of the Plymouth documents to confirm Hubbard's state-

nace, sailed across the bay to Nantasket.* Tarrying there but a twelvemonth, he pushed on to Cape Ann; where, finding a knot of fishermen who resided there permanently, occupying themselves in curing fish in the absence of the smacks of their fellow-*voyageurs*, he resolved to pause. While sojourning here, the English merchants who had sent out these fishermen who here stood huddled together on the cape, appointed Conant their agent; whereupon he, "not liking the present site, transported his company to Naumkeag, some five leagues distant, to the southwest of Cape Ann."†

But neither removal nor Conant's energy saved this venture from financial collapse;‡ and the brave pioneer, in 1625, found himself deserted by most of his companions and without an occupation, in the midst of the tenantless huts of frustrated trade. Then religious sentiment came to his rescue. "To the eye of faith, mountains are crystal, distance may be shaken hands with, oceans are nothing." So now old John White of Dorchester, in England, "a famous Puritan divine of great gravity, presence, and influence," zealous to "spread the gospel and to establish his way," looking across the

---

ment, that Conant was one of Lyford's party at Plymouth. Though historians have adopted that *ipse dixit*, it rests on his word alone. But since Hubbard and Conant were afterwards neighbors and friends, he is likely to have been well informed." Palfrey, vol. 1, p. 205, note.

* Elliot. Hubbard's Hist. of New England, chap. 18.
† Hubbard, chap. 9. Palfrey, Elliot.
‡ Palfrey, vol. 1, p. 286.

Atlantic, descried Conant, a lonely sentinel of Puritanism on the northern shore.* The sagacious pastor saw in Naumkeag a *point d'appui*. He at once wrote Conant: "I have been apprized of the failure of the merchants; but do not desert your post. I promise that if you, with Woodbury, Balch, and Palfrey, the three honest and prudent men lately employed in the fisheries, will stay at Naumkeag, I will procure a patent for you, and likewise send you whatever you write for, either men, or provisions, or goods wherewith to begin an Indian trade."†

Surprised and reinvigorated, Conant prevailed, though not without difficulty, on his companions to remain with him, and they all "stayed at the peril of their lives."‡

In 1627, Woodbury sailed for England in quest of supplies.§ Meantime "the business came to agitation in London; and being at first approved by some and disliked by others, by dint of much argument and disputation, it grew to be well known; insomuch that, some men showing affection for the work, and offering the help of their purses if fit men might be procured to go over, inquiry was made whether any would be willing to engage their persons in the voyage. Thus it fell out that at last they lighted, among others, on John Endicott, a

---

* Elliott, vol. 1, p. 139.
† Hubbard, chap. 17.
‡ Conant's petition of May 28, 1671, in Mass. Hist. Archives.
§ Palfrey, vol. 1, p. 287.

man well known to divers persons of good repute. He manifested much willingness to accept of the offer as soon as it was tendered, which gave great encouragement to such as were still doubtful about setting on this work of erecting a new colony on an old foundation."*

Under the patronage of Dudley, and Saltonstall, and Eaton, and Pyncheon, and Bellingham, men of substance and "gentlemen born," men willing and able to offer "the help of their purses," reinforced by the good wishes of Puritanism at large, the new scheme soon got upon its working feet, and walked forward to success. But so far the project rested on parchment. It must be vivified, and sheltered beneath the *imprimatur* of a hostile government. "Many riddles must be resolved," said old Shirley, "and many locks must be opened by the silver, nay, the golden key."† So they purchased of the Council for New England "a strip of land, in width three miles, north of the Merrimack, and three miles south of the Charles river, and running back from the Atlantic to the Western ocean; so that they were not likely to be crowded."‡ Thus, though it might say as the chief captain Lysias said to Paul, "With a great sum of money obtained I this freedom," the new colony had "a local habitation and a name" ere it was launched.

It has been well said, that Endicott was just the man to lead this venture; firm, rugged, hopeful,

---

* Planters' Plea, chap. 9.   † Cited in Bradford, p. 251.
‡ Elliot, vol. 1, pp. 139, 140.

zealous, devout, he knew no such word as fail. So on the 20th of June, 1628, he took his wife and children, and "not much above fifty or sixty other persons," and plunged across the water.*

They reached New England in the autumn†— that hazy, glowing, golden season, when the woods hang out their myriad-tinted banners to the wind, when the streams gurgle most laughingly, when Nature claps her hands with joy, and the

"Hills, rock-ribbed and ancient as the sun,"

smooth their wrinkled fronts into unwonted softness. Endicott must have had quite a different idea of the western wilds from that which stern, icy December daguerreotyped upon the minds of Bradford and his coadjutors.

At once fraternizing with Conant's sentinel squad—apprized of their coming by Woodbury, who had returned ere Endicott sailed—the newcomers proceeded to put up additional cottages; and they called the nascent hamlet *Salem*, "for the *peace* which they had and hoped in it."‡ Like their brothers at Plymouth, they immediately began to explore the surrounding country. Imagine their surprise when, on one occasion, they stumbled across "an English palisaded and thatched house." Approaching cautiously, they heard the ringing music of an anvil. Here, in the heart of the wilderness, lived Thomas Walford, a hermit smith who had

---

* Planters' Plea, chap. 9. Johnson's Wonder-working Providence. Belknap's Biography, p. 249. Hubbard's Hist.

† Ibid.   ‡ Mather's Magnalia, vol. 1, pp. 67, 68.

won wide favor with the Indians by his skill in working metals.*

From this and kindred incidents, historians have loved to draw a moral, depicting the excess of individuality which marks the Teutonic races. The Saxon inevitably individuates. He can stand alone; is self-reliant and aggressive; asks only, with the old cynic, that intruders shall get out of his sunlight. He does not gather into cities because he is weak, nor because he is social. He is willing, for a purpose, to go out from men, and to create a society patterned on his own model. 'T is a high quality when properly attempered, making individuals kings and nations independent. It explores and subdues unknown and dreaded continents, and is the father of that marvellous enterprise which today realizes Puck's prophecy, and "puts a girdle round the earth in forty minutes."

Walford's hermitage was in Mishawam. The locality seemed favorable for a settlement. The explorers returned to Salem with their report; and ere long " a portion of the colonists established themselves around the forge of the sturdy blacksmith; and with the old patriotic feeling, which neither wrongs nor sufferings could altogether root out, they named the new settlement *Charlestown*, in honor of a king whose severities had driven them from the land of their fathers."†

The report of Endicott's successful colonization,

* Charlestown Records, Palfrey, Elliot, Everett's Address.
† Wilson's Pilgrim Fathers, p. 483.

which reached England early in 1629, encouraged White, "the main promoter and chief organizer of this business," to plant the adventure upon a broader, firmer foundation. The original company was but a voluntary, unincorporated partnership.* This was now "much enlarged" by recruits from the Puritans "disaffected to the rulers in church and state."† The next step was, to get a charter and an incorporation. This was solicited, and after some little difficulty and delay, obtained. On the 4th of March, 1629, Charles I. affixed the royal seal to a parchment which erected White's coterie into a body politic, under the title of "The Governor and Company of Massachusetts Bay, in New England."‡

"The patent passed the seals a few days only before Charles I., in a public state paper, avowed his design of governing England without a Parliament."§ It was cherished by the colonists for more than half a century as a most precious boon; and the old charter‖ is the germ of that "bright, consummate flower," the later constitution.¶

"The administration of the affairs of this puissant corporation," remarks Bancroft, "was intrusted to a governor, a deputy, and eighteen assistants,

---

* Palfrey, vol. 1, p. 290.

† Colony Records. Cradock's Letter in Young's Chronicles.

‡ Prince; Hazard. Hubbard's Hist. Memoir of J. Endicott, Salem, 1847. § Bancroft, vol. 1, p. 342.

‖ This is filed in the State-House in Boston, and is printed in Colony Laws, in Hutchinson's Call, and in Hazard. Bancroft.

¶ Palfrey, Wilson.

who were to be annually elected by a general vote of the members of the body politic. Four times a year, or oftener if desired, a general assembly of the freemen was to be held; and to these assemblies, which were invested with the necessary powers of legislation, inquest, and superintendence, the most important matters were referred. No provision required the assent of the king to render the acts of the colonial authorities valid. In his eye it was but a trading corporation, not a civil government. Its doings were esteemed as indifferent as those of any guild in England; and if grave powers of jurisdiction in America were conceded, it was only because successful trade demanded the concession."*

Nothing was said of religious liberty. The crown may have relied on its power to restrain it; the emigrants may have trusted to distance or obscurity to protect it.† But enough was gained. The charter necessitated full liberty. "If you plant an oak in a flower-vase," says Goethe, "either the oak must wither or the vase must crack." The Puritans meant to let it crack. It is singular that neither Charles nor his lynx-eyed ministers should have detected the freedom or scented the heresy which lurked in the broad terms of the glorious old parchment.

In the old legend, a fisherman took a casket out of the sea, and found on its cover the seal of Solomon. He broke it, and out of the slender casket

* Bancroft, vol. 1, pp. 342, 343.   † Palfrey, vol. 1, p. 291.

rose a giant till he lifted into colossal shape, and raised his right hand to crush the interloper. So now Charles broke the Solomon-seal of his coercion, and enabled this young giant of the West to rise to its legitimate proportions, clutching in its right hand the wholesome sceptre which should crush all obstacles to progressive liberty. In the fable, the fisherman, by a cunning story, lured the giant to go back into the casket, which he then tossed back again into the sea. But neither Charles nor his successors could ever persuade America to go back into the box.

CHAPTER XXI.

"FAREWELL, DEAR ENGLAND."

"With news the time's in labor, and throws forth
   Each minute some."   SHAKSPEARE.

"Why should we crave a hallowed spot?
  An altar is in each man's cot;
  A church in every grove that spreads
  Its living roof above our heads."
              WORDSWORTH.

WITH the precious charter in its pocket, the complacent Massachusetts Company strode out of the royal antechamber, and proceeded at once to effect an organization. Matthew Cradock was elected to the gubernatorial chair; and to Endicott, as deputy, was delegated the government of New England.*

A letter of instructions was indited. It was unique, and highly illustrative of the benevolent spirit of these builders of states—*Conditores Imperiorum*—to whose brotherhood Lord Bacon, in "the true marshalling of the sovereign degrees of honor," assigns the highest place.† Let us cull some specimen paragraphs from the old parchment: "If any of the savages"—such were the orders long and uniformly followed and placed on record more than

---

* Young's Chronicles, Prince, Mass. Hist. Coll.
† Bacon's Works, vol. 2.

half a century before William Penn proclaimed the principles of peace on the borders of the Delaware*—"pretend right of inheritance to all or any part of the lands granted in our patent, we pray you endeavor to purchase their title, that we may avoid the least scruple of intrusion."† Elsewhere the colonial authorities were bidden "particularly to publish, that no wrong nor injury be offered to the Indians."‡

Tobacco was held in especial abhorrence, and denounced as "a trade by this whole Company disowned, and utterly disclaimed by some of the chiefest, who absolutely declare themselves unwilling to have a hand in the plantation, if the intention be to cherish or permit the culture thereof."§

Endicott was authorized to expel the incorrigible, using force when necessary. It was also appointed that all labor should cease at "three o'clock on Saturday afternoon, in preparation for the Sabbath."‖

The colonial seal was an Indian erect, with an arrow in his right hand, and the motto, "Come over and help us," peculiarly appropriate in that age. The old seal has been retained by Massachu-

---

* Bancroft, vol. 1, p. 346.
† Prince's Chronicles, p. 247.   ‡ Ibid.
§ Cited in Elliot, vol. 1, p. 142. "In a subsequent letter this is reiterated thus: 'We especially desire you to take care that no tobacco be planted under your government, unless it be some small quantity for mere necessity, for physic, or the preservation of health; and that the same be taken privately by old men, and no other.'" Ibid.
‖ Young's Chronicles, p. 141. Hazard, vol. 1.

setts; but the motto has been superseded by Algernon Sydney's famous Latin, *Sub libertate quietem.**

"No idle drone may live amongst us;" so ran the colonial statute; and it "was the spirit as well as the law of the dauntless community which was to turn the sterility of New England into a cluster of wealthy, cultured, model states."

The charter had been granted to the Massachusetts Company in March; in April preparations were hastening for the embarkation of fresh emigrants.† It was not difficult to get recruits; for the pinchers of tender consciences grew daily more rigorous. Puritanism saw popery preparing to spring upon it upon one side; it felt the ravenous bite of the Conformists on the other side. It was worse than folly to look to the government for redress; that was the engine of the persecutors. Villiers of Buckingham, that volatile madman, who was

"Every thing by turns, and nothing long,"

as Pope has painted him, had been recently assassinated. His place in the king's confidence was now filled by Strafford, the systematizer of tyranny in England, whose audacious genius impelled him to attempt to nationalize despotism, and erected the tenets of absolute power inside of constitutional forms.‡ By his side stood Laud, his Siamese twin, a prelate who assumed to ransack the universe—

---

* Bancroft. † Ibid., vol. 1, p. 345.
‡ History of the English Puritans, American Tract Society, N. Y., 1867.

> "Whose tongue
> Outvenomed all the worms of Nile."

The statesman and the priest carried it with a high hand;* and the time was not yet when Cozens could say, "The king has no more authority in ecclesiastical matters than the boy who rubs my horse's heels."†

The suffering Non-conformists, "meted and peeled" at home, heard with rapture of that Puritan colony in the wilderness, governed by men whose opinions accorded with their own, and sheltered beneath the ægis of a royal charter. Emigration began to assume unprecedented proportions;‡ and the Company might have its pick of the best men in the island. But much good seed was left; enough to grow Cromwell, and nourish Hampden, and succor Pym.

By the middle of April, 1629, six ships were ready to sail; and under license from the Lord Treasurer, these were freighted with "eighty women and maids and twenty-six children"—hostages of the fixed attachment of the emigrants to the New World—"and two hundred men, with victuals, arms, tools, and necessary wearing apparel."§ They also took on board "one hundred and forty head of cattle, and forty goats.‖

As this was a religious enterprise, care was taken

---

* Hist. of the English Puritans, ut antea.
† Hume, Hist. of Eng., vol. 2, p. 253.
‡ Perry, Eccl. Hist., vol. 1.
§ Mass. Col. Rec., vol. 1. Palfrey.
‖ Palfrey, vol. 1, p. 293.

"to make plentiful provision of godly ministers."* Four clergymen now embarked for Massachusetts Bay. Two of these made no figure on the north shore of New England. Bright was a strict Conformist; and not liking the ecclesiastical proceedings of his comrades, he returned to England in the succeeding summer.† Smith was a Separatist; and since these Puritans were not yet "Come-outers," they were shy of him, so that in landing he went to Nantasket,‡ where we shall meet him again. The remaining two were Mr. Higginson and Mr. Skelton; the first of Leicestershire, the other of Lincolnshire.§ They were both ardent Puritans, who had held livings in the Church of England, and been silenced for non-conformity.|| On receiving an invitation to accompany this expedition, they had "esteemed it a call from heaven," and joyfully assented.¶ "Both of these men," says Cotton Mather, "were eminent for learning and virtue; and being thus in a sense driven out of England, they sought graves on the American strand, whereon the epitaph might be inscribed that was on Scipio's: *Ingrata patria, ne mortui quidem habebis ossa.*"** But unlike the ill-used

---

* Palfrey, vol. 1, p. 293. Mather's Magnalia.
† Higginson's New England Plantation. Palfrey.
‡ Bradford, p. 263. Palfrey, vol. 1, p. 294.
§ Mather's Magnalia.
|| Ibid., vol. 1, p. 68. Palfrey, vol. 1, pp. 294, 295.
¶ Hutchinson's Coll., 24, 25. Hubbard, Bancroft.
** Mather's Magnalia, ut antea. "*Ungrateful country of my birth, thou shalt not possess even my lifeless bones.*"

pagan, they had no taunts for their erring country. "We will not say," cried Francis Higginson, as he stood on deck off the Isle of Wight, and looked back on the receding shores of the fast-anchored island—"We will not say, Farewell, Babylon, Farewell, Rome! but, Farewell, dear England!"*

"England did not regret the departure of these Christian heroes, because she did not know her best men. What nation does? To materialists and politicians, these Pilgrims seemed to be visionaries and idealists; impracticable, and in the way. Yet this class is always the life of a nation. We can look back upon them, and surfeit them with praise; but we cannot easily see their mates walking amongst us, treading our own sidewalks, and so learn to cherish, and not kill the prophets."†

Higginson, Skelton, and their future parishioners, landed at Salem "in the last days of June."‡ Their friends already on the spot gave them a hearty pioneer welcome. Higginson employed his first leisure moments in writing home a transcript of the situation: "When we came first to Naumkeag, we found about half a score of cottages, and a fair house built for the governor. We found also abundance of corn planted by those here, very good and well-liking. The two hundred passengers whom we brought were, by common consent of the old planters, combined together into one body politic,

---

* Mather's Magnalia, vol. 1, p. 74. Uhden, pp. 63, 64.
† Elliot, vol. 1, p. 150.
‡ They landed on the 24th of June, 1629. Uhden, Hutchinson.

under the same governor. There are in all of us, both old and new planters, about three hundred; whereof two hundred are planted at Naumkeag, now called Salem, and the rest have settled at Massachusetts Bay, beginning to build a town there, which we call Charlestown. But that which is our greatest comfort, and our means of defence above all others, is, that we have here the true religion and holy ordinances of Almighty God taught amongst us. Thanks be to God, we have here plenty of preaching and diligent catechizing, with strict and careful exercise and good and commendable order to bring our people into a Christian conversation with those with whom we have to do withal. And thus we doubt not but God will be with us; and if God be with us, who can be against us?"*

On their arrival at Salem, these Massachusetts Pilgrims found no church. It was their first care to erect one; and in the prosecution of this work, they had recourse to the devout Plymouth colonists, their brothers in the faith. Cordial greetings had already been exchanged between these sister colonies. About the time of the arrival of Higginson, "an infection had spread among the northern pioneers, of which many died; some of the scurvy, others of a hectic fever."† Endicott had sent a missive to Plymouth at this time, requesting medical aid, as he had no leech with him. Bradford imme-

---

* Higginson's New England Plantation, pp. 123, 124.
† Bradford, pp. 263, 264.

diately sent Thomas Fuller, physician to his plantation, and the first in New England—for he was a comer in the "Mayflower"—to the relief of the Salem sufferers, and armed him with an affectionate letter of condolence and Christian sympathy.*

These lines, and the prompt despatch of the surgeon, Endicott thus acknowledged:

"Right Worthy Sir—It is a thing not usual that servants to one Master and of the same household should be strangers; I assure you, I desire it not; nay, to speak more plainly, I cannot be so to you. God's people are all marked with one and the same mark and sealed with one and the same seal, and have, in the main, one and the same heart, guided by one and the same Spirit of truth; and where this is, there can be no discord; nay, here must needs be sweet harmony. And the same request, with you, I make unto the Lord—that we may, as Christian brethren, be united by a heavenly and unfeigned love, bending all our hearts and forces in furthering a work beyond our unaided strength, with reverence and fear, fastening our eyes always on Him that is able to direct and prosper all our ways.

"I acknowledge myself much bound to you for your kind love and care in sending Mr. Fuller among us, and rejoice much that I am by him satisfied touching your judgments of the outward form of God's worship. It is, so far as I can gather, no other than is warranted by the evidence of truth,

* Bradford, pp. 263, 264.

and the same which I have professed and maintained ever since the Lord in mercy revealed himself to me; being far from the common report that hath been spread of you touching this particular.* But God's children must not look for less here below than ill-report and slanderous gibes; and 't is a great mercy that he strengthens them to go through with it. I shall not need, at this time, to be tedious unto you, for, God willing, I purpose to see your face shortly. In the mean time, I humbly take my leave of you, committing you to the Lord's blessed protection and rest.

"Your assured Friend,
"JO. ENDICOTT.
"NAUMKEAG, May 11, 1629."†

The chain of friendship thus early welded had an additional link added to it when the Leyden exiles, borne to America in company with Higginson and Skelton, landed from the same flotilla, and pushed from Salem on to Plymouth. Bradford, in reciting this incident, says finely, "Their long stay and keeping back was recompensed by the Lord to their friends here with a double blessing, in that they not only enjoyed them now beyond their late expectation, but with them many more godly friends and Christian brothers, as the beginning of a larger harvest unto the Lord, in the increase of his churches and people in these waste parts, to the admira-

* In allusion to the widespread charge of Brownism, and bigoted exclusion of all other sects from Christian fellowship.
† Bradford, pp. 264, 265.

tion of many and the wonder of the world; and that here should be a resting-place for so many of God's children, when so sharp a scourge came upon their own land. But it was the Lord's doing, and it ought to be marvellous in our eyes."*

Higginson and Endicott had reached Salem in the latter part of June, 1629. Some twenty days later, Endicott "set apart a solemn day of humiliation for the foundation of a church and the choice of a pastor and a teacher."† The elder Pilgrims at Plymouth were invited to be present, and lend their countenance to the unique ceremony.‡

The 20th of July arrived. The first part of the day was spent in prayer and preaching; the latter portion was devoted to the ecclesiastical election.§ "It was after this manner," says Gott—who had come over with Endicott, and was afterwards a deacon in the Salem church—in a letter to Bradford rehearsing the proceedings: "the persons thought of, who had been ministers in the English Establishment, were questioned concerning their calling to preach. They acknowledged that there was a twofold calling, the one inward, when the Lord moved the heart of man to take that calling upon him, and fitted him with gifts for it; the other outward, and from the people, when a company of believers are united in a covenant to walk together

---

* Bradford, p..245.
† Higginson's New England Plantation. Gott's letter to Bradford; cited in Bradford, pp. 265, 266.
‡ Palfrey. § Ibid., Bradford, Gott, etc.

in all the ways of God, and all the male members are given a free voice in the choice of their church officers. Now we, being persuaded that these two men were so qualified as the apostle speaks to Timothy, 'A bishop must be blameless, sober, apt to teach,' we think we may say, as the eunuch said unto Philip, 'What should hinder my being baptized, seeing there is water?' and he believed. So those servants of God, clearing all things by their answers, and being thus fitted, we saw no reason why we might not freely give our voices for their election. Therefore every fit member wrote in a note the name of him whom the Lord moved him to think fit for a pastor; and so likewise the name of him whom they would have for a teacher. Mr. Skelton was chosen pastor, and Mr. Higginson teacher; and they accepting the choice, Mr. Higginson, with several others, laid hands on Mr. Skelton, using prayer therewith; after which there was an imposition of hands on Mr. Higginson by Mr. Skelton and the rest."*

Bradford, "and some others with him, coming by sea," and being "hindered by cross-winds," could not reach Salem in the beginning of the ceremony, but "came into the assembly afterwards, and gave them the right hand of fellowship, wishing all prosperity and a blessed success unto such good beginnings."†

Some days after this election, Mr. Higgin-

---

* Gott's Letter to Bradford.
† Morton's Memorial, p. 146. Hubbard, Prince.

son drew up "A Confession of Faith and Church Covenant." Thirty persons assented to it, and a self-constituted church was planted in the wilderness.* This transaction has determined and colored the whole religious constitution of New England. It was a bold and aggressive act. But the Pilgrims had always objected to the ceremonial law of the home Establishment; and now, being in the Western wilds, they felt free to form their ecclesiasticism on what they conceived to be a more authentic model. "In their position, such words as 'Non-conformity' and 'Separatism' ceased to be significant. It was only important that they should conform to their view of the Bible; and their determination to do so was not shaken by the thought that in doing so they must separate, not in spirit, but in discipline and usage, from a church three thousand miles away."†

The New England theocracy was begotten of these proceedings.‡ "The emigrants," remarks Bancroft, "were not so much a body politic as a church in the wilderness, with no benefactor around them but Nature, no present sovereign but God. An entire separation was made between church and state—at least in theory; religious worship was established on the basis of the independence of each separate religious community; and these

* See the Covenant in Neale's History of New England, vol. 1, pp. 141–143. The subordinate church officers were not chosen till later. See Bradford's Letter-book.
† Palfrey, vol. 1, p. 298.
‡ Uhden's New England Theocracy.

rigid Calvinists, of whose rude intolerance the world had been filled with malignant calumnies, subscribed a covenant cherishing, it is true, the severest virtues, but without one tinge of fanaticism. It was an act of piety, not of study; it favored virtue, not superstition; inquiry, and not submission. The communicants were enthusiasts, but not bigots."* They declared that "the Holy Scriptures only were to be followed, and no man's authority, be he Augustine, Tertullian, or even Cherubim or Seraphim."†

This entire transaction gave dissatisfaction to some at Salem. Finally, John and Samuel Brown, " two brothers, the one a merchant, the other a lawyer, both men of parts, estate, and figure in the settlement, gathered a company separate from the public assembly.‡

Mutual bickerings ensued. A breach of the peace was threatened.§ Then Endicott interposed. He sent the Browns home to England, and thereby restored quiet.‖

The brothers Brown, on reaching England, carried a lusty impeachment to the archiepiscopal throne, then occupied by Laud.¶ The Massachusetts Company, alarmed by the clamor, wrote letters of caution to Endicott: "Beware! 'tis possi-

---

* Bancroft, vol. 1, p. 348. † Mather's Magnalia.
‡ Ibid., vol. 1, p. 72.
§ Ibid., Morton, Prince, Young, Cheever.
‖ Young's Chronicles, p. 288.
¶ Mass. Col. Rec., vol. 1, p. 408.

ble some undigested counsels have been too suddenly put in execution, which may have ill-construction with the state here, and make us obnoxious to any adversary;"* which shows, not that the island Puritans did not sympathize with bluff Endicott's action, but that they dreaded lest it might provoke a hostile government to give their pet colony its *coup de grâce*.

* Mass. Col. Rec., vol. 1, p. 408.

CHAPTER XXII.

THE ARBELLA.

"We will renew the times of truth and justice,
  Condensing into a fair free commonwealth,
  Not rash equality, but equal rights,
  Proportioned like the columns of the temple,
  Giving and taking strength reciprocal,
  And making firm the whole with grace and beauty,
  So that no part could be removed without
  Infringement of the general harmony."
  Byron's *Doge of Venice*.

The success of Endicott and the supplementary success of the detachments despatched to reinforce him—success which at the very outset had left the older settlement at Plymouth, plodding on under a heavy load of debt and odium, far behind—stirred English Puritanism as with the blast of a trumpet. So intense was the interest in the new colony, throughout the realm, that a tract descriptive of New England, written by Higginson, and sent over to England, in manuscript, was printed, and ran through three editions in as many months.* In every hamlet, on every street-corner, eager groups met and discussed the right and the policy of emigration; and the most scrupulous consciences met the query, "Is it permitted that men fly from persecution?" by responding, "Yes; for persecution may lead our posterity to abjure the truth."

* Bancroft, vol. 1, p. 350.

Soon this stir had an effect. Some of the purest, wealthiest, and best-educated men in England agreed to embark for America. One thing only had made them hesitate; the colonial government resided in England, and was only sifted into New-England by delegation. The charter empowered the company, and not the colonists, to transport persons, establish ordinances, and settle government.* It was a chrysalis; it had the face of a commercial corporation, but was pregnant with the essence of an independent provincial government. Like the mermaid, it had a human head, but its body was the body of a fish. This puissant possibility—who should evoke it? Who should utter the talismanic words fit to set free the hidden spirit of self-government? Matthew Cradock, the governor of the company, pronounced the "open sesame." He saw, as did other sagacious men, that the residence of the corporate authority in England embarrassed emigration, barred prosperity, and opened the door to discord. The colonists sighed for a real governor, not one in masquerade; and all began to realize that a government three thousand miles away could not successfully legislate for a settlement whose growing necessities came as quickly and changed as rapidly as the combinations of a kaleidoscope.

So Cradock, with generous self-abnegation, himself proposed the transfer of the charter to such of the freemen of the company as should themselves

* See the *ipsissima verba* of the charter. Mass. Hist. Col.

inhabit the colony.* A heated debate ensued. Both *pros* and *cons* had their say, and the formers of the project strengthened their argument by pointing to such men as Winthrop, Saltonstall, Johnson, Dudley, and Humphrey, all of whom had recently bound themselves at Cambridge to sail for Massachusetts Bay, accompanied by their families, provided the colonial government should be transferred to the Plantation.†

This decided the company, and a general assent was given to the alienation of the patent.‡ Then came an obstacle. The crown lawyers said, "It is not so nominated in the bond; you have no right, standing under this corporation charter in London, to transfer your power." Our fathers replied: "King Charles has granted us certain authority, but our charter does not bind us to exercise that authority in England; locality is not specified. We choose to vote that emigrants shall be freemen, and to summon a meeting beyond the Atlantic. You say this was not contemplated; but where is it forbidden? If you can quibble, so can we. If we have not the right, we will create it. In the light of our success lawyers may read the reason and hunt up a precedent fifty years hence."

It was thus that Puritanism, strong in faith, bold in emergencies, met the exigencies and trod down the difficulties of its epoch. "The corporation did not sell itself—it emigrated. The patent could not

---

* Hutchinson's Hist. of Mass., vol. 1, p. 13. Bancroft, Grahame. † Ibid. ‡ Ibid. Young's Chronicles, p. 88.

be assigned; but the patentees could call a legal meeting in the metropolis, or on board ship in an English harbor; and why not in the port of Salem as well as at the Isle of Wight? in a cabin or under a tree at Charlestown as well as at the house of Goffe in London?"

Thus it was that a unique and daring construction transformed a trading company into a municipality — a change fraught with momentous consequences. Before this decision all hesitation fell. The Cambridge friends announced their readiness to sail, and the old authorities of the Company at once resigned, in order that their offices might be filled by the chief emigrants.* John Winthrop was elected governor; John Humphrey was appointed deputy; and these were reinforced by eighteen assistants.† Just on the eve of embarkation, Humphrey's place was supplied by Thomas Dudley, he being for a space unavoidably detained in England.‡

Winthrop at once accepted the charge; and when he informed his son of the decision, the younger Winthrop replied: "I shall call that my country where I may most glorify God and enjoy the presence of my dearest friends. Therefore herein I submit myself to God's will and yours, and dedicate myself to Heaven and the Company, with the whole endeavors both of mind and body. The motives for emigration are unimpeachable; and it cannot but be a prosperous action which is so well allowed by the

---

* Hutchinson, Winthrop, Palfrey, Bancroft. † Ibid.
‡ Palfrey, vol. 1, p. 302.

judgment of God's prophets, undertaken by so religious and wise worthies in Israel, and indented to God's glory in so special a service."*

And now preparations for an extensive emigration were ardently pushed. The finances of the Company were put on a new basis. All contributors to the fund were *ipso facto* entitled to a share in the profits of the colonial trade and to a grant of Massachusetts land.† "The outlay was distributed in such proportions that it was not burdensome in any quarter. The richer emigrants submitted to it joyfully, from public spirit; the poorer as a panacea for existing evils."‡

Early in the spring of 1630, ten vessels were ready to weigh anchor. Richer than the argosies of the old Venetian or Genoan merchants, this fleet was freighted with the seed of a future empire; with the planters of a renovated England, secure in freedom, firm in religion; with the builders of a transatlantic Saxon state, bound to realize in its beneficent order the noblest dreams of English patriots and sages. Troops of ministering angels hovered round it to ward off danger, and God's own benediction sealed and sanctified the daring venture.

Let us descend into the little cabin of the "Arbella," and scan the faces and take the hands—if we are worthy—of some of the most famous personages of this august Company of devout *voyageurs*. The cabin is long, and low, and dark. But 'tis

---

* Cited in Hutchinson, in Winthrop, vol. 1, pp. 359, 360, and in Bancroft.   † Palfrey, vol. 1, p. 310.   ‡ Ibid.

lighted now, somewhat dingily, indeed, yet still sufficiently to enable us to discern a table covered with maps and legal parchments, round which are ranged a score of deeply-interested talkers.

That tall, handsome, gentlemanly man, who sits at the head of the table, is John Winthrop, the new governor. See what an easy grace there is in his every movement; he has the port of one habituated to command, yet he is very gentle withal. His hair is just touched with silver, and he is in the prime of life—just forty-two, ripe and mellow. Winthrop is not a needy, sour adventurer; he comes of an ancient family long seated at Groton, in Suffolk, where he has a property whose income yields him six or seven hundred pounds a year—the equivalent of at least ten thousand dollars now-a-days. Evidently he quits England from some higher motive than to fatten his exchequer. This is he whom Cotton Mather terms the "Lycurgus of New England;" "as devout as Numa, but not liable to any of his heathenish madnesses; a governor in whom the excellences of Christianity made a most imposing addition unto the virtues wherein even without these he would have made a parallel for the great men of Greece and Rome whom the pen of Plutarch has eternized."* A calm, unobtrusive, able gentleman, Winthrop had "studied that book, which, professing to teach politics, had but three leaves, and on each leaf but one word—MODERATION." He had been initiated into the mysteries of state-craft when

* Magnalia, vol. 1, p. 107.

a boy, for from his youth he had moved in the circles where the highest questions of English policy were discussed and elaborated by the familiar associates of Whitgift, and Bacon, and Essex, and Cecil Burleigh.*

At the right of Winthrop and chatting pleasantly with him, stands Thomas Dudley. He is short and thickset in stature, and stern in expression; a man fit to lead a forlorn hope. Quick and irascible in temper, uncompromising when he esteems himself in the right, every word he utters has the ring of authority. He is a man who speaks bullets. His head is grayer than Winthrop's, but he is still robust, and he walks with a martial air—and no wonder, for he is a soldier. Thirty years before he had borne arms under Henri Quatre in the ranks of the Huguenots, a service which had indoctrinated him in the love of civil and religious liberty;† and he was old enough to have seen Sir Philip Sidney, heard Spencer recite verses to Elizabeth, and lent a shrill voice to the wild huzza at the defeat of the Spanish Armada.‡

But who is this that glides up to Winthrop, and, touching him upon the shoulder, speaks a word in his ear? It is John Humphrey, "a gentleman of special parts, of learning and activity, and a godly man."§ He does not sail now, but is here to bid his friends God speed.

---

* See Winthrop's Life, by R. C. Winthrop, Boston, 1866. Mather's Account, Hutchinson's Sketch, Palfrey, etc., etc.

† Palfrey, vol. 1, p. 303.   ‡ Ibid. Elliot, Wilson.

§ Winthrop's Hist. of New England, vol. 1, p 332.

See, yonder, leaning with graceful negligence against the wainscot of the cabin, lounges a pale, thoughtful, intellectual young man, with a fine head and a face whose expression is that of lovable seriousness. This is Isaac Johnson, the wealthiest of the Pilgrims, a land-owner in three counties.* But profoundly impressed with the importance of emigration, and aware of the necessity of an example, he has risen from the lap of artificial and patrician life and flung away the softness of a luxurious home to battle with the rigors of a wilderness. Like Humphrey, who now approaches to shake hands with him, he is a son-in-law of the earl of Lincoln, the head in that day of the now ducal house of Newcastle,† and also, like his relative, he has been the familiar companion of the patriotic nobles.‡

Johnson now goes out as one of Winthrop's assistants, as does also Sir Richard Saltonstall, of Halifax, in the West Riding of Yorkshire, a bountiful contributor to the finances of the emigration.§ This little man, whose keen, searching eyes take in every thing without an effort, as he sits quietly on the left side of the table, is Theophilus Eaton, an eminent London merchant, but accustomed to courts, as he had resided at Copenhagen as English minister to Denmark.‖ That grave, sedate gentleman, directly opposite Eaton, is Lucien Bradstreet, son of a dissenting minister in Lincolnshire, and grand-

---

* Mass. Hist. Col. Palfrey, Prince, Mather.   † Ibid.
‡ Palfrey, vol. 1, p. 303.   § Ibid.
‖ Hume, Hist. Eng. Mather, Prince.

son of a "Suffolk gentleman of fine estate," and was graduated at Emanuel College, Cambridge. By his side sits William Vassall, an opulent West India proprietor.* These, and some others known to fame, now stood clustered in the cabin of the "Arbella"—a little ship of three hundred and fifty tons burden†—forming one of the grandest collections of friends on any historic canvas.

Nor were they alone. Many of the settlers had their families with them.‡ The enterprise was still further hallowed by the unshrinking devotion of unselfish women. These, inspired by piety and love, gave up all that is most dear and most essential to their lives, "security and the comfort of homes in England, to brave the stormy, frightful sea, to land on these bleak, wild shores, to front the miseries and trials of pioneer life, and to sink into untimely graves, as so many did. These were the martyrs who laid down their lives for freedom and for us; to them, therefore, let us uncover our heads."§

> "By fairy hands their knell is rung,
> By forms unseen their dirge is sung;
> There Honor comes, a Pilgrim gray,
> To bless the turf that wraps their clay;
> And Freedom shall awhile repair
> To dwell, a weeping hermit there."

* Archæologia Americana, vol. 3, 47, et seq. From this work most of the above facts have been cited.

† Formerly the "Eagle;" she was a naval vessel, and carried twenty-eight guns. She had been recently bought by the Company. Palfrey.   ‡ Winthrop's Hist. of New England.

§ Elliot, vol. 2, pp. 16, 17.

Foremost among these noble women, in position, in culture, and in sacrifice, stood the Lady Arbella* Johnson. Her heroism has thrown a halo of poetry around a venture which needed no additional ray to make it bloom in immortal verse. The daughter of Earl Lincoln, the idol of her associates, she was yet a Puritan. Married to Isaac Johnson, she was indeed a *helpmeet*, sharing in his feelings and animating him to loftier exertions. When her husband resolved to emigrate, she determined to share his peril, and though ill-fitted to brave the rigors of an inclement wilderness by her delicate nature, she answered all objections by saying, "God will care for me, and I must do my duty." An exile voyage was her wedding tour; and so touched were the Pilgrims by her devotion, that they named their vessel after her, the "Arbella."†

Such was the character, such the home position, of Winthrop and his coadjutors. Even the prejudiced and reluctant pen of that high Tory, Chalmers, though essaying a sneer, had half of its curse turned into a blessing, for he was compelled to write, "The principal planters of Massachusetts were English country gentlemen of no inconsiderable fortunes; of enlarged understandings, improved by

---

* The most common orthography is *Arabella*, but later writers almost unanimously reject this spelling, which is founded on the often erring authority of Mather in the Magnalia, and of Josselyn, and accept that of John Winthrop in his Diary, of Johnson in the "Wonder-working Providence," and of Dudley's Epistles. All of these men were personally intimate with Mrs. Johnson, and they must have known her name. See Winthrop, p. 1, note.

† Mather, Winthrop, Palfrey, Elliot, Hutchinson, etc., etc.

liberal education; of extensive ambition, concealed under an appearance of religious humility."*

On the 29th of March, 1630, the "Arbella" sailed from Cowes, off the Isle of Wight, and speeding down the channel, stopped at Yarmouth to join her consorts, the "Talbot," the "Jewel," the "Ambrose," and the rest.† Here the self-banished devotees penned a farewell to their brothers in the faith who remained in England. Their noble letter concludes thus: "Wishing our heads and hearts may be as fountains of tears for your everlasting welfare, when we shall be in our poor cottages in the wilderness, overshadowed by the spirit of supplication, through the manifold necessities and tribulations which may not altogether unexpectedly, nor, we hope, unprofitably, befall us, we shall ever rest assured friends and brethren."‡

This done, all was done; then, in the early days of April, favored by the breath of budding spring— fit season in which to sail—the flotilla lifted anchor and left Yarmouth, where the feet of these Pilgrims pressed the soil of their dear England for the last time.§ "Sadness was in their hearts, and tears dimmed their eyes, for they loved the land of their fathers; they could not forget the tender associations of youth, nor the holier associations of manhood, when leaving it forever. But 'as the hart

---

* Hist. of the Result of the American Colonies, vol. 1, p. 58.
† Winthrop's Diary.
‡ This address is said to have been drawn by Mr. White. Palfrey. § Elliot.

panteth for the water-brook,' so their souls longed for Liberty and God, and they went out full of hope. With a fair wind they passed the Needles, St. Albans, Portland, Dartmouth, and the Eddystone, with its fiery eye, watching for ships over the broad sea. The Lizard, and at last the Scilly Islands disappeared, went down day by day in the blue distance, and were left with the past, till, on Sunday, the 11th of April, 1630, the little fleet stood out bravely into the stormy Atlantic."*

* Elliot,

CHAPTER XXIII.

THE ARRIVAL.

> "Here the architect
> Did not with curious care a pile erect
> Of carvéd marble touch, or porphyry,
> But built for God and hospitality."
> CAREW.

NINE weeks the "Arbella" tossed on the Atlantic; then the lookout descried the New England coast-line, and shouted, "Land ho!" "About four in the morning," was Winthrop's entry in his diary under date of June 12th, "we neared our port, and shot off two pieces of ordnance."* A little later, Endicott entered a shallop and was rowed out to the incoming ship.† Greeting the new governor cordially, he at once conducted him to Salem, where all "supped on a good venison pastry."

Winthrop found disease stalking among the settlers, and provisions nearly spent; but all were hopeful, though the winter had been hard.‡ The stores he brought were not unwelcome, but these were not more heartily received than were those who brought them; for pioneer life brings out hospitality and good fellowship; and besides, these men had common hopes and fears, and were united in faith and practice.

---

* Winthrop's Diary, p. 31. † Ibid.
‡ Ibid., Palfrey. Bancroft.

THE ARRIVAL.

The governor seems not to have been quite satisfied with Salem as a definitive settlement; for, pausing there but a week to recruit after the tedious voyage, he pushed on in search of another place to "sit down."* Sailing up a bay "made by a great number of islands, whose high cliffs shoulder out the sea," the explorers finally decided upon a spot on the banks of Charles river, and a settlement was commenced where Cambridge now stands.†

Busy days followed. Land was allotted, hunting parties were sent out; Indians were chatted with; and thanksgivings for the past and prayers for the future were offered.‡ But, enfeebled by fevers and enervated by the scurvy, while the deceitful river and the marshy ground in its vicinity bred contagious and miasmal vapors to enshroud them nightly, the emigrants made little progress in their most important work, the erection of a town.

Daily the sickness increased, and it haunted Salem as well as infant Cambridge. In August there was a large mortality; but September was the most dreary month. Francis Higginson, who had been for some time slowly wasting away with a hectic fever, died in this sad autumn;§ but "in the hour of his death the future prosperity of New England and the coming glories of its many churches floated in cheerful visions before his eyes."‖ Then

---

* Winthrop's Journal, p. 32.
† Dudley's letter to the countess of Lincoln, cited in Hutchinson.   ‡ Hubbard, Mass. Col. Rec., Archæol. Am.
§ Ibid.   ‖ Bancroft. vol. 1, p. 350.

death struck another shining mark. The Lady Arbella Johnson's fragile frame, coming "from a paradise of plenty and pleasure into a wilderness of wants,"* succumbed shortly to the dread epidemic,† to the infinite sorrow of her loving friends. Her death broke the heart of her devoted husband. His sorrow was too full for utterance; or he might have hymned it in that verse of Dr. Watts, so pregnant with tenderness and pathos:

> "I was all love, and she was all delight;
> Let me run back to seasons past;
> Ah! flowery days when first she charmed my sight,—
> But roses will not always last."

Isaac Johnson survived the beautiful victim but a few weeks,‡ then he followed her to immortality through the grave.

> "He tried
> To live without her, liked it not, and died,"

said Mather, quaintly.§ Winthrop, through his tears, wrote his assistant's epitaph: "He was a holy man and wise, and died in sweet peace."‖

And now the mortality was fearful. Eighty of Endicott's colonists had been buried ere the coming of Winthrop;¶ in the summer and autumn succeeding his arrival over two hundred died.** Death reaped its hecatombs and battened on corpses. The Pilgrims wailed out their grief in God's ear, and

---

* Hubbard, p. 133. † Ibid. Prince, Winthrop.
‡ Ibid. § Magnalia, vol. 1, p. 77.
‖ Winthrop, vol. 1, p. 34.
¶ Palfrey, Bancroft, Archæol. Am.
** Ibid. Mass. Hist. Col.

kept fasts and appointed days of humiliation. But He "who doeth all things well" had his own purpose to subserve, and his hand was not stayed from smiting till the chill December skies mantled the earth with snow.*

Early in September the colonists determined to desert the pestilential river banks; a few went back to Salem, some paused at Charleston; others, led by Winthrop, planted themselves on that neck of land which is now called Boston.†

Ere long this peninsula came to be thought the fittest site for the erection of a colonial capital, and the 17th of September, 1630, was formally set apart as the date of its settlement.‡ The spot was then called *Shawmut*,§ and it was picturesquely seated on a surface which swelled into rising grounds of considerable height, which have since become famous as Copp's hill, Fort hill, and Beacon hill.‖ Rome sits upon seven hills; Boston is a trimountain city.

Why was it called Boston? Because Boston in England, a prominent town in Lincolnshire, some five score miles north of London, had played no inconsiderable part in the drama of this colonization, giving to the enterprise some of its chiefest pillars, among others, Dudley, and Bellingham, and Leverett, and Coddington.¶ The grateful Pilgrims thought that they owed the old English city a rec-

---

* Dudley's Letter to the Countess of Lincoln. Prince's Chronology. † Winthrop's Hist. of New England. Hutchinson.
‡ Ibid. § Shawmut, or the Settlement of Boston, p. 2.
‖ Drake's Hist. of Boston. ¶ Ibid. Elliot.

ognition and a tribute; so they gave to their capital the familiar name of *Boston*.*

Shawmut had an occupant previous to its hasty adoption by the deserters from Cambridge. William Blackstone, who had come over with Endicott, found himself cramped even in sparsely-settled Salem; so he pushed on to Shawmut neck and became sole proprietor of the whole peninsula, which was afterwards bought of him. Here he lived ten years, and saw the foundations of society laid. He was an eccentric character; and though an ordained clergyman of the English church, he had Puritan proclivities. As he had been pinched at home by conformity laws, he had exiled himself that he might secure elbow-room for his sentiments. But he loved liberty so well that he never would unite with the New England church. "No, no," he always replied, when solicited to do so, "I came from England because I did not like the lord-bishops; and I cannot join you, because I would not be under the lord brethren."†

---

* Drake's Hist. of Boston. Elliot.

† "Blackstone retained nothing in America of his ministerial character but his canonical coat. He devoted himself to the cultivation of the six or seven acres of land which he retained in his possession, and planted, it is said, the first orchard of apple-trees in New England. He left Boston because he was annoyed by its strict sectarian laws. Banishing himself again to the wilderness, he settled in a place now called Cumberland, on the banks of the Pawtucket river. Here he built a house in the midst of a park, planted an orchard near it, and divided his time between study and labor. He called his retreat "Study Hill," and resided there until his death in May, 1675.

"He was a man of a kind and benevolent heart; and when he went to Providence to preach, as he did occasionally, notwithstand-

THE ARRIVAL.

The Pilgrims went to work in Boston with a will. Winter impended; a shelter must be provided against the December sleet and the chilly braw. But the task was hard; the *vis inertiæ* of nature was to be overcome; and, without tools, carts, or experienced joiners, all hands began to realize that the carpenter was not inferior to the priest or the poet.*

Some few grew discouraged. Of the seven hundred whom Winthrop brought out, ninety went back to England.† But this gap was soon closed by fresh arrivals. Quite a fleet lay moored in Massachusetts bay; from Beacon hill seventeen ships might have been counted, all of which came in 1630;‡ and these had disgorged some fifteen hundred earnest, devout emigrants, "the best" that Britain could produce.§

As a body, the Pilgrims were full of courage, and their faith at all times bubbled over into song or into prayer. "We here enjoy God and Jesus Christ," wrote Winthrop to his wife, whom sickness had detained in England, "and is not that enough? I thank God I like so well to be here as not to

---

ing his disagreement in opinion with Roger Williams, he would carry with him some beautiful apples as a present to the children, who had never seen such fruit before. Indeed, the kind called Yellow Sweetings were first produced in his orchard; and the older inhabitants, who had seen apples in England, had never before seen that sort." Shawmut, or the Settlement of Boston, p. 27.

* Elliot, vol, 1, p. 152.
† Bancroft, p. 359. Palfrey, vol. 1. p. 313.
‡ Hutchinson, Prince, Hubbard.
§ Ibid. Charlestown Records.

repent coming. I would not have altered my course, though I had foreseen all these afflictions. I never had more content of mind."*

Before such a spirit—the right spirit—all obstacles were certain to succumb. It was sure to

———"sway the future,
While God stood behind the shadow,
Keeping watch above his own."

* Mass, Col. Rec., Bancroft.

CHAPTER XXIV.

THE CHARTER POLITY.

"And then we'll raise, on these wild shores,
A structure of wise government, and show
In our New World a glorious spectacle
Of social order."
            Mrs. Hale's *Ormond Grosvenor*.

The fundamental law of the colonies of Massachusetts Bay was the charter, which bore the crown seal. The old parchment contained a permit and a fiat. It gave the corporation the right to enlarge or decrease its numbers at its option, and to establish the terms on which new members should be admitted to its franchises. It decreed that the governor and his assistants should be elected by the suffrages of the Company at large. Every freeman, as the members of the corporation were called, was entitled to vote.*

On the 3d of August, 1630, at Charlestown, Winthrop convened his assistants, and held the first court under the transferred charter.† It was the earliest baby-cry of the provincial government. Administrative functions were at once assumed. Measures were initiated which looked to the support of ministers; the question of wages was adjusted; and an order was issued for the arrest of

---

* Bancroft, Story, Palfrey. See the Charter, in Massachusetts Hist. Col.   † Winthrop, Hutchinson, Hubbard.

Thomas Morton,* who, through the carelessness of Allerton, the Plymouth agent, had returned to New England, and once more "hied to his old nest" at Merry-mount, only to renew his godless pranks.†

"Such was the first colonial legislation, and such the first legislative body. No heralds, no wigs, no cannon, no gilding, were necessary to impose upon the senses or give majesty and authority to law."

Two months later,‡ a general assembly of the freemen of the colony was convened at Boston.§ In the Assembly the charter vested the fundamental legislative authority.‖ It was the colonial Parliament. At this session more than a hundred planters were admitted to the franchises of the corporation;¶ and since this accession increased the preëxisting inconvenience of gathering the whole Company for purposes of legislation, the freemen ceded to the governor and his assistants the whole political power, reserving only the right to supply vacancies.** The tenure of office was unlimited;†† perhaps it was tacitly understood to be, as in the old English law, "during good behavior"—*quamdiu se bene gesserint*. For a season the government was an elective aristocracy. It was oligarchical, like that of Venice.

This endured but little more than a twelve-

---

* See chap. 19, pp. 245 et seq.
† Bradford, Winthrop, Hubbard.   ‡ On the 19th of Oct.
§ Winthrop, Hutchinson.   ‖ See the charter.
¶ Bancroft, vol. 1, p. 359.   ** Ibid.   †† Ibid., p. 360.

month. In May, 1631, the freemen met again, "after corn was set," and revoked a part of the authority of which they had been too lavish. The government was curbed by a reservation to the commons of the right to make such annual changes as the majority should desire.*

"At this same time a law was established pregnant with evil, and with good. 'To the end that the body of the commons may be preserved of honest and good men'—so runs the old text—'it is ordered and agreed that, for the time to come, no man shall be admitted to the freedom of this body politic but such as are members of some of the churches within the corporate limit.' This rule stood unchanged until after the Restoration. Thus was the elective franchise narrowed. The polity was a sort of theocracy; God himself, speaking through the lips of his elect, was to govern his people. An aristocracy was founded; but not on wealth, or blood, or rank. The servant, the bondman, might be a member of the church, and therefore a freeman of the Company. Other states have limited the possession of political rights to the opulent, to freeholders, to the first-born. The colonists of Massachusetts, scrupulously refusing to the clergy the least shadow of political power, established the reign of the visible church, a commonwealth of the chosen people in covenant with God."†

But we must not let the boldness and presump-

---

* Bancroft, vol. 1, p. 360.
† Bancroft, vol. 1, pp. 360, 361.

tion of this act blind us to its inconsistency and its evil tendency. If men might enjoy the franchise only by uniting with the church, ambitious men, wicked men, might become hypocrites, that they might get power. When church-membership became the road to political authority, there was danger that audacious and unchastened interlopers might usurp the government, as they did in England under Whitgift, and Williams, and Laud.

This law was an inconsistency, because it was a radical departure from the primal principle of Massachusetts ecclesiasticism, the separation of church and state, and the complete independence of the individual churches.* Now it was affirmed that the state must unfold within the church.† Indeed, a kind of state church was developed.‡ This is evident from two facts. The clergy were to be supported, not merely by the contributions of actual church-members, but it was decreed that "all who are instructed in the word of God must contribute for those by whom they are taught in all good things."§ The government was empowered to curb ecclesiastical errorists; and "if any church should grow schismatical, rending itself from the communion of other churches, or should walk incorrigibly and obstinately in any corrupt way, contrary to the word of God, in such case the civil

---

* Uhden's New Eng. Theocracy, p. 68. Dexter's Congregationalism.
† Ibid., p. 71.   ‡ Ibid., Bancroft.
§ Ibid. Vide Cambridge Platform.

magistrate was directed to put forth his coercive power."*

Thus individual religious independence, child of the Protestant principle, was strangled. Our fathers honestly erred. Purity of religious worship was their goal; and in order to that, they desired the unclogged enjoyment of what they esteemed the divinely-appointed means of grace. Their model was the Mosaic code. They did not remember that God had superseded it by a new dispensation.

The Pilgrims were wise and devout men, and in most respects they were a century in advance of their generation; but as a body, they did not understand the golden rule of toleration. Divorcing church and state in theory, in practice they married them.

"It is folly," remarks an English scholar who has himself rehearsed the story of the Pilgrims, "for either British or American encomiasts to seek to disguise this fact. It is on record. All may read it. Impartial history is compelled to acknowledge that very few, even of the foremost thinkers and moralists of the seventeenth century, had any just conception of that grand principle, the outgrowth of the New Testament, which acknowledges God as the sole Judge of human faith, and interferes with opinions or creeds only when they run to

---

* Vide the Cambridge Platform, 1648. "This Confession of Faith belongs, indeed, to a later period, but it expresses throughout the principles of the early colonists unchanged." Uhden, p. 68.

seed in riot, and develope consequences inimical to social virtue and political order."*

But notwithstanding the fact that the Pilgrims erected a theocracy, and by conferring upon the civil arm jurisdiction in religion, opened the way to unjust persecution, it is also true that they "builded better than they knew;" for the principles they professed eventually forced their children to a broader platform. They secured the future. They were the acorn; let the nineteenth century be the oak.

> "For we doubt not, through the ages
> One increasing purpose runs;
> And the thoughts of men are widened
> With the process of the suns."

* Wilson's Pilgrim Fathers, pp. 487, 488.

CHAPTER XXV.

INCIDENTS.

"He cometh unto you with a tale which holdeth
Children from play and old men from the chimney-corner."
                                    SIR PHILIP SIDNEY.

THE life of the Pilgrim Fathers in these first years of their settlement was full of incident. They could not assent to Solomon's *dictum*, that "there is nothing new under the sun." Here they found a new heaven and a new earth; all things were strange. Their only acquaintance in the western wilds was God; and they never wearied of investigation. Their first move, after thanking God for preservation and a safe voyage, was to explore. They loved to "guess" out enigmas. They were always analyzing the soil, and speculating on the prospects of storms, and dickering with the Indians. From the homeliest and most commonplace circumstances, they did not disdain to gather wisdom or "to point a moral and adorn a tale." They had a teachable spirit, and were ardent students in the school of nature.

The unbroken forest especially possessed an unfading charm in their eyes. They were fascinated both by its freedom and its vastness; for in England, whatever patches of wood existed were enclosed in the parks of the exclusive nobles, and a bitter code of game-laws barred all entrance. But while a source of pleasure, it was also often a source of anxiety.

One pleasant afternoon Winthrop took his gun and strolled into the woods for a short walk. He lost his way, and night overtook him. Kindling a fire, he prepared to "camp out." He spent the hours till dawn in walking up and down and "singing psalms." Next morning he reached home safely, much to the delight of his neighbors, who had passed the entire night in the forest, hallooing and shooting off guns, in the hope that the lost governor might hear them.*

On another occasion one of the settlers lost a calf. Hearing the wolves howl in the night, he got up and shot off his musket several times in rapid succession, to frighten them away. The wind carried the report to all the settlements; every one was aroused; drums were beaten; messengers were despatched to spread the alarm; every bush was taken for an Indian. "But next morning the calf was found unharmed, the wolves and the colonists being well frightened. The former had disappeared, and the latter went 'merrily to breakfast,' esteeming their alarm a good joke, and quaintly rallying one another on the 'great fear that had come upon them, making all their bones to shake.'"† But their fright was not foolish; it was bred of caution and a knowledge of their situation. They remembered with old Ben Johnson, that

* Winthrop's Journal, † Elliott, vol. 1, pp. 155, 156.

> "A valiant man
> Ought not to undergo or tempt a danger,
> But worthily, and by selected ways;
> He undertakes by reason, not by chance."

At Plymouth the Pilgrims had been longer in America, and the first flush of initial excitement had abated. The pulse-beat there was calmer, for they were more learned in woodcraft than the later comers. Yet even at Plymouth the jog-trot of events was occasionally broken. There is a traditionary anecdote, illustrative of the danger of one gentleman's commissioning another to do his wooing for him, which doubtless created an unwonted stir in the sedate old town at the time. It seems that Miles Standish had buried his wife some time after his arrival in New England; on which he thus communed with himself:

> " 'T is not good for a man to be alone, say the Scriptures.
> This I have said before; and again and again I repeat it;
> Every hour in the day I think it, and feel it, and say it.
> Since Rose Standish died, my life has been weary and dreary.
> Sick at heart have I been, beyond the healing of friendship.'"

So Standish resolved to wed again. He had already taken a fancy to Miss Priscilla Mullins, one of the sweetest of the Puritan maidens; and he said:

> " 'Oft in my lonely hours have I thought of this maiden, Priscilla.
> She is alone in the world. Her father, and mother, and brother,
> Died in the winter together. I saw her going and coming,
> Now to the grave of the dead, and now to the bed of the dying;
> Patient, courageous, and strong, and said to myself, that if ever
> There were angels on earth, as there are angels in heaven,

Two have I seen and known; and the angel whose name is Priscilla
Holds in my desolate life the place which the other abandoned.'

Therefore the captain resolved to woo her. But,

"Being a coward in this, though valiant enough for the most part,"

he decided to do it by proxy; so he selected John Alden, his secretary—

"Fair-haired, azure-eyed, with delicate Saxon complexion,
Having the dew of youth, and the beauty thereof, as the captives
Whom St. Gregory saw, and exclaimed, 'Not Angles, but angels.'
Youngest of all was he of the men who came in the Mayflower."

"John," said he,

"'Go to the damsel Priscilla, the loveliest maiden of Plymouth;
Say that the blunt old captain, a man not of words, but of actions,
Offers his hand and heart—the hand and heart of a soldier.
You, who are bred as a scholar, can say it in elegant language,
Such as you read in your books of the pleadings and wooings of lovers;
Such as you think best adapted to win the heart of a maiden.'"

Now it happened that poor John Alden was himself enamoured of the lovely Puritan maiden, and he listened to this request aghast. But Standish, unaware of this fact, urged the unwelcome mission on his blushing scribe, and demanded his acceptance of it in the name of friendship. Alden determined to perform the mission, and to do it faithfully; so he hied him through the forest to Priscilla's dwelling. Entering without ado, he at once broached the subject, and flung forth a glowing record of his master's virtues. Priscilla heard him awhile in ominous silence, and then interrupted him by this query:

> "'If the great captain of Plymouth is so very eager to wed me,
> Why does he not come himself, and take the trouble to woo me?
> If I am not worth the wooing, I surely am not worth the winning.'"

Alden tried to explain and smooth the matter;

> 'But as he warmed and glowed in his simple and eloquent language,
> Quite forgetful of self, and full of praise of his rival,
> Archly the maiden smiled, and, with eyes overrunning with laughter,
> Said in a tremulous voice, 'Why do n't you speak for yourself, John?'"

The bewildered but happy secretary at once took the hint. Returning to Standish, he reported his failure. Then he *did* "speak for himself," and to such purpose that he was soon married. There were no horses in the wilderness; so after the nuptials,

> "Alden, the thoughtful, the careful, so happy, so proud of Priscilla,
> Brought out a snow-white bull, obeying the hand of his master,
> Led by a cord that was tied to an iron ring in its nostrils,
> Covered with crimson cloth, and a cushion placed for a saddle.
> She should not walk, he said, through the dust and heat of the noonday;
> Nay, she should ride like a queen, not plod along like a peasant.
> Somewhat alarmed at first, but reassured by the others,
> Placing her hand on the cushion, her foot in the hand of her husband,
> Gayly, with joyous laugh, Priscilla mounted her palfrey.
> Like a picture it seemed of the primitive, pastoral ages,
> Fresh with the youth of the world, and recalling Rebecca and Isaac;
> Old, and yet ever new, and simple and beautiful always,

Love immortal and young, in the endless succession of lovers.
So through the Plymouth woods passed onward the bridal procession."*

But sometimes events of ruder and less joyous significance came to stir a ripple on the placid sea of frontier life. Even among these Pilgrims there were laws to be enforced and bad men to be curbed. Thomas Morton was one. This irrepressible torment was once more engaged at "Merry Mount" in selling guns and "fire-water" to the Indians; nor did he hesitate to "shoot hail-shot into them," because they refused to bring him a canoe in which to cross the river. He was apprehended on their complaint, and because he "discredited the whites." His den was burned in the presence of the natives whom he had maltreated; and he himself, after being for a while "set in the bilboes," was sent once more a prisoner to England.†

This occurred at Boston. At Plymouth a still more emphatic and sombre scene was enacted. John Billington, always a pest, of whom Bradford had said, "He is a knave, and so will live and die,"‡ was convicted of wilful murder. Conference was held with the most judicious men of Massachusetts Bay as to the disposition to be made of him. Winthrop and the rest favored his execution, basing the right to inflict that penalty, not so much on the English common law as on the code of Moses: "Whoso

* Longfellow's Courtship of Miles Standish. See, also, Banvard and Thatcher.
† Elliot, vol. 1, p. 154. Winthrop, Bradford, Prince.
‡ Ibid., p. 68. Banvard, Thatcher, Morton.

sheddeth man's blood, by man shall his blood be shed."* Under this decision Billington was hung; and this was the first capital punishment ever inflicted in New England.

These magisterial rigors did not suffice to quell the evil-doers; for shortly afterwards Philip Radcliff ventured to revile the "powers that be;" nor did he scruple to asperse the colonial churches. For this misdemeanor he was condemned to lose his ears. This did not subdue him; so he was whipped and banished. All which processes did not serve to increase his affection for the Pilgrims. Landing in England, he did them what mischief he could.†

Then came another rogue. This was Sir Christopher Gardiner, "one of those mysterious visitors whose appearance in remote settlements so easily stimulates the imaginations of men of more staid habits and better mutual acquaintance."‡ It was not known who he was, nor whence he came, nor why. It has been conjectured that he was a spy of Sir Ferdinand Gorges and other foes of Puritanism in England.§ Bradford says, "He came into these parts on pretence of forsaking the world, and to live a private life in a godly course. He had been a great traveller, was a Knight of the Holy Sepulchre, and a relative of that Gardiner who was so bitter a persecutor under "Bloody Mary." Now

* Elliott, vol. 1, p. 68. Banvard, Thatcher, Morton. This was in 1630. † Winthrop's Journal.
‡ Palfrey, vol. 1, p. 329. § Ibid.

he avowed himself penitent for his past ill life, offered to join the churches here, and said he was willing to apply himself to any employment."*

Soon, however, he fell under suspicion at Massachusetts Bay. He was suspected of living in concubinage with "a comely young woman whom he had brought over with him," and whom he called his cousin, "after the Italian manner." Being cited to answer these charges, he decamped. Soon Winthrop received letters which showed that this "knight" had "two wives living in London."† An order was issued for his apprehension. Eventually he took refuge at Plymouth. Here he chanced to drop his diary; and in this was found a "memorial showing what day he was reconciled to the pope and the church of Rome, and in what university he took his scapula and such and such degrees."‡ So Bradford sent the unmasked Jesuit, with the unfortunate diary, to Winthrop;§ who, in his turn, presently sent him back "to the two wives in Old England, that they might search him further."‖ On reaching the island, he was not restrained of his liberty, but roaming at large, soon found out the enemies of the colonies; and he, with Radcliff, actively engaged in intrigues to its prejudice.¶

"So difficult was it," observes Elliot, "to get away from the wickedness of Satan, who, even in this

---

* Bradford, p. 294. † Winthrop's Journal.
‡ Bradford, p. 295. § Ibid.
‖ Winthrop's Journal. ¶ Palfrey, vol. 1, p. 330.

virgin land, and among these godly Puritans, would thrust himself in where his company was in no way wanted. But now one more rascal was exported and sent home, where, with his two wives and his 'Italian manner,' and his popery, he would not poison Massachusetts."*

Yet, spite of these isolated instances of riot, insubordination, and disturbance, the Puritan settlements were in the main models of industry, sobriety, and good order. "I have read," says Cotton Mather, "a printed sermon which was preached before 'both Houses of Parliament, the lord-mayor and aldermen of London, and the Westminster assembly of divines,' the greatest audience then in the world; and in that sermon the preacher had this passage: 'I have lived in a country where, in seven years, I never saw a beggar, nor heard an oath, nor looked upon a drunkard.' That Utopia was New England."† Mather adds sadly: "But they who go hence now must tell another story."‡

What was the secret of such prosperity? When Demosthenes was asked what it was that so long preserved Athens in a flourishing state, he replied, "The orators are men of learning and wisdom; the magistrates do justice; the citizens are quiet, and the laws are kept among them all."§ 'T was a glorious record for the immortal city, and the same secret gave the settlements of the Pilgrim fathers substantial peace and happy order.

* Elliot, vol. 1, p. 155. † Magnalia, vol. 1, p. 103.
‡ Ibid., p. 97. § Orations, N. Y., 1855.

Winthrop relates that once "at Watertown there was, in the view of divers witnesses, a great combat betwixt a mouse and a snake; and, after a long fight, the mouse prevailed and killed the snake. The pastor of Boston, Mr. Wilson, a very sincere, holy man, hearing of it, gave this interpretation: the mouse was a poor contemptible people, brought by God hither, who should overcome Satan here, and dispossess him of his kingdom. Upon the same occasion he added: 'I dreamed before coming to this country, that I was here and saw a church rise out of the earth, which gradually expanded into a colossal shape'—as pray God ours may."*

Winthrop's prayer seemed even then in the way to exact fulfilment. Many earnest, devoted Pilgrims, continued to pour into New England. In 1631, Eliot, the famous apostle to the Indians, landed at Salem.† Full of love and full of hope, he soon entered upon those labors which have immortalized his name on earth, and enrolled it on the heavenly records as a teacher and benefactor of his race.‡

---

* Winthrop's Hist., vol. 1, p. 97. † Ibid., p. 76.

‡ Eliot spent the first years of his transatlantic life as a preacher at Roxbury. Here he was engaged with Weld and Richard Mather in compiling the first book published in New England—"The Psalms in Metre"—which appeared in 1640. In 1645, he became deeply interested in the work of evangelizing the Indians, "those ruins of mankind." Into this labor he threw his whole heart; and he never relinquished it until God called him home; for he believed with the psalmist, that Jehovah was perpetually saying, "Ask of me, and I will give thee the heathen for thine inheritance."

Going into the wilderness, he preached his first Indian sermon in October, 1646, in a wigwam at Nonantum, near Watertown. He had already familiarized himself with the aboriginal languages;

A little earlier, Roger Williams was wafted to these shores, where, in his May of youth, he found a glorious destiny awaited him.*

and since the New England tribes—loosely estimated at a united membership of forty thousand—were a part of the Algonquin race, whose tongues were similar, this acquisition was not as difficult as it might seem. Eliot had the happiness to witness several conversions as the result of his first essay; and from that moment he worked on with a resolution and self-abnegation above all earthly praise. The "Apostle," as he soon came to be called, at once commenced several translations. Two catechisms were done into the Indian dialects. A primer, the Psalms, and Baxter's Call, followed; and finally, an Indian Bible, a marvellous monument of patience, industry, and faith, appeared in 1663. Of course, this work necessitated money. Eliot appealed for aid. The English Parliament granted, in 1649, a special sum for the promotion of the gospel among the aborigines. Large collections were made throughout England for the same purpose; and even infant Boston contributed twenty-five hundred dollars in its poverty. The zeal of Eliot and the funds of the godly were not in vain expended. A number of Indians were hopefully converted, and these were colonized into separate towns. The chief seat of the "praying Indians" was Natick, settled by them in 1651. There Eliot erected his headquarters; and he gave his converts "the same advice as to government that Jethro gave to Moses; so they assembled, and chose their rulers of hundreds, fifties, and tens, and proclaimed, 'that God should rule over them.'" Their houses were Indian cabins, built of bark, except the meeting-house, which was fashioned after the churches of the pale-faces. In this latter building Eliot had a bed and a room. Natick then contained one hundred and fifty-two persons. Eliot saw that civilization was necessary for his dusky *protegés*, both as a bond of union and as a fulcrum for his gospel lever. He knew also that responsibility educates. So he was careful to induct into offices of honor and responsibility those of his converts who seemed the most trusty, energetic, and intelligent. Such commissions were highly esteemed by the Indians, and sometimes they performed their official duty with amusing formality. On one occasion, a native magistrate named Ilihoudi,

* Ibid., p. 49. He came February 11, 1630.

The Pilgrims made the best of every thing—saw only the good of the land. Even the climate of New England did not lack encomiasts. Wood had issued the following warrant, directed to an Indian constable: "I, Hihoudi, you, Peter Waterman. Jeremy Wisket,—quick you take him, fast you hold him, straight you bring him before me. Hihoudi!"

Natick was a nucleus settlement. Soon a number of supplementary colonies were grouped about it, and these embraced, some sixty, some seventy, some eighty, "praying Indians," all provided with churches, schools, and the rude initial apparatus of civilization. In 1674, there were eleven hundred Christian Indians who were possessed of fixed homes within the jurisdiction of Massachusetts. And Eliot enumerated twenty-five hundred more to Boyle, as settled in Plymouth, Nantucket, and Martha's Vineyard. The usual exercises were praying, reading the Bible, and preaching—sometimes by a white teacher, sometimes by a native missionary. Then all united in singing; and we are told that "sundry could manage to do so very well." After this, some were catechized. Then, says Eliot, "if there was any act of public discipline—as divers times there was, since ignorance and partial barbarism made many stumblers—the offender was called forth, exhorted to give glory to God, and urged to confess his sins." King Philip's war partially paralyzed these efforts of Eliot and his compeers; it robbed them of the sympathy of the whites, and roughened their path; but they persevered; and even after Eliot's decease, in 1690, God put it into the hearts of some to carry on his work, and efforts continued to be made towards the evangelization of the natives as far down as the year 1754. At that time the Rev. Mr. Hawley was "set apart" for that special work, in the "Old South Church," in Boston, and Deacon Woodbridge and Jonathan Edwards were enlisted in the same good cause. Roger Williams had been an active co-worker with Eliot, and a little later the Mayhews gleaned their rich harvest at Martha's Vineyard. Indeed, the Mayhews were so successful that on the single little island where they labored, six meetings were held in as many different places every Sabbath, and there were ten native preachers, who, according to the testimony of Thomas Mayhew, were of "good knowledge and holy conversation."

But the missionaries did not find it plain sailing. Besides the

been "carefully hatched," yet in England disease sapped his life. While in America, he wrote: "Scarce do I know what belongs to a day's sickness."*

An English churchman, who had not Wood's motive for liking New England, saw with different eyes: "The transitions from heat to cold are short, sudden, and paralyzing. We are sometimes frying, and at others freezing; and as some men die at their labor in the field of heat, so some in winter are frozen to death by the cold."† No doubt.

> "Oh, who can hold a fire in his hand
> By thinking of the frosty Caucasus?"

The Puritans saw New England as the refuge of the godly, and looking at it through the mirage of sentiment, its sky rivalled that of Italy in soft incessant jealousy between the whites and the aborigines, they had to encounter the natural repugnance of the Indian to desert the blind faith of his fathers and accept the God and Saviour of the white men. Massasoit, spite of his friendship for the whites, lived and died a strict unbeliever. Philip, his son, was equally obstinate, saying on one occasion, after listening to an exhortation from Eliot, and placing his hand on a button on the Apostle's coat: "I care no more for the gospel than I care for that button." The Narragansetts went so far as to prohibit preaching within their borders. Yet still the missionaries went on, and, with God's blessing, they harvested many souls, long before good Bishop Berkeley launched his noble but abortive scheme for the conversion of the red men. Those readers who are desirous of studying this subject in detail, are referred to Sparks' Life of Eliot; Mayhew's Indian experiences; Mansell's recent reprint at Albany of tracts concerning Eliot's Indian missions; R. Williams' Key; Hubbard's Hist.; Mather's Magnalia; Gookin, in Mass. Hist. Col., etc., etc.

* Wood's New England Prospect, p. 4.
† J. Macpherson's America Dissected, 1752.

beauty. To the churchman it seemed a rugged wilderness in very deed. It was a difference of standpoint.

But mild or severe, the Pilgrims loved this adopted mother on whose breast they lay, and their settlements began to increase in number. A brood of eight little towns, or *townlets*, now nestled under the wings of the Massachusetts charter;* while Plymouth already began to think of equipping a new colony,† and annexing the Connecticut.

The western wilds were no longer tenantless, or what is equivalent to that, held only by prowling barbarians. The French, who had been hovering over the coast ever since their rout from L'Acadie, in 1613, by Sir Samuel Argall, had recently acquired Canada by purchase.‡ The wise statesmanship of Richelieu had bought from Charles I.—busy in a fatal attempt to enforce ceremonialism,

"Rending the book in struggles for the binding,"—

one of the finest provinces in the known world for fishing, masts, harbors.§ Already the Latin provinces had begun to string a chain of citadels westward along the banks of the St. Lawrence and the borders of the lakes to the valley of the Mississippi,

"toppling round the dreary west
A looming bastion fringed with fire."

---

* Palfrey, vol. 1, p. 323. These were Salem, Charlestown, Watertown, Boston, Roxbury, Dorchester, Mystic, and Saugus.
† Bradford, p. 311. ‡ Elliot, vol. 1, p. 1
§ Prince, Bancroft, Hutchinson.

INCIDENTS. 313

The Spaniard was in Florida.* The Dutchman smoked his pipe on the banks of the Hudson.† English adventurers held Virginia.‡ The Pilgrims had clutched New England. Labor was vocal on every hill-side; the whole continent began to echo to the civilizing stroke of the woodman's axe.

* Bancroft, vol. 1, chap. 2. passim.
† Brodhead's Hist. of New York. Dunlap.
‡ Chalmers, Hening.

CHAPTER XXVI.

THE ADVANCE OF CIVILIZATION.

> "So work the honey-bees—
> Creatures that, by a rule of nature, teach
> The art of order to a peopled kingdom.
> They have a head and officers of sorts,
> Where some, like magistrates, correct at home;
> Others, like merchants, venture trade abroad;
> Others, like soldiers, armed in their stings,
> Make boot upon the summer's velvet buds;
> Which pillage they with merry march bring home
> To the tent royal of their emperor,
> Who, busied in his tent, surveys
> The singing mason building roofs of gold;
> The civil citizens kneading up the honey;
> The poor mechanic porters crowding in
> Their heavy burdens at his narrow gate;
> The sad-eyed justice, with his surly hum,
> Delivering o'er to executors pale
> The lazy, yawning drone."
>
> SHAKSPEARE'S *Henry V.*

FROM the year 1630—before that, but more perceptibly after—the advancing march of civilization carried all before it in New England. There were, indeed, occasional oscillations in its career of triumph; but always, when its genius seemed to balk, it ended by bearing off a trophy.

At Plymouth, all the social and religious forces had "settled down into fixed ways." Justice was administered, order was preserved, education was provided for.* The old town began to prosper. The busy hum of men and the laughter of successful trade echoed through the streets; and Bradford wrote, "Though the partners have been plunged into great engagements and oppressed with unjust debts, yet the Lord has prospered our traffic so that our labor is not for naught. The people of this plantation begin to grow in their outward estates, by reason of the flowing of many into the province, especially into the settlements on Massachusetts Bay; by which means corn and cattle have risen to a great price, whereby some are much enriched, while commodities grow plentiful."†

As property and a sense of security increased, the Plymouth Pilgrims began to show a disposition to disperse, for the convenience of better pasturage and ampler farm-room. So the three hundred inhabitants, esteeming themselves crowded, separated, and a new church and hamlet were planted on the north shore of the shallow harbor.‡ "The town in which all had lived very compactly till now," observes the old Plymouth governor somewhat ruefully, "was left very thin by this move." In Bradford's eyes, it was the beginning of a movement pregnant with evil.§ He thought, somewhat plausibly, that strength and safety lay in the close union of the scattered colonists. Yet that idea was fatal to colonization, and bolder theorists deter-

---

* Thatcher's Plymouth. † Bradford, pp. 255–310.
‡ Palfrey, vol. 1, p. 336. § Bradford, p. 301.

mined to educate communities by responsibility, the best of school-masters. They said,

"Out of this nettle, danger, we pluck this flower, safety."

For several years the church at Plymouth had enjoyed the ministrations of an ordained clergyman. That Separatist, Mr. Smith, who had crossed the water with Higginson and Skelton in 1629, perceiving that he was looked upon with some suspicion by his brother Pilgrims on account of his "come-outism," an aroma which they were not then prepared to exhale, went immediately to Nantasket, sojourning there "with some stragglers" for several months.* One day a Plymouth boat happened to touch at that port, whereupon Mr. Smith "earnestly besought the crew to give him and his, with such things as could be readily carried, passage to Plymouth, as he had heard that there was likelihood that he might there find house-room until he could determine where to settle; for he said he was weary of the uncouth place in which he found himself, where his house was so poor that neither himself nor his goods could keep dry."†

He was brought to Plymouth, where he "exercised his gifts"—which were rather "low"‡—being "kindly entertained and sheltered," and finally "chosen into the ministry;"§ so that Brewster once again found respite. A little later, Smith's labors and gifts were supplemented by Roger Will-

---

* Chap. 21, p. 264.   † Bradford, p. 263.
‡ Elliot, vol. 1, p. 119. Young's Chronicles, Morton's Memorials, etc.   § Bradford, p. 263. Morton.

iams—why and how long we shall in due time discover.

In 1632, an event of no little interest occurred. Governor Winthrop went to Plymouth to exchange fraternal greetings with Governor Bradford, and mutual inquiries of "What cheer?" were passed. Winthrop has related the incident. Let us open his record: "The governor of Massachusetts Bay, with Mr. Wilson, pastor of Boston, and some others, went aboard the 'Lion' on the 25th of October, and thence Captain Pierce carried then to Wessagusset, where is now a prosperous settlement of a graver sort than the old ones. The next morning the governor and his company went on foot to Plymouth, and came thither within the evening. The governor of Plymouth, Mr. William Bradford, a very discreet and grave man, with Elder Brewster and some others, came forth and met them without the town, and conducted them to the governor's house, where they were very kindly entertained, and feasted every day at several houses.

"On the Lord's Day there was a sacrament, of which they partook; and in the afternoon Mr. Roger Williams, according to the Plymouth custom, propounded a question, to which the pastor, Mr. Ralph Smith, spoke briefly; then Mr. Williams prophesied;* and after, the governor of Plymouth spoke to the question; after him, the elder; then some two or three more of the congregation. Then the elder desired the governor of Massachusetts Bay

* The old form of expression for *exhort* or *expound*.

and Mr. Wilson to speak to it, which they did. When this was done, Mr. Fuller, their surgeon, put the congregation in mind of their duty of contribution; whereupon the governors and all the rest went down to the deacon's seat, and put into the box, and then returned.

"On Wednesday, the 31st of October, at about five o'clock in the morning, the governor and his company came out of Plymouth; whose governor, pastor, elder, and others, accompanied them nearly half a mile in the dark. Lieutenant Holmes, one of their chiefest men, with two companions and Governor Bradford's mare, came along with them to a great swamp, about ten miles. When they came to the great river,* they were carried over one by one by Luddam, their guide, as they had been when they came, the stream being very strong, and up to the crotch; so the governor called that passage 'Luddam's Ford.' Thence they came to a place called 'Hue's Cross.' The governor being displeased at the name, because such things might hereafter give the papists occasion to say that their religion was first planted in these parts, changed the name, and called it 'Hue's Folly.' So they came that evening to Wessagussett, where they were bountifully entertained, as before; and the next day all came safe to Boston."†

This was the first interchange of gubernatorial civilities ever known in America. It was certainly

---

* Now called "North river," near Scituate. Massachusetts Hist. Col. 4. † Winthrop, vol. 1, pp. 108-111.

unique. One governor lent the other his mare to ride home upon, gave him a guide on whose shoulders he could be ferried across a rapid stream, and entertained his guest by beseeching him to "prophesy" on the Sabbath, and by gently reminding him that the contribution-box was empty.

Such was the homely, hearty, frank hospitality of the Pilgrim fathers over two hundred years ago. Such were the manners and customs of New England when Brewster "prophesied" and when Winthrop and Bradford governed. Looking back across two centuries, we smile; but perhaps, with all its super-refinement, modern hospitality is no whit in advance of that which contented Winthrop, and of which it may be said,

> "There was no winter in't; an autumn 't was,
> That grew the more by reaping."

In this same year of Winthrop's visit to Plymouth, the Pilgrims had their first boundary quarrel with the French. The extent of Acadia to the west was long a subject of dispute.* The lands which bordered on the rival boundaries became a "debatable" ground. Bradford and his coadjutors had erected a trading station on the Penobscot. This was now assaulted, and "despoiled of five hundred pounds worth of beaver-skins, besides a store of coats, rugs, blankets, biscuits;" and insult was added to injury; for the cavalier Frenchmen bade the tenants of the plundered post tell the English

---

* Palfrey, vol. 1, p. 337. Hubbard, Prince.

that "some gentlemen of the Isle of Rhé had been there to leave their compliments."*

This taunt was not instantly responded to. Indeed, it was put out at interest, and remained unsettled until the next century, when these "religious English" gave the intruders indefinite leave of absence from Canada, and settled the boundary question by annexing the whole territory.

As an offset to their loss on the eastern rivers, the Plymouth Pilgrims began to push their enterprise towards the west. "Rumor, with its thousand tongues," had frequently hymned the praises of the Eldorado of Connecticut. The phlegmatic Dutchman, so cold on other themes, kindled on this, and actually took his pipe out of his mouth, that he might speak more freely. The taciturn Indian melted into profuse and graphic eloquence when he painted the beauty and fertility of these western bottom-lands.†

These glowing reports at length won the Pilgrims, tied at first by the necessity of overcoming a contiguous wilderness, to scout in that region. Parties visited the banks of the "Fresh river," as the Dutch styled it,‡ or the *Connecticut*, as it soon came to be called, "not without profit," finding it "a fine place both for planting and for trade."§

In 1633, Bradford and Winslow, who had him-

---

* Bradford, p. 294.

† Ibid., p. 311. Winthrop, Hubbard, Thatcher.

‡ Brodhead's N. Y.; the Dutch claim to have discovered it. Brodhead. § Bradford, ut antea.

self bathed in the waters of the silvery river, went up to Boston to solicit from Winthrop a united effort to colonize the Connecticut valley. In the first spring after Winthrop's landing, a Connecticut sachem, expelled from his hunting-grounds by the prowess of the Pequods, a fierce and numerous tribe, as powerful in New England as the "Six Nations" were in New York,* had come across the country to offer the pale-faces a settlement on the banks of the beautiful river, together with the alliance of his warriors and a yearly tribute of corn and beaver.† The Indian negotiator was well received, but Winthrop declined to accede to his request, since, "on account of their so recent arrival, they were not fit to undertake it."‡ The Plymouth diplomats received the same answer; and returning home, they resolved to push into the Connecticut forests unassisted.§

Meantime the Dutch, hearing of this purpose and preparation, decided to preoccupy the land, and so, by antedating the Pilgrim settlement, claim the soil by priority.‖ They did indeed purchase, from a Pequod chief, a spot of land where Hartford now stands, and erecting a "slight fort" in June, 1633, planted cannon, and forbade any Englishman to pass.¶

Undeterred by threats, the Pilgrims perfected

---

* Trumbull's Connecticut. † Winthrop, vol. 1, p. 52.
‡ Bradford, p. 312. § Ibid.
‖ Brodhead's N. Y., Bradford, Hubbard.
¶ Ibid., Palfrey.

14*

their arrangements, and in October sailed by the "Good Hope" of the Dutch, after a parley and mutual threats*—in which they were struck only by a few Dutch oaths—and planted at Windsor the first English colony in Connecticut.† A twelvemonth later, a company of seventy Dutchmen quitted New Amsterdam with the avowed purpose of expelling the Pilgrim pioneers. But after observing the spirit and preparation of the little garrison, they concluded to end their war-trail in a reconciliation, and retired without violence.‡

In the midst of their hardy enterprise, while the door of civilization was just ajar in Connecticut, an infectious fever came to scourge the Pilgrims. "It pleased the Lord to visit those at Plymouth," says Bradford, "with a severe sickness this year, of which many fell sick, and upwards of twenty, men, women, and children, died; among the rest, several of those who had recently come over from Leyden; and at the last, Samuel Fuller, their surgeon and physician. Before his death, he had helped many and comforted all; as in his profession, so otherwise, being a deacon in the church and a godly man, forward to do good, he was much missed. All were much lamented, and the sadness caused the people to humble themselves and seek God; and towards winter it seemed good to him to stay the sickness.

* Brodhead's N. Y., Bradford, Hubbard. Palfrey.
† Palfrey. vol. 1, p. 340.
‡ Winthrop, vol. 1, pp. 105-113. Bradford, pp. 311-314. Brodhead. Hist. N. Y., vol. 1, pp. 235-242

"This disease swept away many of the Indians in that vicinage; and the spring before, especially all the month of May, there was such a quantity of strange flies, like wasps in size, or bumblebees, coming out of holes in the ground, spreading through the woods, and eating up every green thing, as caused the forest to ring with their hum ready to deafen the hearers.* They have not been heard or seen since; but the Indians then said their presence foretokened sickness, which indeed came in June, July, August, and the chief heat of summer."†

At this period in colonial history, the tide of emigration seemed to flow at one time and to ebb at another. It was governed by the increase or the slack of persecution in England. In 1630, the date of the alienation of the provincial government, it was at the flood; in the succeeding year it actually receded. "Climate and the sufferings of the settlers were against free emigration; and besides, Morton, Radcliff, and Gardiner, were busy in the island against the colonists. In 1631, only ninety persons came over. But in 1632, the sluggish current quickened, and again set westward. Spite of threats, the Pilgrims had not been molested, and as Laud's pesterings grew in virulence, many ships then prepared to start, and some of Britain's noblest sons were about to desert her; among them

---

* "The insect here described," remarks Judge Davis, "is the *Cicada Septendecim* of Linnæus, commonly called the *locust*. They have frequently appeared since, indicated by Linnæus' specific name." Davis' edition of the Mem., p. 171.

† Bradford, pp. 314, 315.

Lord Say, Lord Rich, the 'good Lord Brooke,' Hazlerigge, Pym, Hampden, and Oliver Cromwell. But on the 31st of February, 1633, the king, in council, issued an order to stay the flotilla."*

'T is a high fact, and shows upon what slight hinges the weightiest events turn. The very foremost chiefs of the maturing revolution were at this time not only anxious to emigrate, but had actually embarked for America. Well would it have been for Charles, had he said to the disaffected Puritans,

> "Stand not upon the order of your going,
> But go at once."

Had some good genius nudged the elbow of the king, on that critical morning when his breathless messenger was hastening to stay the emigrant flotilla, urged him to say Yes, to its sailing, and foretold the future, how eagerly the fated monarch would have caught the cue, and torn that parchment, so pregnant with mischief, which forbade their departure; and offered the immortal junto jewels of gold and precious stones as an inducement to be gone, and cried, "Egypt is glad," when they set out.

But God made the wrath of man praise him. He struck the besotted court with judicial blind-

---

* Elliot, vol. 1, pp. 160, 161. Hist. Eng. Puritans, Am. Tract Soc., N. Y., 1866. Arch. Am. Mather's Magnalia, vol. 1, p. 97. Rev. J. S. M. Anderson's Hist. of the Col. Chh. of the B. Emp., vol. 1, p. 175, note. The fact of this embarkation of Cromwell and Hampden has been questioned by some careful writers. See Forster's British Statesmen, in loco. Also, Sanford's Ill. of the Fr. Rev., Lond., 1858.

ness. Neither Charles, nor Strafford, nor Laud could read the hand-writing on the wall. They could not foresee events which were ere long to

> "Fright the isle
> From her propriety."

These "fanatics" were not needed in New England. Their fellows had already commenced to build, at Plymouth and at Massachusetts Bay, for God and liberty. So they were detained to organize "resistance to tyrants" in the senate-house, and to give the arbitrary principle its death-blow at Naseby and Long Marston Moor.

But though the court, frightened at the prodigious extent of an emigration which threatened to depopulate the kingdom, had fulminated a decree against colonization, the departure of Pilgrims was only hindered, not stayed. They continued to cross the water until, in 1640, this pattering emigration had rained four thousand families and upwards of twenty thousand settlers into New England.* Then for a few glorious years the exodus ceased. The prospect of reform in England caused men to remain at home, "in the hope of seeing a new world" without passing the Atlantic.

In the summer of this same year which witnessed the detention of Cromwell, and Pym, and Hampden, and Hazlerigge, and Lord Brooke, a ship was freighted for America; and with two hundred other passengers, it bore to these shores three men who became as famous on this side the water

* Hutchinson, vol. 1, p. 93.

as the revolutionists did on the other—John Haynes, John Cotton, and Thomas Hooker.* On board the "Griffin" at this same time was another eminent minister, Mr. Stone; "and this glorious triumvirate coming together," remarks Cotton Mather, "made the poor people in the wilderness say that God had supplied them with what would in some sort answer their three great necessities; *Cotton* for their clothing, *Hooker* for their fishing, and *Stone* for their building."†

Haynes, afterwards governor both of Massachusets and Connecticut, was "a man of very large estate, and still larger affections; of a 'heavenly' mind and a spotless life; of rare sagacity and accurate but unassuming judgment; by nature tolerant; ever a friend to freedom, ever conciliating peace. He was an able legislator, and dear to the Pilgrims by his benevolence and his disinterested conduct."‡

Cotton and Hooker speedily became the most revered spiritual teachers of two commonwealths; Cotton shaped and toned Massachusetts ecclesiasticism; Hooker was the Moses of Connecticut. Both were well born; both had been clergymen of the English church; both had been silenced for non-conformity; both were consummate scholars—in Mather's strong phrase, *walking libraries;* both had won wide fame at home, which, like Joseph's bough, "ran over the wall" of the Atlantic ocean,

---

* Bancroft, vol. 1, p. 362.   ‡ Bancroft, ut antea.
† Magnalia, vol. 1, p. 265.

and made their names familiar in every cabin on the eastern coast.

"Cotton was acute and subtile. The son of a Puritan lawyer, he had been eminent at Cambridge as a student. He was quick in the nice perception of distinctions, and pliant in dialectics; in manner persuasive rather than commanding; skilled in the fathers and the schoolmen, but finding all their wisdom compactly stored in Calvin; deeply devout by nature as well as habit from childhood; hating heresy and still precipitately eager to prevent evil actions by suppressing ill opinions, yet verging in opinion towards progress in civil and religious freedom. He was the avowed foe of democracy, which he feared as the blind despotism of animal instincts in the multitude. Yet he opposed hereditary power in all its forms; desiring a government of moral opinion, according to the laws of moral equity, and 'claiming the ultimate resolution for the whole body of the people.'"*

Cotton was, if not the originator, then the main mover of the theocratical idea. "When he came," says Mather, "there were divers churches in America, but the country was in a perplexed and divided state; points of church order he settled with exactness; and inasmuch as no little of an Athenian democracy was in the mould of the colonial government, by the royal charter which was then acted upon, he effectually recommended that none should be electors or elected except such as were visible

* Bancroft, vol. 1, p. 363.

subjects of Christ personally confederated in the church. In this way, and in others, he propounded an endeavor after a theocracy, as near as might be to that which was the glory of Israel."*

Cotton was a man of much personal humility. "He learned the lesson of Gregory, 'It is better, many times, to fly from an injury by silence, than to overcome it by replying;' and he used that practice of Grynæus, 'To revenge wrongs by Christian taciturnity.' On one occasion he had modestly replied to one that would much talk and croak of his insight into the revelations: 'Brother, I must confess myself to want *light* in these mysteries.' The man went home and sent Cotton a *pound of candles.*"†

He was iron in his doctrines, but personally he had the *nimia humilitas* which Luther sometimes lamented in Staupitz; so much so, indeed, that Mather marvels that "the hardest flints should not have been broken on such a soft bag of cotton."‡

Cotton, on landing, in 1633, at once assumed that leading position to which his intellect entitled him, and his pulpit at Boston speedily became a leading power in Massachusetts.

Hooker was settled, during his sojourn in the Bay plantation, at Cambridge.§ He was a man "of vast endowments, a strong will, and an energetic mind. Ingenuous in temper, he was open in his

---

* Magnalia, vol. 1, pp. 265, 266. † Ibid, p. 277. ‡ Ibid., 276.

§ Mather's Magnalia, vol. 1, p. 343. Mr. Stone was his assistant.

professions. He had been trained to benevolence by the discipline of affliction, and to tolerance by his refuge from home persecution in Holland. He was choleric in temper, yet gentle in his affections; firm in faith, yet readily yielding to the power of reason; the peer of the reformers, without their harshness; the devoted apostle to the humble and the poor, severe only to the proud, mild in his soothings of a wounded spirit, glowing with the raptures of devotion, and kindling with the messages of redeeming love. His eye, voice, gesture, and whole frame, were animated with the living vigor of heart-felt religion; he was public-spirited and lavishly charitable; and 'though persecution and banishment had awaited him as one wave follows another,' he was ever serenely blessed with 'a glorious peace of soul'—fixed in his trust in Providence, and in his adhesion to the cause of advancing civilization, which he cherished always, even while it remained to him a mystery.

"This was he whom, for his abilities and services, his contemporaries placed 'in the first rank' of men; praising him as the one rich pearl with which 'Europe more than repaid America for the treasures from her coast.' The people to whom Hooker had ministered in England had preceded him in exile; as he landed, they crowded about him with their cheery welcome. 'Now I live,' exclaimed he, as with open arms he embraced his flock, 'now I live if ye stand fast in the Lord.' "*

* Bancroft, ut antea.

Hooker was an apostle of great boldness and of singular charity. He had fine tact and a habit of discrimination. He had a saying that "some were to be saved by compassion, others, by fear, being pulled out of the fire." He knew how to reach the heart; once, when a settlement twenty leagues from his habitation was suffering from hunger, he sent a ship-load of corn to relieve the sufferers, thus demonstrating his Christianity by what Chrysostom calls "unanswerable syllogisms."*

Whitfield once said of him: "Hooker is one in whom the utmost learning and wisdom are tempered by the finest zeal, holiness, and watchfulness; for, though naturally a man of choleric temper, and possessing a mighty vigor and fervor of spirit, which as occasion served was wondrous useful to him, yet he had as much government of his choler as a man has over a mastiff dog in a chain; he could let out his dog or pull him in, as he pleased."†

Mather records that some one once, seeing Hooker's heroism and persistent goodness, said: "He is a man who, while doing his Master's work, would put a king in his pocket."‡

Of this there was an instance. It chanced once that on a fast-day kept throughout England, the judges on their circuit stopped over at Chelmsford, where Hooker was to preach. Here, before a vast audience, and in the presence of the judges, he freely inveighed against the sins of England, and foretold the plagues that would result. Charles had

---

* Magnalia, vol. 1, p. 346. † Ibid., p. 345. ‡ Ibid.

recently married a papist princess. The undaunted apostle in his prayer besought God to set in the heart of the king what His own mouth had spoken by his prophet Malachi, as he distinctly quoted it: "An abomination is committed; Judah hath married the daughter of a strange god; the Lord will cut off the man that doeth this." Though the judges turned to and noted the passage thus cited, Hooker came to no trouble; but it was not long before England did.*

Hooker and Cotton have been well called the Luther and Melancthon of New England; each became the oracle of his plantation.

And now "the prophets in exile began to see the true forms of the house." They already held the soil by a twofold title: the royal charter had granted it to the patentees called the "Massachusetts Company," "to be held by them, their heirs and assigns, in free and common soccage; paying, in lieu of all services, one fifth of the gold and silver that should be found."† And this vestment the conscientious Pilgrims had been careful to supplement by actual purchase from the aborigines.‡

Every day the old trading corporation assumed new prerogatives, verging more and more towards a representative democracy. Winthrop was timid, and doubted the legality of this popular movement. Cotton was alarmed; and on one election day he essayed to check the democratic tendency by preach-

* Magnalia, vol. 1, p. 345. † See the Charter.
‡ Chap. 21, pp. 260, 261; also chap. 27, p. 342.

ing to the assembled freemen against rotation in office, arguing that an honest magistrate held his position as a proprietor holds his freehold. But the voters were deaf to the fears of the government, and careless, for once, of the decision of the pulpit. Dudley succeeded Winthrop in the gubernatorial chair;* legislation was intrusted to representatives chosen by the several towns of Massachusetts Bay;† it was decreed that the freemen at large should be convened only for the election of magistrates.‡ Thus, in 1634, the electors exercised their "absolute power," and "established a reformation of such things as they judged to be amiss in the model of government."§

Now the colonial authority was divided between two branches. The representatives were the legislative, the magistrates were the executive arm. Both sat together in the outset, forming what was called "The General Court." Finally, the magistrates grew discontented; as the towns increased, so did the representatives; and they found themselves outvoted; so they pressed for separate houses, each with a veto on the other. It was granted. The *deputies* and the *council* were inaugurated;‖ and these, under the Republic, have become the Representatives and the Senate.

Next, a law was framed which forbade arbitrary taxation; it was decreed that "the deputies alone

* Winthrop's Journal. † Colony Records. Winthrop.
‡ Ibid. § Winthrop, Hutchinson, Hubbard.
‖ Ibid., Elliot.

were competent to grant land or raise money."* Already "the state was filled with the bane of village politicians; 'the freemen of every town in the Bay were busy in inquiring into their liberties.' With the important exception of universal suffrage, in our age so happily in process of complete establishment, representative democracy was as perfect two centuries ago as it is to-day. Even the magistrates who acted as judges held their office by annual popular election. 'Elections cannot be safe there long,' sneered an English lawyer, Leckford, with a shrug. The same prediction has been made these two hundred years. The public mind, in perpetual agitation, is still easily shaken, even by slight and transient impulses; but after all its vibrations, it follows the laws of the moral world and safely recovers its balance."†

The test of citizenship was indeed exclusive. But the conception which based the ballot on goodness of the highest type, goodness of such purity and force that nothing save faith in Christ could create it—which conferred political power on personal character, was noble, even while impracticable. But God commissioned an American reformer to plant the seed of a larger growth by a vehement and potent protest.

* Elliot, Bancroft. † Bancroft, vol. 1, p. 365.

CHAPTER XXVII.

ROGER WILLIAMS.

"I venerate the man whose heart is warm,
  Whose hands are pure, whose doctrine and whose life,
  Coincident, exhibit lucid proof
  That he is honest in the sacred cause."
                                    Cowper's *Task*.

The Pilgrim Fathers were enamoured of the Mosaic code. They esteemed it to be a diamond without a flaw. Their constant, persistent effort was to naturalize the Jewish ritual in New England. For this their statesmen planned and their divines dogmatized. They did not remember that the judicial government which fitted the world in its infancy had been outgrown, and now sat awkwardly upon Christendom twenty-one years of age. They did not remember that Christ had "rung out" the old dispensation and "rung in" a grander and broader one.

Of course, in standing under the Mosaic code they were perfectly sincere; and to their sincerity they wedded a Titanic earnestness. They regarded toleration as a snare and a curse. It was either the badge of indifference or the corslet of Atheism; therefore a vice entitled to no terms. The advocates of toleration in the seventeenth century may be counted on the fingers of one's two hands. The most advanced thinkers of that epoch scarcely ventured, even in their most generous moments, to hint at a toleration of all creeds—each man responsible alone to God. The Romanist denied it amid the crackling flames of his *auto da fé*, and held with the Sorbonne and with Bossuét, that the stake is bound to extirpate heresy.* The Protestant urged exceptions when he asked for toleration; and, with Cartwright, forsook those who came under his ban, " that they might not corrupt and infect others."†

Tindale appealed not to the Pope, or to councils, or to the king, but to the Bible. So did Latimer; so did the Ridleys; so did Cranmer; so did Bradford: all of whom were blessed martyrs: yet none of these believed in full toleration; they had not yet reached it. They accepted what was behind them; they had a shadowy conception of what was in advance; but they feared, and were tolerant only up to their own position, while they cried "halt!" to a farther progress.

This European wave of sentiment swept in strong eddies to America; and in New England Cotton wrote: "It was toleration that made the world anti-Christian; and the church never took harm by the punishment of heretics."‡ The cobbler of Agawam§ responded: "Yes: to authorize an untruth

* Bossuét.
† Reply to Whitgift, cited by Stowell in his History of England. Puritans.
‡ "Bloody Tenet;" see Cotton's Controversy with Roger Williams.
§ Rev. Mr. Ward, in 1647.

by a toleration of state, is to build a sconce against the walls of heaven, to batter God out of his chair."*

Therefore, the Pilgrim Fathers, backed by the public opinion of Christendom, tabooed toleration, and gave it no place under the theocracy. When Roger Williams landed with his wife at Boston, in 1631, this was the sentiment and so stood the law.

He was a Welchman—for he had been cradled in the crags of Carmarthen—some thirty years of age, ripe for great acts, and though sometime a minister of the English church, he had thrown up his living because he could not, in Milton's phrase, "subscribe him slave," by conforming to Laud's idea.†

He had heard of America as a land of splendid possibilities—as the Holy Land of a grander crusade than that which had been launched to clutch the East from beneath the Saracenic scimetars; for this meant not empty sentimentality, it was an effort to win the wilderness for God. In that essay he longed to share; and his quick-flowing blood, his bold energy, and what Winthrop called his "godly fervor," united to decide him to quit England, cramped in forms and chained in wrongs, for the young, elastic, unbounded freedom of the west of the Atlantic.

Roger Williams was an earnest seeker after

---

* Cited in Elliot, vol. 1, p. 190.
† Knowles' Life of Roger Williams.

truth. Like Robinson, he smiled at the idea that the acme of knowledge had been reached. He knew, moreover, that his goal was to be run for "not without toil and heat." He was romantically conscientious; but he held to his opinions with grim determination, while the slowly-ripening principles of the English revolution of 1640 had already flowered in his brain. Now, in New England, he longed to set his ideas on two feet, and bid them run across the continent.

Like all positive characters, the young Welchman speedily attracted attention and made himself felt. His clear, ringing heel had scarce sounded in Boston streets ere he was cordoned by friends and surrounded by foes.* His opinions were novel; some of them have been grafted into the fundamental law of our Republic, and are now justly considered the palladium of religious peace; others are still unsettled and partly unaccepted, being held by certain sects, and rejected by several as the *disjecta membra* of divinity; but to the Pilgrims they were alike odious and revolutionary.

But the principle upon which hangs his immortality of fame is that of complete toleration. "He was a Puritan, and a fugitive from English persecution," remarks Bancroft, "but his wrongs had not clouded his accurate understanding. In the capacious recesses of his mind he had revolved the nature of intolerance, and he, and he alone, had arrived at the grand principle which is its sole effec-

* Knowles, ut antea. Colony Records, C. Mather, etc.

tual remedy. He announced his discovery under the simple proposition of the sanctity of conscience. The civil magistrate should restrain crime, but never control opinion; should punish guilt, but never violate the freedom of the soul. The doctrine contained within itself an entire reformation of theological jurisprudence; it would blot from the statute book the felony of non-conformity; would quench the fires that persecution had so long kept burning; would repeal every law compelling attendance on public worship; would abolish tithes and all forced contributions to the maintenance of religion; would give an equal protection to every form of religious faith; and never suffer the authority of civil government to be enlisted against the mosque of the Mussulman, or the altar of the fire-worshipper; the Jewish synagogue, or the Roman cathedral. It is wonderful with what distinctness. Roger Williams deduced these inferences from his central tenet, the consistency with which, like Pascal and Edwards, those bold and profound reasoners on other subjects, he accepted every fair inference from his doctrine, and the circumspection with which he repelled every unjust imputation. In the unwavering assertion of these views he never changed his position; the sanctity of conscience was the great tenet, which, with all its consequences, he defended as he first trod the shores of New England; and in his extreme old age it was the last pulsation of his heart. But it placed the young emigrant in direct opposition to the whole system on which Massachusetts was founded; and forbearing and forgiving as was his temper, prompt as he was to concede every thing which honesty permitted, he always asserted his belief, however unpalatable it might be, with temperate firmness and an unbending benevolence."* And just here, it is only fair to add, that his opponents, on their part, usually applied their principles without personal animosity. Between Williams and his great antagonist, Cotton, there was always, in their most heated moods, a substratum of cordial respect, while Winthrop, though consenting to the banishment of the pioneer American reformer, continued his fast friend through all.†

This principle of toleration, together with several other obnoxious tenets, all of which Williams avowed with frank courage, soon brought him under the frown of the colonial authorities—a frown which deepened when he refused to unite with the church at Boston " because its members would not make public declaration of their repentance for having communion with the church of England before their emigration."‡

This declaration—and the same thing may be said of several of his tenets—looks narrow and bigoted in our eyes; but Roger Williams had an undoubted right to cherish his own views under the very principles which he first of all men in America pro-

* Bancroft, vol. 1, pp. 367, 368.
† Elliot, vol. 1, p. 188. Palfrey, vol. 1, p. 406, et seq.
‡ Winthrop, vol. 1, p. 53.

claimed, that "the public or the magistrate may decide what is due from man to man, but when they attempt to prescribe a man's duties to God, they are out of place, and there can be no safety; for it is clear, that if the magistrate has the power, he may decree one set of opinions or beliefs to-day and another to-morrow; as has been done in England by different kings and queens, and by different popes and councils in the Roman church; so that belief would become a heap of confusion."*

Be this as it may, the Pilgrims came to regard Roger Williams as a dangerous heresiarch; as "unsettled in judgment;"† as carrying "a windmill in his head."‡ Indeed, so strong was this feeling that many years afterwards Cotton Mather headed his account of Williams' advent, in the "Magnalia," with this Latin : "*Hic se aperit Diabolus*"—Here the devil shows himself.§

Under these circumstances, we may easily imagine the consternation which reigned in Boston, when, in April, 1631, it was rumored that Roger Williams was about to be installed in the vacant place of Francis Higginson at Salem as assistant to Mr. Skelton.‖ The court was convened; and a letter was at once indited to John Endicott, "one of the chief promoters of the settlement," in which, says Winthrop, the judges "marvelled that he should countenance such a choice without advising with

---

* See Williams' "Hireling Ministry." † Bradford, p. 310.
† Mather's Magnalia, vol. 2, p. 495.   § Ibid.
‖ Winthrop. Hubbard, Mather's Magnalia, Hutchinson.

the Council; and withal desiring him to use his influence that the Salem church should forbear till all could confer about it."*

In that day good ministers were not common in New England; and, moreover, the Salem churchmen liked Williams; so, without heeding the remonstrance of the authorities, they proceeded to settle the teacher of their choice. He at once began to preach; but with the advance of summer the temper of the government grew hot with the season, and finally he decided to bid Salem farewell and take refuge at Plymouth.† This he did, being soon after elected assistant to Ralph Smith.‡ At Plymouth as at Salem, he made many friends, and Bradford bears witness that he was " a man godly and zealous, having many precious parts."§ But his "strange opinions" were not fully approved; and consequently, when, after the death of Mr. Skelton, in 1633, the Salem church urged their truant pastor to return to them, Williams acceded. He was dismissed, as Brewster counselled, from the Plymouth church, but was followed back to Salem by a bodyguard of devoted admirers, "who would have no other preacher."‖

It was during his sojourn at Plymouth that Roger Williams began to cement that famous friendship with the Indians which was one day to stand

---

* Winthrop's Journal, pp. 63, 64.
† Knowles' Life, Savage on Winthrop, Magnalia, etc.
‡ Bradford, p. 310. § Ibid.
‖ Morton's Memorial, p. 151. Bradford, p. 310.

him in such good stead.* "My soul's desire," he said, "was to do the natives good."† And later, when

> "Declined
> Into the vale of years,"

he wrote again: "God was pleased to give me a painful, patient spirit, to lodge with them in their filthy, smoky holes, to gain their tongue."‡ In this way he became acquainted with Massasoit, the chief of the Wampanoags, and with Canonicus and Miantonomoh, the sachems of the Narragansetts, among whom, in after-years, he sought and found a home.

On his return to Salem his struggle with the government recommenced. While at Plymouth he had written a pamphlet against the validity of the colonial charter, and submitted it to Bradford.§ Now he published it. He said: "Why lay such stress upon your patent from King James? 'Tis but idle parchment: James has no more right to give away or sell Massasoit's lands, and cut and carve his country, than Massasoit has to sell James' kingdom or to send his Indians to colonize Warwickshire."‖

Since the Pilgrims had legalized their title to the land *in foro conscientiæ*, by actual purchase from the aborigines,¶ it is somewhat difficult to conceive

---

* Prince, Elliot, Banvard.
† Cited in Elliot, vol. 1, p. 199.   Banvard, p. 160.   ‡ Ibid.
§ Palfrey, Knowles. Winthrop, vol. 1, pp. 143, 144.
‖ Elliot, vol. 1, pp. 197, 198.
¶ Knowles' Life of Williams, Mather's Magnalia, Dwight's Tracts, ante chaps. 21 and 26, pp. 260, 261.

why Williams, already staggering under a load of odium, should have added to the pack by a declaration entirely useless, yet certain to kindle anger because it was looked upon as treason against the cherished charter.*

The fact should seem to be that he had the *certaminis gaudia*—the joy of disputation; common to intellectual gladiators. Occasionally this got the better of his prudence; and when it did, like a skilful rider, he soon recovered the reins of his caution and made glad amends. On this occasion, he confessed his penitence for the ill which had arisen from the unfortunate polemic, and offered to burn the manuscript if the authorities chose to countenance the bon-fire.†

Roger Williams next pronounced himself upon an exciting local question. It was then a mooted point at Salem whether women were commanded to appear at church veiled.‡ Singularly enough, the radical Williams said Yes, and the conservative Cotton said No; the historic opponents for once changed places; and Cotton, going to Salem, handled the subject so convincingly in his morning sermon, that the ladies came to church in the afternoon unveiled; upon which "Williams, though unconvinced, desisted from opposition."§

Behind these frivolities were graver issues. In

---

* Bancroft, vol. 1, p. 368.
† Winthrop, vol. 1, pp. 145, 146. Palfrey, vol. 1, p. 409.
‡ See 1 Corinthians 11:5.
§ Magnalia. Palfrey, vol. 1, p. 409.

1633, trouble seemed brewing between England and the Pilgrim colonists. Charles, Laud, and Strafford, had hinted at a "commission" for the regulation of the non-conforming American plantations; and the Privy Council had commanded Cradock to order the colonial charter home, to be "regulated." The ex-president of the Massachusetts Company did write for it in 1634, and in 1635 "quo warranto"* was issued. But the provisional authorities, while answering Cradock's missive, declined to return the charter.†

Affairs looked black indeed. Resistance was seriously contemplated; what was called the "freeman's oath," which bound the colonists to allegiance to the colony rather than to the king, was ordered to be subscribed throughout Massachusetts Bay; and at the same time it was decided to "avoid and protract."‡ Nothing prevented England from launching her cohorts upon the plantations but the presence of those home troubles which now began to press the royalist party as closely as the serpents enveloped Laocöon. It was a time of general anxiety, and men cried Hush! and held their breath to see what should next occur.

But "Williams could not keep quiet in this seething world," affirms Elliot; "nor could Endicott. Both of them saw the inevitable tendencies

---

* A writ requiring a person to show by what right he is doing a special thing.

† Elliot, vol. 1, p. 200. Bancroft, Hubbard.

‡ Ibid., Hutchinson, Knowles.

of the Roman church; and feeling that such a church was dangerous to their infant liberties, they decided that the symbol under which the pope and Laud marched should not be their symbol: so Endicott cut the cross out of the king's colors. At such a crisis, when the aim was to 'avoid and protract,' this audacious act of course made trouble; and Endicott, at the next court, was 'sadly admonished,' and disabled from office for a year.* Williams held peculiar views respecting oaths, and cited the Scripture command—'swear not at all.' And as the freeman's oath clashed with the oath to the king, he also spoke against that, and dissuaded some from taking it."†

Besides this, Roger Williams was an avowed democrat. He proclaimed this truth: "Kings and magistrates are invested with no more power than the people intrust to them."‡ And he said again: "The sovereign power of all civil authority is founded in the consent of the people."§ Republicanism was the logical sequence of religious liberty—came from it as naturally as the bud expands into the flower. Yet it startled the Pilgrims. They were constantly making forays into the domain of absolutism. They never scrupled, when they had a chance, at clutching popular prerogatives. They were always busy in enacting democracy into law;

---

* Williams' connection with this act is but distant and oblique, if he had any. See Knowles, Winthrop, Hubbard, Palfrey, etc. † Elliot, vol. 1, p. 201.
‡ Williams' "Bloody Tenet." § Ibid.

but they were shocked when Roger Williams put it into propositions.

"Had Cromwell been in power at the time, with his republican bias," remarks Felt, "these sentiments would have been crowned with approbation; but being uttered under one of the Stuarts, they were hissed as the expression of sedition. It has ever been in accordance with the spirit of human policy, that principles under the circumstances of one period are accounted patriotism, which under the circumstances of another era are denounced as treason."[*]

Thus it was that the theories of Roger Williams "led him into perpetual collision with the clergy and the government of Massachusetts Bay. It had ever been their custom to respect the church of England, and in the mother-country, they had frequented its service; yet its principles and its administration were still harshly exclusive. The American reformer would hold no communion with intolerance; for, said he, 'the doctrine of persecution for conscience' sake is most evidently and lamentably contrary to the doctrine of Jesus Christ.'

"The magistrates insisted on the presence of every man at public worship; Williams reprobated the law; the worst statute in the English code was that which did but enforce attendance upon the parish church. To compel men to unite with those of a different creed, he regarded as an open violation of their natural rights; to drag to public wor-

[*] Felt's Hist. of New England, vol. 1, p. 175.

ship the irreligious and the unwilling, seemed like requiring hypocrisy. 'An unbelieving soul is dead in sin'—such was his argument. 'And to force the indifferent from one worship to another, is like shifting a dead man into several changes of apparel.' He added: 'No one should be forced to worship, or to maintain a worship against his own consent.' 'What!' exclaimed his antagonists, amazed at his tenets, 'is not the laborer worthy of his hire?' 'Yes,' replied he, 'from those who hire him.'

"The magistrates were selected exclusively from the church members; with equal propriety, reasoned Williams, might 'a doctor of physic or a pilot' be selected according to his skill in theology and his standing in the church. It was objected, that his principles subverted all good government. 'Oh no,' said he; 'the commander of the vessel of state may maintain order on board the ship and see that it pursues its course steadily, even though the dissenters of the crew be not compelled to attend the public prayers of their companions.'"*

The Pilgrims heard all this aghast. Soon they wearied of discussion; they invoked the syllogism of the law to rebut the heresies of the bold declaimer. Williams was cited in 1635, to appear before the General Court at Boston, for examination. Taking his staff in his hand, he set out. The session was stormy. Cotton argued; others scolded; Winthrop pleaded; Endicott was wrenched away from Williams' side; but Williams, while

* Bancroft, vol. 1. pp. 372, 373.

maintaining some odd opinions, spoke boldly for God and liberty that day, and "maintained the rocky strength of his grounds."*

"To the magistrates he seemed the ally of a civil faction; to himself he appeared only to make a frank avowal of the truth. The scholar who is accustomed to the pursuits of abstract philosophy, lives in a region of thought quite remote from that by which he is surrounded. The range of his understanding is aside from the paths of common minds, and he is often the victim of the contrast. 'T is not unusual for the world to reject the voice of truth, because its tones are strange; to declare doctrines unsound, only because they are new; and even to charge obliquity or derangement on a man who brings forward principles which the average intelligence repudiates. 'T is the common history; Socrates, and St. Paul, and Luther, and others of the most acute dialecticians, have been ridiculed as drivellers and madmen."†

Roger Williams now evinced his kinship with the martyrs for human progress, by suffering that rejection common to those who venture to project their revolutionary thoughts from the front of a century's advance. Misunderstood and condemned, he was commanded to abjure his heresies or else expect "sentence."‡

Of course, he could not reject himself; therefore,

* Winthrop, Hutchinson, Hubbard, Knowles, Elton's Life.
† Bancroft, ut antea.
‡ Winthrop, Colonial Records, Knowles.

saying with Job, "Though I die, I will maintain my integrity," he uncovered his head with serene patience to "bide the pelting of the pitiless storm." The thunderbolt soon fell. The church at Salem was coerced into abandoning the immortal pastor; and in November, 1635, he was ordered "to depart out of the jurisdiction of Massachusetts Bay within six weeks;"* a sentence which is said to have been mainly due to Cotton's eloquence.†

Finally, Williams was permitted to remain at Salem until the following spring, as the season then shivered on the verge of winter.‡ Then the Pilgrims grew alarmed; the reformer's opinions were contagious; they thought, after all, that it would be best to send Williams home to England. A ship was about to sail; a warrant was issued; officers were despatched to arrest the disturber of that Israel. But on coming to his house and opening the door, they found "darkness there, and nothing more." Roger Williams, apprized of the change of purpose, had quitted Salem "in winter snow and inclement weather."§ On, on he pressed, for Laud and the Tower of London were behind him. Without guide, without food, without shelter, he suffered tortures. "For fourteen weeks I was sorely tossed in a bitter season"—so he wrote in the evening of his life—"not knowing what bread or bed did

* Winthrop, Colony Records, Knowles.
† Bancroft, vol. 1, p. 377.
‡ Ibid., Hubbard, Hutchinson.
§ Knowles, Elton's Life, Hutchinson, etc.

mean."* "But," said he sweetly, "the ravens fed me in the wilderness;"† and he often made his habitation in the hollow of a tree. But nothing could daunt him. His cheerful faith,

> "Exempt from public haunt,
> Found tongues in trees, books in the running brooks,
> Sermons in stones, and good in every thing."

So he fled on, on, through the snow, the darkness, the dreary forest; "fled from Christians to the savages, who knew and loved him, till at last he reached the kind-hearted but stupid Indian heathen Massasoit."‡

This winter banishment of Roger Williams was cruel and bigoted, but it was not without palliation. He had run a tilt against the law and order of his time; he had sneered at the validity of the charter, then the fundamental law; he had impeached the theocracy; he had the dangerous advantage of being personally equipped with those gifts which win and "grapple to the soul with hooks of steel." Every motive of worldly prudence seemed to dictate banishment. These things extenuate, but they do not excuse; because we are bound to impeach an untrue order. Paul cried, "God is God," and trampled wicked laws beneath his feet. The catacombs of Pagan Rome were choked with martyrs who went against the law and order of their time. Huss and Wickliffe, Latimer and Ridley, violated law precisely as Roger Will-

---

* Roger Williams in Mass. Hist. Col., vol. 1, p. 276.
† Ibid. ‡ Elliot.

iams did. The law-breaker is not necessarily immoral and a pest. Society is bound to see that the statute-book does not fetter the human conscience. If society is recreant to its duty, individuals must not be false to God. Therefore, in this matter of opposing the colonial law, we hide Roger Williams behind the apostles, and enclose him within the leaves of the New Testament.

After months of vicissitude, the great exile reached the shores of Narragansett Bay, and founded Providence. As he floated down the stream in his canoe, and neared the site of the beautiful city born of his piety, the Indians shouted, "Wha-cheer, friend; wha-cheer?" and grasped his hand with cordial sympathy as he stepped ashore.* A large grant of land was easily obtained from Canonicus and Miantonomoh—easily obtained because of the love and favor which they bore him, since Williams says that money could not have bought it without affection and confidence†—and as the whole domain was his, he might have lived as lord-proprietor; but principle forbade. "On the hill the forests, just clothed in their full leafage, bowed their heads to this fugitive, the hero of a great idea, and whispered 'Liberty!'"‡

He heeded that whisper, and dedicated the infant state to the most radical idea of liberty; so that it became the asylum of the oppressed; and

---

* Knowles, Elliot, Judge Durfee's poem, "What Cheer?"
† Knowles, p. 270. ‡ Elliot.

as the Hebrew prophet always prayed with his window open towards Jerusalem, so distressed consciences, when they felt the sting of persecution, murmured, Providence.

Roger Williams planted a democracy—a government of the people, by the people, for the people.* He cemented his state by toleration. "The removal of the yoke of soul-oppression," said he, "as it will prove an act of mercy and righteousness to the enslaved nations, so it is of binding force to engage the whole and every interest and conscience to preserve the common liberty and peace."†

So it proved; for, spite of Cotton Mather's epigram, that it was "*bona terra, mala gens*"‡—a good land and a wicked people—it increased and prospered from the outset, justifying the motto of the commonwealth, *Amor vincet omnia*.§

While Roger Williams believed in toleration, he did not believe in license, but was always earnest for liberty regulated by law. Thus when the *Ranters* appeared and railed against all order, he invoked the judicial arm to suppress their madness.‖ But when the Quakers invaded the state, he attacked them only with syllogisms. He was ardently opposed to their tenets; but he essayed to "dig George Fox out of his burrows" with words only, and returned a stern "No" to the thrice-repeated request

---

* Knowles, p. 120.   Elton, Hutchinson.
† Cited in Bancroft, vol. 1, p. 371.
‡ Magnalia, vol. 1, p. 497.   § Love will overcome all things.
‖ Winthrop, Hutchinson, Hubbard.

of Massachusetts that they be expelled from his jurisdiction.* "We find," he wrote, "that where these people are most of all supposed to declare themselves freely, and are only opposed by argument, there they least of all desire to come."†

In 1643, Williams went to England to obtain a charter for his plantation. He "found all in a flame; civil war raging, Hampden just killed, Charles fled from London, and the city and the government in the hands of the Parliament." Here he lived on intimate terms with Sir Harry Vane and Milton, kindred spirits, who were doing in England what he had done in America. His mission was successful, and a twelvemonth later he returned to Providence with a liberal patent, the free-will offering of jubilant democracy across the water.‡

Eight years later, under the Protectorate, Roger Williams once more visited England on colonial business; and his admission and recognition among the foremost thinkers of the time were general and hearty. The acquaintance with Vane and Milton was continued, and Marvell and Cromwell were added to his list of friends.§ But his heart was in America, and in 1654 he came back to Providence;‖ whereupon he was elected president of the cluster of plantations which, in after-days, were moulded into the little state of Rhode Island.¶

* Knowles. p. 295. † Elton, p. 127. Hutchinson, Elliott.
‡ Ibid. Knowles, Hist. Col., vol. 2, p. 121. § Ibid.
‖ Ibid. ¶ Rhode Island Colony Records.

For many years Williams and his colony were under the frown of their brother Pilgrims; but through it all they bore cheerily up, trusting to God, time, and success, to remove all prejudice, and "keeping always to that one principle, 'that every man should have liberty to worship God according to the light of his own conscience.'"*

Roger Williams had learned that most difficult of lessons, to return good for evil. He never wearied in well-doing; and his fine tact, broad statesmanship, and friendly zeal, on more than one occasion came between the colonists who had flung him into dishonorable banishment and impending harm.† With the Indians he was singularly influential, and frequently his presence at their camp-fires and in their wigwams served to explode a maturing conspiracy.‡

On the Restoration, an event occurred which finely illustrates the beautiful text, that "He who goeth forth and weepeth, bearing precious seed, shall doubtless come again with rejoicing, bringing his sheaves with him." The American republican had been the warm friend and coadjutor of Cromwell, and Milton, and Pym. When Charles II. came to the throne, all looked to see his hand stretched across the Atlantic to menace and chastise. It was outstretched, but only to bless; for the foppish Stuart actually renewed the charter

---

* Morton's Memorial, p. 154.
† See Hutchinson, vol. 1, p. 38.
‡ Elton's Life of Williams, p. 54. Knowles, Winthrop.

which the wise Protector had first granted to the Providence plantations. He paid unconscious homage to the principle of Roger Williams, and assented to what Gammel calls "the freest paper that ever bore the signature of a king—the wonder of the age."*

Such was one instance of the influence of a man whose beneficent career is at once an example and an inspiration; not because he was always right or always wise, but because he was always true to his own ideal. Roger Williams was the initiator of many changes; and he, first of all in America, boldly framed the creed of democracy. But the brightest jewel in his crown is that he, taking his life in one hand and his good name in the other, "was the first reformer in modern Christendom to assert in its plenitude the doctrine of the liberty of conscience, the equality of all opinions before the law. At a time when Germany was the battle-field for all Europe in the implacable wars of religion; when even Holland was bleeding with the anger of vengeful factions; when France was still to go through a fearful struggle with bigotry; when England was gasping under the despotism of intolerance; almost half a century before William Penn became an American proprietary; and two years before Descartes founded modern philosophy on the basis of free reflection," Roger Williams demanded the enfranchisement of the human soul.

"We praise the man who first analyzed the air,

* Gammel, p. 182.

or resolved water into its elements, or drew the lightning from the clouds, even though the discoveries may have been as much the fruits of time as of genius. A moral principle has a much wider and nearer influence on human happiness; nor can any discovery of truth be of more direct benefit to society than that which establishes perpetual religious peace, and spreads tranquillity through every community and every bosom.

"If Copernicus is held in everlasting reverence because, on his death-bed, he published to the world that the sun is the centre of our system; if the name of Kepler is preserved in the annals of human excellence for his sagacity in detecting the laws of planetary motion; if the genius of Newton has been almost adored for dissecting a ray of light and weighing heavenly bodies in a balance—let there be for the name of Roger Williams at least some humble place among those who have advanced moral science, and made themselves the benefactors of mankind."*

* Bancroft, vol. 1, pp. 376, 377.

CHAPTER XXVIII.

AN ARRIVAL, A UNIVERSITY, AND A STATE.

"Three things are of the first importance—good men, education, and a settled commonwealth."
LORD BACON.

SPITE of internecine struggle and transatlantic intrigue, New England walked steadily on in the path towards material prosperity. It was inevitable; for the parents of success were within her borders: essential godliness was in her right hand, and the habit of thrift was in her left. It is very probable that prosperity was helped instead of hindered by the agitation which was begotten of the official acts of the colonial government. The stir served to keep Christendom agog for the latest news from America. "What are these Pilgrims now at?" was the inquiry incessantly on every lip. Thus it was that the name and action of New England became as prominently familiar in the *salons* of the ultramontanists in Europe, and in the club-rooms of the riotous cavaliers, as in the humble dwellings of the godly Puritans.

Besides, agitation in its turn begot progress. Where there is silence there is death. If the Alps, piled in cold, still sublimity, are the emblem of fat and contented despotism, the ocean is the symbol of democracy; for it is pure and useful only because never motionless.

At all events, the progress of New England was unique and unprecedented. "*Nec minor ab exordio,*" says Cotton Mather, "*nec major incrementis ulla.*"* Never was any thing more lowly in inception or more mighty in increase. In 1635, twenty ships dropped anchor in Boston and Plymouth harbors;† and in that single year three thousand new settlers were added to the Pilgrim colonies.‡ Men came over fast and

> "Thick as autumnal leaves that strow the brooks
> In Vallambrosa, where the Etruscan shades,
> High overarched, imbower."

And these, like their predecessors, were of "the best."§

With them landed an illustrious *trio*—Hugh Peters, the younger Winthrop, and Sir Harry Vane.‖ The fiery Peters came from one exile to another; for he had been pastor of an English church at Rotterdam. He was an enlightened republican, public spirited, prodigiously energetic, and eloquent, already endowed with those high qualities which soon afterwards pushed him into prominence in the English civil war as the coadjutor of Cromwell, the jailor of Charles I., and an echoer of the regicidal verdict.¶

---

* Magnalia, vol. 1, p. 80.   † Ibid., p. 136.
‡ Bancroft, vol. 1, p. 383,   § Winthrop's Journal.
‖ Ibid., Bancroft, Elliot, Palfrey, Hutchinson. They landed in October, 1635.
¶ See Encyclopedia Americana, Appleton's Encyclopedia, English Encyclopedia.

During his seven years' sojourn in New England, Hugh Peters was settled at Salem as the successor of Roger Williams.* At once his restless and various activity bubbled over into works of utility.† He was minister, he was politician, he was factotum. He saw the commercial capabilities of America, and set himself to develop them. He "went from place to place," says Winthrop, "laboring both publicly and privately to raise men up to a public frame of spirit, and so prevailed, that he procured a good sum of money to set on foot a systematic fishing business."‡

The younger Winthrop was Hugh Peters' *compagnon de voyage*. 'T is related of a son of Scipio Africanus that, proving degenerate, the scoffing Romans forced him to pluck off a signet-ring which he wore, with his father's face engraved upon it. There was no occasion for such public discipline in this case, for young Winthrop was, in Cotton Mather's phrase, *Bonus a bono, pius a pio*, the son of a father like himself. After an exemplary and studious boyhood, he had followed the elder Winthrop to New England; where, dowered with the advantages of extensive travel and consummate education, he had been annually elected one of the gubernatorial assistants—an honor which was continued even when he returned to Europe for a space.§

He now came armed with the authority of Lord

---

* Mather's Magnalia, Palfrey, etc.
† Palfrey, vol. 1, p. 436.   ‡ Winthrop, p. 170.
§ Ibid., p. 173. Palfrey, Trumbull's Hist. Conn., Elliot.

Say and the "good Lord Brooke," the original patentees of Connecticut, to plant a new colony, of which he should be governor.* "But inasmuch as many good people from Massachusetts Bay and Plymouth had already taken possession of a part of his demesne, this courteous and godly gentleman would give them no molestation; but saying, 'the land is broad,' he accommodated the matter with them, and then sent a convenient number of men to erect a town and fort at the mouth of the Connecticut, which he called, after the patrons of the enterprise, *Say-brook*. By this happy action, the planters farther up the river had no small kindness done them; while the Indians, who might else have been even more troublesome than they soon proved, were kept in some awe."†

Winthrop was one of the few early Pilgrims who had been graduated at a university, yet was not won to lay aside his layman garb for the clerical robe. "It is a singular fact," observes Elliot, "that, possessed as he was of scholarly and scientific tastes, he took hold resolutely of the material life of his plantation at Saybrook, and worked to shape it well, as the base of the superior structure which he meant to rear upon it. He appreciated what scholars and idealists are prone to forget, the prime value of a good material foundation. For many years he was chosen governor of the colony, and in that position he gave universal satisfaction. For

---

* Trumbull, Mather's Magnalia.
† Mather's Magnalia, vol. 1, p. 158.

his vices and his enemies, if he had either, they are forgotten.

"He was too large a man to engage in the persecution of the Quakers, which he always opposed; and if he believed in witchcraft, a rank superstition at that time common, it was as a query, not as a fact. His leisure hours were devoted to science; and his contributions to the old 'Royal Society of London,' of which he was an early member, were highly valued. Indeed, Boyle and other scientific scholars at one period had a plan for joining their fellow-student in the New World, for the purpose of pushing their investigations of natural knowledge."*

The last member of this famous group, Sir Harry Vane junior, was at this time but twenty-three,† and he came out much against the wishes of a father who stood as high in the confidence of the queen of England as Strafford did in the affections of the king.‡ "Let him go," said Charles to the perturbed courtier, when he learned that Harry had turned Puritan and proposed to emigrate—"Let him go; my word for 't, he'll soon sicken on 't and be back, if you give him consent to remain in those parts for three years."§

So the devout boy embarked. On reaching Boston, he was saluted with enthusiasm. His high

* Elliot, vol. 1, pp. 249, 250.
† Palfrey, Bancroft, Hubbard.
‡ Palfrey, Winthrop, Elliot, Bancroft.
§ Mather's Magnalia, vol. 1, p. 136.

birth, his sacrifices, his Puritanism, his splendid talents, every thing about him, served to enlist the sober Pilgrims in his favor; and this effect was heightened by his personal beauty, singular learning, and ingratiating manners.* As the Bostonians knew him better they liked him better; soon he was the most popular man in the colony; and in 1636 he was elected to fill the gubernatorial chair—elected over the heads of Winthrop, and Dudley, and the elders of our Israel, which they might and did look upon as a freak of democratic strategy quite superfluous.†

The first public act of the three friends was, to placate a long smouldering feud between Winthrop and Dudley. Winthrop was accused of over-leniency in his politics; Dudley was charged with undue severity. A friendly convention was held; the questions at issue were kindly talked over. Vane and Peters counselled mutual forbearance; and the quarrel ended with a "loving reconciliation" never afterwards broken.‡

Some little time after Winthrop and Dudley, under Vane's auspices, had given each other the kiss of peace and gone home arm in arm, with the fire of their differences definitively quenched, measures were matured to plant a college in New England. Nothing more finely exhibits the wisdom of the Pilgrim Fathers than their watchful and ample provision for education, which Bacon has fitly termed the "sheet-anchor of peaceful common-

* Elliot, Hubbard.   † Ibid.   ‡ Winthrop, pp. 177–179.

wealths." In their estimation, its importance was second to nothing but religion, whose handmaid it was.

They longed to rear a race of cultured men—to plant a school which should elbow out of America those wicked universities which were then the pests of Europe—vicious sinks which Beza called *Flabella Satanæ,* Satan's fans; and which Luther styled *Cathedras pestilentiæ et antichristi luminaria,* seats of pestilence and beacons of antichrist; where, under the tuition of the Jesuits, immorality was made a fine art, and ferocity was taught as a cardinal virtue.

With this two-fold object, a public school was called into life at Cambridge in 1636; and in that same year the General Court made a grant of four hundred pounds, which formed the legs on which the infant university first toddled.* Later, John Harvard bequeathed eight hundred pounds and his library to help forward the scholastic venture; whereupon the grateful authorities eternized the donor's name by calling the school HARVARD COLLEGE.†

Henceforth New England had a "city of books." Harvard college speedily became a nursery of piety, and was to America, as Livy said of Greece, *sal gentium.*‡ In narrating this achievement, the quaint divine who heaped together the mingled wheat and chaff of the *Magnalia,* cites triumphantly the lan-

---

* New England's First Fruits, vol. 1, Quincy's Boston, etc.
† Ibid., Hutchinson, Hubbard, Mather's Magnalia.
‡ The nation's safety. See Magnalia, vol. 2, p. 1.

guage of the orator who chanted pæans to the English Cambridge: "We have now provided—and let envy be as far removed from this declaration as is falsehood—that in popular assemblies stone shall not talk to stone; that the church shall not lack priests, or the bar jurists, or the community physicians; for we have supplied the church, the government, the senate, and the army, with accomplished men."*

Thus the new university was rightly esteemed an ornament and a civilizer; for learning, as the poet has hymned it,

> "Chastens the manners, and the soul refines."†

The school is at once preserver and benefactor; it is *urbis medicus*, the physician of the state.

And now the settlements along the coast-line of Massachusetts were become "like hives overstocked with bees; and many of the new inhabitants began to entertain the thought of swarming into plantations farther in the interior." The fifteen thousand settlers in Massachusetts felt crowded. They longed to imitate the Plymouth Pilgrims, who had sent out a forlorn hope to colonize Windsor, and the venture of the younger Winthrop at Saybrook. They too, longed

> "To descry new lands,
> Rivers and mountains, in this spotty globe."

As early as 1634, Hooker's parishioners, at Cambridge, had petitioned the General Court to permit

---

* See Magnalia, vol. 2, p. 1.
† "Emollit mores, nec sinit esse feros." HORACE.

them "to look out either for enlargement or removal."* The authorities withheld their assent at the outset; but when, in 1636, the motion was renewed, they said Yes.†

Hooker—whom Morton calls "a son of thunder"‡—and Haynes were the chief promoters of this project to remove.§ The winter of 1635-6 was spent in active preparation. Scouting parties were thrown forward. In the opening of the year, Hartford was settled, government was organized, civil order was established.‖ At the same time pioneers went out from Dorchester, and pushing the earlier Plymouth settlers from the ground, usurped Windsor in the name of Massachusetts Bay.¶ Others quitted Watertown, and sat down at Wethersfield;** while some left Roxbury, and were enchurched at Springfield, which was afterwards found to lie within the boundary of the old Bay State.††

But this emigration was merely preliminary; it was the first patter of the coming shower; it was the scouts of the Pilgrims, making an initial survey of the new Hesperia of Puritanism. In June, 1636, the principal caravan, led by Thomas Hooker and John Haynes, began its march. "There were of

* Winthrop, p. 132.
† Ibid., Palfrey, Bancroft, Trumbull.
‡ Memorial, pp. 239, 240.
§ Trumbull, Winthrop, Hutchinson.
‖ Bancroft, vol. 1, p.396.
¶ Trumbull, vol. 1. Mather's Magnalia, vol. 1, p. 81.
** Bradford, Hubbard, Morton.   †† Magnalia, ut antea.

the company about one hundred souls, many of them persons accustomed to the affluence and ease of European life. They drove before them numerous herds of cattle; and thus they traversed the pathless forests of Massachusetts, advancing hardly ten miles a day through the tangled woods, across the swamps and numerous streams, and over the highlands that separated the intervening valleys; subsisting, as they slowly wandered along, on the milk of the kine, who browsed on the fresh leaves and early shoots; having no guide through the nearly untrodden wilderness but the compass, and no pillow for their nightly rest but heaps of stones. How did the hills echo with the unwonted lowing of the herds! How were the forests enlivened by the fervent piety of Hooker! Never again was there such a pilgrimage from the seaside 'to the delightful banks' of the Connecticut."*

The Pilgrims paused at Hartford, which the presence of Hooker and Haynes soon lifted into the foremost importance, and it became the Jerusalem of the west. The government was similar to that which Winthrop, and Endicott, and Cotton had shaped at Boston, except that now the church-membership test was omitted, church and state were half-divorced, and all freemen were citizens†—liberality which placed the new-born state close beside the Providence plantations in magnanimous catholicity. Indeed, Haynes, whose plastic hand mould-

* Bancroft, vol. 1, p. 396.
† Palfrey, Trumbull, Bancroft, Elliot, etc.

ed the primitive constitution of Connecticut, had gone through a bitter experience in the trial and banishment of Roger Williams; and his wiser statesmanship bade him beware lest, in steering clear of the Scylla of anarchy, he should ground his politics on the Charybdis of bigotry. His wise tact saved him from both perils, and enabled him, while never interrupting the *entente cordiale* with Massachusetts, to open a friendly intercourse with the Rhode Island " heretics."*

A twelvemonth after the arrival of the Pilgrims at Hartford, the pioneers were flanked by an invasion of brother Puritans fresh from England. New Haven was planted; and in 1637, Guilford was colonized, and then Milford was settled.† These were independent of Connecticut, and for upwards of forty years formed a separate colony, called New Haven.‡ "The settlers," says Cotton Mather, "were under the conduct of as holy, and as prudent, and as genteel persons, as ever visited these nooks of New England; and though they, in a manner, stole out of Britain, being forbidden to sail, yet they dropped here a plantation constellated with many stars of the first magnitude; for if Theophilus Eaton and John Davenport were not blazing lights, where shall we hunt for meteors?"§

The New-Haveners were traders; they believed more in commerce than in husbandry, and so they

* Hubbard, Palfrey, Elliot, Mather.
† Trumbull, vol. 1. Hubbard, Hist. Col.
‡ Ibid. § Magnalia, vol. 1, p. 88.

"went down to the sea in ships." But in the wilderness traffic did not yield the dividends which it gave on 'change in London, or on the Rialtos of the world; so that in half a decade their stock was spent, and they so nearly touched bottom that they gladly turned for help to despised agriculture,* the surest base for new states to build on.

For some months New Haven lacked a charter, and so floated rudderless. But eventually the settlers formed themselves into a body politic by mutual consent, and signed a kind of constitution in a barn;† and this is the first political paper that was ever cradled in a manger. It was generally *secundum usum Massachusettensem*,‡ to follow Cotton Mather's barbarous Latin; or, in plain English, after the model of the Bay State theocracy.

"Thus it was," exclaims a jubilant old chronicler, "that Jesus Christ was worshipped in churches of an evangelical character in the outermost wilderness; and from thence, if the inquirer were inclined to make a sally across the channel to Long Island, he might have seen the congregations of our God taking root in those wild wastes."§

The New Haven and Connecticut colonists were for many years on the verge of a quarrel with the Dutch at New Amsterdam, who felt that in this territorial race they had been outstripped and outwitted, and were consequently lifted out of their

---

* Hubbard, p. 321.   Hazard.
† "The settlers met in Mr. Newman's barn," etc.   Elliot, vol. 1, p. 242.   ‡ Magnalia, vol. 1, p. 83.   § Ibid.

wonted phlegm by irritation. The "Yankee" and the Dutchman carried on a lusty war of words about their boundary lines, and for this good reason, there were none. Irving tells us that the Dutch disliked the smell of onions; and that the keen Yankee, knowing this, planted his rows each year a little farther west, and before this invasion of onions the sad Dutchman always retired with tearful eyes, leaving the polluted soil to the onion planters.

But bright as seemed the portents, the colonists soon found themselves environed by danger—girdled by a wall of fire. The hostile Dutchman scowled in the west. The untrodden wilderness stretched away on the north. Scores of weary, pathless miles separated them from their brothers on the Atlantic coast. The vengeful Pequods were panting for war in the southeast. They had found, not peace, but a sword; their painful enterprise seemed but "a lure to draw victims within the reach of the tomahawk." Premonitory symptoms gave warning that danger lurked in the covert beside every log-house beyond the mountains. Soon the woods were ambuscaded, "and the darkness of midnight began to glitter with the blaze of the frontier cabins." Then shrieked the ghastly Pequod, smeared in his horrid paint. "Fathers found the blood of their sons fattening the wasted cornfields; mothers were frozen by the war-whoop which disturbed the peaceful slumber of the cradle."

CHAPTER XXIX.

ON THE WAR-TRAIL.

> " The shout
> Of battle, the barbarian yell, the bray
> Of dissonant instruments, the clang of arms,
> The shriek of agony, the groan of death,
> In one wild uproar and continued din,
> Shake the still air."
>
> Southey's *Madoc*.

'Tis related of a certain keeper of wild beasts at Florence, that, after he had entertained the spectators in the amphitheatre with their encounters on the stage, he had a strange device for forcing them back into their dens. A wooden machine, painted in the image of a great green dragon, with two lighted torches protruding from its sockets as eyes, and vomiting sulphurous flame, was wheeled into the midst of the herd, and before this onset the fiercest animal crawled howling to his cell.

'Tis an emblem of despotism; it is government coercing men by fraud and fear, by appeals to the ignorant and brutish instincts. The Pilgrim Fathers took a long stride away from that ugly ideal. They developed a nobler type of civil polity; and in nothing was their temper and Christianity more firmly shown than in their treatment of the Indians, whom they regarded as the orphaned wards of civilization. They were uniformly gentle and obliging to the savage tribes, and they were invariably and inflexibly just in treatment and in requisition. Take this for an illustration: In 1636, an Indian who had been on a trading tour to the pale-face settlements, seated himself towards evening on the day of his return in the woods on the edge of a swamp. He had with him a parcel of coats, and five pieces of wampum, the peaceful trophies of his barter. Soon he was accosted by four white men who happened to pass. A friendly chat ensued; the pipe of peace was passed; when suddenly the whites saw the coats and the wampum. At once that meanest, most unscrupulous imp in Satan's brood, the devil of avarice, entered their hearts—avarice, of which Decker has said,

> "When all our sins are old in us,
> And go upon crutches, covetousness
> Does but then lie in her cradle."

They determined to assassinate the dusky trader and filch his goods. Under pretence of shaking hands with him, one of the ruffians stabbed him in the thigh; this blow was followed by another, and yet another; whereupon the death-smitten savage fled. The murderers also departed; and when they were gone the Indian crawled back from his forest hiding-place and stretched himself across the trail, that he might be discovered and receive help.

This scene was enacted at Pawtucket, near Providence, but then within the precincts of Plymouth colony. Some hours after the affray, Roger Williams learned from an Indian runner that some pale faces were at Pawtucket almost starved. He at once sent the sufferers food and spirits, and a cordial invitation to visit his cabin. After some delay they came, enlisting the sympathy of their kind host by a pitiful tale of loss of way and hunger in the forest. Towards ten o'clock all retired. At midnight a loud cry was heard. The Indians clamored at the door for admittance, and to Roger Williams' queries they replied by informing him that one of their brothers lay almost dead in the woods from wounds inflicted by a party of pale-faces. "Have you seen them?" they shouted.

Meantime, the murderers, awakened by the cries, had fled. They were pursued, and three of the four were captured, and arraigned for trial at Plymouth. A jury was empannelled, and among the twelve "good men and true" were Bradford, and Standish, and Prince, and Winslow.* No delay was suffered, but the trial was fair and open. The guilt of the assassins was clearly proved, and they were sentenced to be hung.† Three limp forms suspended from the gallows-tree a little later, gave most palpable evidence that justice covered even the tangled wilderness morasses with its ægis. It was as certain death to kill an Indian in the forests of America, as to slay a noble in the crowded streets of London.

The effect of this execution was salutary. Its strict impartiality pleased the shrewd red men. It

* Bradford, Morton's Memorial, Thatcher, Banvard.
† Ibid., Prince, Hazard.

convinced them of the certainty of the colonial protection. And kindred acts before had won them to surrender that most prominent trait in their habits, the evenging of their personal wrongs; they adjourned their injuries to the justice of the Pilgrim courts and invoked the statute, sure that

> "The good need fear no law;
> It is his safety, and the bad man's awe."

But now this old epoch was buried: a new one dawned. The Indian surveyed the in-coming paleface tide which seemed always to flow and never to ebb. The hunting grounds of his people began to disappear. His own domain was restricted—there was no longer free range. A farm was here; a clearing was there; yonder stood a settler's cabin. The "medicines" of the red men grew alarmed. They asked each other: "Where will this end?" To be sure, the settlers held their estates by purchase; but the Indians did not always understand the value of a bargain from which they reaped no benefit; nor did they at all times recognize the validity of contracts made by their sachems, perhaps without the knowledge of the tribe, and which alienated the forest acres of their immemorial inheritance.

Heated by memory and by fear, and kindled by some occasionally unfriendly acts of the colonists—for in so large a population it was impossible that all should be just and honest—many of the New England tribes grew restless and peevish. A human powder magazine yawned beneath the feet of the

Pilgrims; it needed but some bold hand to drop the spark to cause an explosion which might unhinge a continent.

This the Pequods essayed to do. They had long been fretful. The Connecticut colonists had befriended a rival and hated tribe, the Mohegans.* Sassacus, the sachem of the Pequods, and Uncas, the Mohegan sagamore, were at deadly enmity.† Yet Uncas was the frequent and welcome occupant of pale-face cabins from Providence in the east to the farthest onion rows which troubled the Dutchmen in the west. The Pequods panted for revenge. They began to intrigue for a war of extermination. Embassies were despatched to inveigle neighboring tribes into an alliance against the ever-encroaching pale-faces. At the camp-fires of the Wampanoags, and in the wigwams of the Narragansetts, the Pequod orators pleaded their wrongs, sneered at the whites, and depicted the ferocious pleasures of the war-path to many a credulous and eager listener.

The forests became pregnant with insurrection, and at last a faint whisper of the impending peril reached the settlements. White Massachusetts shivered. Sir Harry Vane, knowing the influence of Roger Williams with the Indians, wrote him urgently to balk the Pequod embassadors among the Narragansetts.‡ At once the founder of Rhode Island set out; alone in his canoe, through a cutting, stormy

---

* Increase Mather's Early Hist. of New England, p. 121, et seq.   † Ibid.

‡ Elton's Life of Roger Williams, p. 54.

wind, he pulled across the bay to the forest haunt of Canonicus and Miantonomoh.*

"The Pequod diplomats were already at work, urging the dark dangers which hung over their united tribes, reiterating the tale of the encroachments of the whites, the chicanery, the insolence, the cruelty, which some had practised, and appealing to the Indian pride of possession and of race. For three days and nights Roger Williams, in the sachem's lodge, mixed with the bloody-minded Pequod embassadors, and pushed his dangerous opposition to the war; and at last his old friendship and superior diplomacy prevailed. Canonicus and Miantonomoh repudiated the Pequod league and refused to dig up the tomahawk."†

The Pequods, no whit disheartened by this balk, determined to fight unassisted, thinking, perhaps, that the precipitation of hostilities would fire the Indian heart.

Sassacus, followed by seven hundred‡ painted and yelling warriors, plunged into the woods and opened the war-path. Winding out of their beautiful nest in southeastern Connecticut, between the rivers Pawcatuck and Thames,§ they spread consternation and the most ghastly form of death north, east, south, west.

According to their habit, the Indians were cau-

---

* Elton's life of Roger Williams, p. 54.   Elliot, vol. 1, p. 210.
† Elliot.
‡ I. Mather's Early Hist., etc.   Palfrey, Bancroft, Elliot, Hutchinson § Ibid.

tious at the outset. Isolated instances announced their hostility. In 1634, Captains Stone and Norton sailed up the Connecticut in a coasting smack, manned by a crew of eight men. They were steering for a Dutch trading station on the river side, when their vessel was becalmed. In a flash a fleet of canoes were launched from either bank of the river, and a swarm of savages surrounded the smack. Suspecting no danger, twelve of them were permitted to board, and Stone engaged two of these to pilot a boat higher up the stream. The guides at night murdered the two sailors in charge of this shallop, and at the same hour their companions on the vessel assailed the sleeping crew. Stone was killed secretly in his cabin, and, to conceal the body, a light covering was thrown over it. Then the massacre extended to the deck and forecastle. Soon all were dead save Norton. "He had taken to the cook-room on the first alarm, and here he made a long and resolute defence. That he might load and fire with the greatest expedition, he placed powder in an open bowl, just at hand, which, in the hurry of action, taking fire, so burned and blinded him that he could fight no longer; whereupon he too was tomahawked."* Then the smack was pillaged and sunk.†

Two years later, John Oldham,‡ while trading fairly on the Connecticut, was suddenly set upon

---

* White's Incidents, p. 59.   I. Mather, Palfrey, Hubbard, Winthrop.   † Ibid.
‡ Chap. 17, p. 215, et seq.

and brained. His companions, two Narragansett Indians and a couple of boys, were kidnapped.*

A few days after this sad catastrophe, an old English sailor, John Gallup, floating on the tranquil bosom of the treacherous river in his little shallop of twenty tons, manned only by himself, his two sons, and one old salt, espied Oldham's pinnace off Block Island. He tacked for it and hailed. No answer; a closer survey showed him a deck crowded with Indians. Gallup's suspicion was aroused, and when the clumsy savages attempted to make sail and get away, he regarded the movement as a cover to foul play.

Then one of the most remarkable instances of gallantry recorded in the annals of border warfare occurred. Gallup, with his single sailor and his two little boys, armed only with a couple of rusty muskets, two pistols, and some buck-shot, prepared for action, and this though fourteen savages, heated by carnage and drunk with blood, stood ready with guns, and pikes, and swords, to repel his assault. The wind was fresh, and the audacious captain steered directly for the pinnace, and striking it stem foremost, nearly upset it; which so frightened the Indians that six of them jumped overboard and were drowned. Repeating this manœuvre—in unconscious imitation of the Athenian naval tactics—he came stem on again; for there were still too many Indians for him to venture to carry the pinnace by boarding. After this thump, Gallup had

* Bradford, Morton's Memorial, Hubbard, White.

the satisfaction of seeing, as he cleared his vessel and stood off once more, four more savages leap into a watery grave—for they all sank. Then he steered for the battered craft for the third time; whereupon the remaining Indians sought refuge in the hold beneath the hatches. Gallup sprang on the deck of poor Oldham's vessel, and there, stretched out before his eyes, was the late owner himself, still warm, but with cloven skull and amputated hands and feet.*

The savages in the hold were now anxious to surrender. Two of them at Gallup's bidding came up and were bound; and then, maddened by the sight of Oldham's disfigured corpse, the sailor plunged the victims into the river. The two remaining savages would not give up their arms or come up from under the hatches. Gallup could not dig them out; so he secured the cargo, buried Oldham, and then tying the pinnace to the stern of his own victorious shallop, he set sail to tow her to the settlements. But in the night it blew hard; his capture was detached, and, drifting to the Narragansett shore, the secreted warriors escaped—two only out of fourteen†—a swift and sweeping retribution.

The knowledge of these dismal tragedies crept slowly into the colonies. News was carried only by some coastwise vessel, whose progress, crab-like, was backwards; by some Indian runner often interested in being sluggish; or by some pale sufferer who, trav-

* Winthrop, pp. 189, 190.   † Palfrey, White, Elliot, etc.

ersing forest, morass, and mountain, was frequently his own messenger of woe; for the Pilgrims had no stage-coaches like their immediate descendants; no good roads, like the men of '76; no railway and no steamboat, like ourselves; and above all, no telegraph, annihilating space, to

> "Speed the swift intercourse from soul to soul,
> Or waft a sigh from Indus to the Pole."

But eventually the colonists learned of these spasmodic outrages; and all promptly decided that justice and the common weal alike dictated punishment. "After consultation with 'the magistrates and ministers,' Sir Harry Vane despatched ninety men down Long Island sound, in three small vessels, to the seat of war—Block island. The expedition was under the chief command of John Endicott, who was assisted by four subordinate officers, one of whom, Captain John Underhill, wrote an account of the foray and of the succeeding and more effective one. A sort of Friar Tuck—devotee, bravo, libertine, and buffoon—Underhill takes a memorable place among the eccentric characters who from time to time broke what has been altogether too easily assumed to have been the dead level of New England gravity in those days. He had been a soldier in Ireland, in Spain, and more recently in the Netherlands, where he 'had spoken freely with Count Nassau.' He came over with Winthrop, who employed him to train the Pilgrims in military tactics."*

* Palfrey, vol. 1, pp. 458, 459.

The expedition, spite of Endicott's skill and Underhill's bravery and the number of men engaged in it, was an essential failure. A few savages were shot; some lodges were burned; several canoes were staved; and a number of acres of corn were despoiled. Indeed, just enough was done to madden the savages, but not enough to intimidate them.*

In the summer of 1636, Endicott sailed into Boston harbor in bloodless triumph. Meantime, his irritating raid was revenged by a wide-spread assault upon the isolated Connecticut colonists.† Every tree became a covert. In the long grass, in the morasses, in the out-buildings of the settlers, lurked the envenomed savages. To step outside those block citadels to which all flocked for safety, was certain death. Men were kidnapped and roasted alive.‡ Traders were waylaid on the rivers and tortured to death; and two victims especially were cut into two parts lengthwise, each half being hung up on a tree by the bank of the Connecticut.§ Women and children were captured and reserved for a fate worse than death. In the winter of 1637, thirty of the two hundred settlers who had colonized Connecticut, fell beneath the hatchets of the Pequods.‖ Everywhere the whites were worsted; even at Saybrook, their chief fort, the garrison was held

---

* Palfrey, vol. 1, pp. 458, 459. I. Mather, Prince, Introduction to Mason's Hist. of the Pequod War. † Ibid.
‡ Gardiner's Relations, etc., in Mass. Hist. Rep., 23.
§ Ibid., p. 143. Trumbull's Hist. Connecticut, vol. 1, p. 76.
‖ Palfrey, vol. 1, p. 462.

in duress by a besieging band of demoniacal red men.*

New England was trembling on the verge of death. For the distressed and harassed Pilgrims there seemed no alternative but speedy extermination, or such an exercise of courage and skill as should effectually overawe the Indians in the full flush of their success. Measures were at once matured. Massachusetts Bay acted with her accustomed vigor. It was declared that "the war, since it was waged on just grounds and for self-preservation, ought to be vigorously prosecuted."† Six hundred pounds were levied; one hundred and sixty men were recruited.‡

At Plymouth similar activity was displayed; and a levy of forty men was made.§ But it was in Connecticut, the menaced spot, that the most herculean exertions were put forth. Hartford, Windsor, and Wethersfield, placed ninety men in the field, under the command of stout John Mason—a sometime soldier in the Low Countries under Sir Thomas Fairfax, who held him in such esteem that in after-years, when at the head of the parliamentary muster, he wrote his truant *protégé* urging his return to England, that he might lend his skilful sword to the patriot cause.‖

Mason, with Hooker's benediction, immediately

---

* I. Mather, Gardiner in Mass. Hist. Col., 23.
† Mass. Hist. Col. Col. Rec., vol. 1, p. 192. ‡ Ibid.
§ Plym. Col. Rec., vol. 1, pp. 60-62.
‖ Palfrey, ut antea. Prince. Introduction to Mason's Hist,

opened a vigorous campaign. Saybrook was reinforced.* A subsidiary detachment of Mohegans, under Uncas, was recruited.† The mouth of the Connecticut was made the base of operations, and thither the united levies of Massachusetts, Connecticut, and Plymouth, were transported. Here a council of war was held. After Stone, the chaplain, had sought the divine direction in prayer, it was decided to march directly upon the Pequod village off Point Judith.‡ All embarked; the objective point was safely reached. Then a storm intervened; it was impossible to land. The next day was Sunday; it was spent devoutly on shipboard; nor was it until Tuesday evening, the third day after they had dropped anchor, that the eager Pilgrims touched land.§

Mason bivouacked on the sea-shore, and in the gray of the next morning commenced the memorable march. "Seventy-seven brave Englishmen— the rest were left in charge of the vessels—sixty frightened Mohegans, and four hundred more terrified Narragansetts, entered the war-trail, and went twenty miles westward towards the Pequod country, to a fort occupied by some suspected neutrals. There a pause for the night was made, and, lest any Indian should give the doomed Pequods the alarm, the citadel was girt by the sentries of the shrewd English captain."‖

* Mason's "Brief Hist., etc. Hubbard.
† Trumbull, Mather.   ‡ Palfrey, vol. 1.
§ Ibid., Hubbard, Trumbull, Mather.
‖ Palfrey, vol. 1, p. 164.

Before noon, on the following morning, they broke camp, and marched fifteen miles farther inland, pausing at nightfall under a hill "which, according to information received from their dusky allies—who had now all fallen in the rear, 'being possessed with great fear'—stood the chief stronghold of the Pequods."[*]

Mason could hear the savage revelry of the ill-fated and unsuspecting Indians very distinctly, as the wind wafted the laughter, the yells, the vaunts, from the village over the little hill. The din sank and fell till midnight. All were enjoying a general guffaw over the English, whose ships they had seen sail eastward on the sound, bearing, as they imagined, the pale-face warriors to tell their squaws of their discomfiture.[†]

The Pequod fort was a citadel of straw. It "was merely a circular acre or two enclosed by trunks of trees some twelve feet high, set firmly in the ground, and so closely ranged as to exclude entrance, while the interstices served as port-holes for marksmen. Within, ranged along two parallel lanes, were upwards of seventy wigwams, covered with matting and thatch. At the two points for entrance or egress, spaces were left between the timbers, the intervals being protected only by a slighter structure, or by loose branches."[‡]

Something of all this the curious eyes of the Pilgrims took in as they patiently waited for the

---

[*] Palfrey, vol. 1, p. 465.   [†] Ibid., Mason, Underhill.
[‡] Palfrey, ut antea.

midnight order to advance. At length it came; the camp was broken; prayers were offered; the Indian allies fell back to a still safer distance. The drowsy Pequod stronghold was surrounded; Mason was on one side, Underhill was on the other. Cautiously the girdling band crept on, on, on, towards the sally-ports, looking like sheeted phantoms in the ghastly moonlight. Their hands were on the gates, when a dog barked. The Indians were aroused. "Owanux! Owanux!" "The Englishmen are here!" came in a hoarse shout from within. Then, with a wild "Huzza!" the Pilgrims plunged themselves like an avalanche upon the frail and creaking fortress, firing the straw in fifty different directions. The rest was death; for it was not a battle—it was a massacre. Shouting the watchwords of the Israelites in Canaan, the Pilgrims smote the Pequods hip and thigh, for they knew that safety and peace dwelt in every blow—that severity was mercy.

Soon the explosion of a powder-train made the village kick the heavens. Then the flames began to wink, and at last to go out. Darkness followed—a darkness made more frightful by the moans of the wounded, the fierce panting of those wretches who still struggled against fate, and the vindictive yell of the Mohegan and Narragansett warriors, now in full cry after the dazed and despairing fugitives.*

At last the sad morning dawned. The dead bodies of seven hundred† Pequods were counted amid

---

* Mason's Brief Account, etc.

† Ibid., Palfrey. Elliot, I. Mather, Winthrop, Hubbard, Hutch-

the *débris* of the carnage. There lay the whole nation,

"In one red burial blent."

But let us turn from the sickening scene. "Never was a war so just or so necessary," remarks Palfrey, "that he who should truly exhibit the details of its prosecution would not find the sympathy of gentle hearts deserting him as he proceeded. Between right policy and the suffering which sometimes it brings upon individuals, there is a wide chasm, to be bridged over by an argument with which the heart does not naturally go. When, for urgent reasons of public safety, it has been determined to take the desperate risk of sending the whole available force of a community into the field to encounter desperate odds, and certain to be set on, if worsted, by neutral thousands, the awful conditions of the venture forbid daintiness in the means of achieving the victory, or about using it in such a manner as to veto the chance of incurring the same peril again. At all events, from the hour of that fatal carnage Connecticut was secure. There could now be unguarded sleep in the long-harassed cabins of the settlers. It might be hoped that civilization was assured of a permanent abode in New England."*

Mason followed up his victory, like an able soldier as he was. After the fatal night attack, Sas-

---

inson. Two of the English were killed, and upwards of forty—more than half of the force—were wounded.

* Palfrey, vol. 1, p. 467.

sacus and the remnant of his undone tribe fled westward.* They were overtaken, and forced to fight in a swamp and in a panic. Then there was another massacre; and two hundred prisoners were captured, besides a booty of trays, kettles, and wampum.† The Pequod chieftain once more baffled fate, and with a body of twenty warriors sought an asylum among the Mohawks, on the banks of the Hudson, where the unhappy sagamore, bereaved of people and of country, was himself treacherously slain, his scalp-lock being sent as a trophy to the pale-face conquerors.‡

At the same time two other chiefs were hunted down at a point east of New Haven. Here they were beheaded; and the spot—now a famous summer resort—has been called since that day "Sachem's Head."§

It is sad to relate that this awful slaughter was crowned by the enslavement of the wretched survivors of the fight. When Mason returned to Hartford, bringing the retinue of his command with him, Massachusetts and Connecticut, needing laborers, and blind to the injustice, divided the human booty; and with Rhode Island, which purchased some of the victims, they must share the guilt.∥ But in this the Pilgrims did not sin against the spirit of their age. It was not an insurrection against the coun-

---

* Mason, Hubbard, Hazard, Trumbull.   † Ibid., Elliot.
‡ Trumbull, Mason, Winthrop, Hist. Coll.
§ Elliot, vol. 1, p. 257.   Trumbull.
∥ Ibid.   Hutchinson, vol. 1. p. 80.   Winthrop, vol. 1.   Palfrey.

science of that epoch, for the flagitious practice was universal. Human slavery had not yet been branded as infamous amid the scornful execrations of mankind.

Thus in death and captivity closed the career of a gallant tribe. They threw themselves before the chariot-wheels of progress, and were crushed; they essayed to check God, and were overthrown. Like ancient Agag, they were hewn in pieces. In its first warlike bout with barbarism, civilization was the victor, and went crowned with bays.

CHAPTER XXX.

DE PROFUNDIS.

"We have strict statutes and most biting laws,
The needful bits and curbs to headstrong steeds."
SHAKSPEARE.

THE Pilgrim Fathers were not students of Godefridus de Valle's odd book, "*De Arte Nihil Credendi*"—The Art of believing Nothing. They did believe, from the bottom of their hearts; and, in obedience to Paul, they strove to "hold fast" that which they esteemed "good." They had two passions, devotion to the common weal as citizens, and to the interests of the church as Christians. "They regarded themselves, not as individual fugitives from trans-Atlantic persecution, but rather as confederates in a political association for religious purposes."* From this idea their mixed government naturally evolved; and this, in its turn, gave birth to the principle that the magistrate was armed with power to suppress all phases of internal opposition to the theocracy; because that type of authority logically carried in its train the necessary conditions of its perpetuity.

They neither invited nor desired the intrusion of elements at variance with their ideas; and to such they said, pointing to the broad continent,

* Uhden's New England Theocracy, p. 135.

"There is room; leave us in peace." And to secure themselves from molestation, it was enacted, in 1637, that "none should be received into the jurisdiction of Massachusetts Bay but such as should be welcomed by the magistrates"*—a provision somewhat analogous to the alien law of England and to the European policy of passports.†

Singularly enough, Massachusetts Bay, spite of its exclusive policy, possessed from the very outset a strong charm in the eyes of those who dissented from its formulas. Like the *Petit Monsieur* who found himself left out of the tapestry which exhibited the story of the Spanish invasion, they longed to work themselves in the hangings of colonial history. They soon swarmed in Boston and Salem; and notwithstanding the banishment of Roger Williams, the "heretics" continued to thrive.

Ere long the public mind " was excited to intense activity on questions which the nicest subtlety only could have devised, and which none but those experienced in the shades of theological opinion could long comprehend; for it goes with these opinions as with colors, of which the artist who works in mosaic easily and regularly discriminates many thousand varieties, where the common eye can discern a difference only on the closest comparison."‡

From this fermentation there bubbled up a profound and bitter struggle. The strife filled the in-

* Winthrop, Hutchinson, Hubbard, Col. Records, etc.
† Bancroft, vol. 1, p. 389. ‡ Ibid., p. 386.

terstices of the Pequod war, whose prosecution it sadly crippled; and indeed, at one time it threatened to rend the colony by civil war.*

Two distinct parties were early developed. One was composed chiefly of the older colonists, headed by Dudley, and Phillips, and Wilson, and Winthrop, an able coalition of clergymen and politicians. These were earnest to preserve the state as it was. They discountenanced innovation, and "dreaded freedom of opinion as the parent of various divisions." They said, "These cracks and flaws in the new building of the Reformation portend a fall."† They were anxious "to confirm and build up the colony, child of their prayers and sorrows; and for that they desired patriotism, union, and a common heart." They dreaded change, because they knew that,

"Striving to better, oft we mar what's well."

The other party was iconoclastic. It was "composed of men and women who had arrived in New England after the civil government and religious discipline of the Pilgrims had been established."‡ They felt cramped under the theocracy; and having come self-banished to the wilderness to enjoy toleration, they resisted every form of despotism over the human mind, and "sustained with intense fanaticism the paramount authority of private judgment." "They came," observes Bancroft, "fresh from the study of the tenets of Geneva, and their

* Uhden, Winthrop, Hutchinson, Hubbard.
† Shepherd's Lamentation, 2. ‡ Bancroft, vol. 1, p. 387.

pride consisted in following the principles of the Reformation with logical precision to all their consequences. Their eyes were not primarily directed to the institutions of Massachusetts, but to the doctrines of its religious system; so to them the colonial clergy seemed 'the ushers of a new persecution,' 'a popish faction,' who had not imbibed the principles of Christian reform; and they applied to the influence of the Pilgrim ministers the doctrine which Luther and Calvin had employed against the observances and pretensions of the Roman church."*

There is an old Latin proverb,

"Nulla fere causa est, in quâ non fæmina litem Moverit."†

The life and soul of the crusade against the theocracy was Anne Hutchinson, whom Johnson styled, "the chiefest masterpiece of woman's wit."‡ Antedating the Cordays, the Rolands, and the De Staels by more than a dozen decades, she was the equal, in tact, and zeal, and honest conviction, of the best of those brilliant women who, in the *salons* of the French capital, inspired the revolution of 1793.

Anne Hutchinson was the wife of a Boston merchant, the daughter of a Puritan preacher in England, and had been one of John Cotton's most devoted parishioners ere he was driven into exile.§

---

* Bancroft, vol. 1, p. 387.
† There are few controversies where a woman is not at the bottom of them. ‡ See Bancroft, vol. 1, p. 388.
§ Palfrey, vol. 1, p. 472, et seq.

In 1634 she followed that eminent divine to America, and was received into his church at Boston,* spite of some strange theories which she had avowed on shipboard.† Her active benevolence and unflagging kindness to the sick soon wedded to her many hearts.‡ She planted herself deep in the affections of the city.

The male members of the Boston church had a habit of taking notes of the sermon on Sunday, and then holding week-day meetings for the recapitulation and discussion of the doctrines advanced§— a very commendable practice. Mrs. Hutchinson, thinking perhaps that woman's influence and intellect were not sufficiently recognized in the church, inaugurated a similar series of week-day conventicles for the ladies of Boston.‖

Mrs. Hutchinson's lectures—for she was ever the chief speaker—attracted crowds, and they were countenanced by Sir Harry Vane, who then occupied the gubernatorial chair, and by his host, John Cotton;¶ below whom stood a crowd of warm adherents, flanked by John Wheelwright the clerical brother-in-law of the lady speaker, and by the hearty influence of John Coddington one of the wealthiest of the colonists.** "Thus the women," says Cotton Mather, "like their first mother, hooked in the husbands also."††

---

* Winthrop, vol. 1, p. 200. † Ibid., Hubbard.
‡ Palfrey, vol. 1, p. 473. § Ibid. Magnalia, vol. 2, p. 516.
‖ Ibid., Elliot, Hutchinson, Uhden.
¶ Palfrey, Winthrop, Elliot, Hubbard, etc.
** Ibid., Col. Records. †† Magnalia, vol. 2, p. 509.

Soon the vigorous and daring mind of Anne Hutchinson struck off new watchwords. Much was said of a "Covenant of Works" and a "Covenant of Grace," and between these many fine distinctions were made. "Under these heads she and her friends classified the preachers of the Bay. Those who were understood to rely upon a methodical and rigid observance of their religious duties as evidence of acceptance with God were said to be 'under a covenant of works.' Those who held to certain spiritual tenets were ranged 'under the covenant of grace.' These phrases began to be bandied to and fro. 'Justification' and 'sanctification' were in all mouths; even children jeered each other; and there was no stemming the heady current of discussion as it swept on."*

Winthrop and his coadjutors looked upon the debate with equal horror and alarm. Two words, which were then common, expressed to them a vague but frightful danger; *Antinomianism* was one, and *Familism* was the other. The *Antinomians* were a sect of German extraction, and their name meant *against the Law;* for they held that "the gospel of Christ had superseded the law of Moses."† But the word had been made the shelter of sad excesses and many base acts, so that it was in bad odor among the Pilgrims, who esteemed Antinomianism to be a cloak to cover the naked form of license.‡

Familism had been nursed into vicious life in

* Elliot, vol. 1, p. 263. † Ibid. ‡ Ibid.

Holland; where, in 1555, Henry Nicholas formed a "Family of Love," who, in their opinions, "grieved the Comforter, charging all their sins on God's Spirit, for not effectually assisting them against themselves."* The Familists had long been numerous, factious, and dangerous, in England, and their practice was even worse than their doctrine; for their laxity of morals made them the sappers of social order.†

Anne Hutchinson does not seem to have been inoculated with the virus of Familism; but she was, of course, an Antinomian, since she assailed the theocratic law; and therefore, to the heated minds of the Pilgrims, she might easily appear to be the fleshly tabernacle of both—the incarnation of heresy.

Meantime the debate grew in bitterness. Mrs. Hutchinson, when taunted with Familism and Antinomianism, retorted by nicknaming her foes *Legalists;* "because," she said, "you are acquainted neither with the spirit of the gospel nor with Christ himself."‡ Boston echoed the phrase with wild delight, and "Legalist! Legalist! Legalist!" was dinned into the ears of the clergy of the Bay.

Winthrop and his friends were exasperated, and they invoked the courts to interfere. Several of the Antinomians were heavily fined.§ Wheelwright, who, in a fast-day sermon, had strenuously main-

---

* Fuller's Ch. Hist. of England, vol. 2, pp. 514, 515, et. seq.
† Ibid.   ‡ Uhden, p. 98.
§ Winthrop, vol. 1, p. 203. Hubbard, Palfrey, Hazard.

tained the Antinomian tenets, was formally censured by the General Court for sedition.*

Then the innovators were, in their turn, angered. "The fear of God and the love of neighbors was laid by;" Mrs. Hutchinson and her adherents clamored all the louder; and Vane, disgusted and dispirited, tendered his resignation, and craved permission to return to England;† but "the expostulations of the Boston church finally turned him from his design," and kept him at his post.‡

Meanwhile Wheelwright, provoked at his censure, had appealed to England. This wrecked Vane's administration, and ruined the Antinomian cause; for the patriotic feeling of the colony ran so high, that "it was accounted perjury and treason to appeal to the king."§ In the elections of 1637 public opinion was made manifest; Winthrop, with the towns and the churches at his back, outvoted Vane, whose sole support was Boston, and the fathers of the colony once more grasped the helm.‖

Winthrop originated, enacted, and defended the alien law.¶ This found in Vane an inflexible opponent; and, using the language of the time, he left a memorial of his dissent. "Scribes and Pharisees, and such as are confirmed in any way of error"— these are the remarkable words of the man who soon embarked for England, where he afterwards

---

* Winthrop, vol. 1, p. 203. Hubbard, Palfrey, Hazard, Col. Records. † Palfrey, vol. 1, pp. 475, 476. Winthrop.
‡ Ibid. § Ibid., Bancroft, Elliot, Hutchinson.
‖ Ibid. Uhden, p. 96. ¶ Winthrop, Palfrey

pleaded in Parliament for the liberties of all classes of dissenters—" all such are not to be denied cohabitation, but are to be pitied and reformed. Ishmael shall dwell in the presence of his brethren."*

Now that the founders of the colony had emerged from their brief eclipse and regained their pristine influence, they decided to initiate measures which should definitely silence the unseemly " noise about the temple." An ecclesiastical synod was convened.† Assembling in the summer of 1637, it branded eighty-two opinions then in vogue as heretical, and summoned Anne Hutchinson, Wheelwright, and others of that "ilk," to their bar for examination.‡

They appeared; and Cotton, who had satisfied his brother clergymen of his orthodoxy, tainted for a space by his connection with the Antinomians, was set to examine Mrs. Hutchinson; "which was hard for him to do, and bitter for her to endure; for she had been his *protegé*."§

This remarkable woman was now in her element. She was calm, and she was firm, and she was keen; for,

> " Spirits are not finely touched
> But to fine issues."

But one bold avowal sealed her doom. "We have," she said, "a new rule of practice by immediate rev-

---

* Cited in Bancroft, vol. 1, p. 390.
† C. Mather's Magnalia, vol. 2, p. 510. Palfrey, Hubbard.
‡ Ibid., Hutchinson's Coll., Neale's Hist. of New England.
§ Elliot, vol. 1, p. 267.

elations; by these we guide our conduct. Not that we expect any revelation in the way of a miracle; that is a delusion; but we despise the anathemas of your synods and courts, and will still follow the whisperings of conscience."*

This speech caused wide-spread alarm. It seemed to squint towards anarchy. "The true parents of the brats began to discover themselves," quaintly comments old Mather, "when the synod lifted the sword upon them."† An insurrection of lawless fanatics, "like a Munster tragedy," seemed brewing. The magistrates decided that the danger was desperate; that Anne Hutchinson was "like Roger Williams, or worse;"‡ and so, says Winthrop, "we applied the last remedy, and that without delay."§

Anne Hutchinson, Wheelwright, and Aspinwall, were solemnly exiled as "unfit for the society" of the Pilgrims; and those of their followers who remained were ordered to deliver up their arms, lest they should, "upon some revelation, make a sudden insurrection."||

Thus ended the *ecclesiarum prœlia.*¶ "And thus," says Cotton Mather, "was the hydra beheaded—*hydra decapitata.*"** "This legislation may be reproved for its jealousy, but not for its cruelty; for it condemned the "heretics" to a ban-

---

* Bancroft, vol. 1, p. 390.
† C. Mather's Magnalia, vol. 2, p. 512.
‡ Winthrop in Hutchinson's Coll.   § Winthrop's Journal.
|| Bancroft, vol. 1, p. 391.   ¶ Battles of the Churches.
** Magnalia, vol. 2, p. 508.

ishment not more severe than many of the best of the Pilgrims had encountered from choice." But it is a sad chapter; and perhaps the old divine was right when he wrote, "What these errors were 't is needless now to repeat; they are dead and gone, and buried past resurrection; 't is a pity to strive to rake them from their graves."*

The exiles, followed by great numbers of proselytes, on quitting Massachusetts Bay, wandered southward, " designing to plant a settlement on Long Island, or near Delaware Bay. But Roger Williams welcomed them to his vicinity," and obtained for them a resting-place. They colonized Rhode Island, or *Aquitneck*, as it was then called. "It was not price nor money that got Rhode Island," wrote Williams; "it was gotten by *love;* by the love and favor which that honorable gentleman, Sir Harry Vane, and myself, had with that great sachem, Miantonomoh."†

Being thus held by the same tenure that Providence owned, Aquitneck was based upon the selfsame principle of intellectual liberty; and though the two were not united in one state until after the Restoration, they clasped hands in equal brotherhood, and were buoyed by toleration.

Thus the principles of Anne Hutchinson, thrown out of Massachusetts, sprouted in Rhode Island,

---

* Magnalia, vol. 2, p. 512.

† Knowles' Life of Williams, Elton. Mrs. Hutchinson, some years after her exile, suffered a melancholy fate, being tomahawked by the savages. See Bancroft, vol. 1, pp. 393, 394.

and grew a well-ordered, sober state. A happy result flowed from an unhappy cause.

And now for a season internecine strife was hushed. All eyes were directed across the water. "The angels of the trans-Atlantic churches, sounding forth their silver trumpets, heard the sound of rattling drums" on every European breeze.* Democracy was about to assert itself in England. The Pilgrim Fathers grasped hands, and silently marked the lesson; which was, that "courtiers, bishops, and kings, too, have a joint in their necks."

* Johnson's Wonder-working Providence, p. 96.

CHAPTER XXXI.

THE CHART AND THE PILOTS.

"And sovereign law, the state's collected will,
   O'er thrones and globes elate,
Sits empress, crowning good, repressing ill."
SIR WILLIAM JONES.

"To do the genteel deeds—that makes the gentleman."
CHAUCER.

'TIS a trite saying, that legislation reflects character. The penal code of a state mirrors the culture, the thought, and the habits of its citizens; because laws grow from men's exigencies. Of course, the Pilgrims had a legal chart, and they wrote its quaint characters in the ink of their peculiarities. Unlike our statute-book, it made no fine distinctions and it used no legal fictions, but was very simple and very plain; results due to the primitive social customs of the colonies, to the lack of lawyers, and to the constant effort to avoid litigation; for in those days they did not mean

   ———"With subtle cobweb cheats,
To catch in knotted law, like nets;
In which, when men are once imbrangled,
The more they stir, the more they're tangled."

The founders of New England had little sympathy with, and made no provision for, legal legerdemain. They were much too earnest and honest to admire that kind of justice which Pope has satirized:

> "Once—says an author, where I need not say—
> Two travellers found an oyster in their way:
> Both fierce, both hungry, the dispute grew strong,
> When, scale in hand, dame Justice passed along.
> Before her each with clamor pleads the laws,
> Explains the matter, and would win the cause.
> Dame Justice, weighing long the doubtful right,
> Takes, opens, swallows it, before their sight.
> The cause of strife removed so rarely well,
> 'There take'—says Justice—'take you each a shell.
> We thrive at Westminster on fools like you:
> 'T was a fat oyster—live in peace—adieu.'"

But while the Pilgrims knew nothing of law as a vehicle for quarrels to ride on and for trickery to drive, they made use of it as a bit to curb disorder. "Some of their enactments exhibit profound wisdom, sagacity, and forecast; others show their strong attachment to the precepts of the Bible; and still others descend to matters of such trivial nature as to appear puerile; yet of these it may be said that they are preventive. The Pilgrims believed in nipping crime in the bud. The things forbidden may have been, in themselves, comparatively unimportant; but their influence, if unchecked, might have led to gross offences. By destroying the seed of wickedness, they labored to prevent the fruits."*

Very evidently the colonists were not free traders, for, three years after the landing at Plymouth Rock, a protective law was passed, by which it was enacted that "no handicraftsmen, as shoemakers, tailors, carpenters, joiners, smiths, and sawyers, be-

---

* Banvard, p. 200.

longing to this plantation, shall work for any strangers and foreigners until the domestic necessities be served."* And at the same time, in order to prevent the return of a famine which had repeatedly visited them, it was enacted that "until farther orders, no corn, beans, or peas, be exported, under penalty of a confiscation of such exports."†

Marriage was held to be a civil contract,‡ and the intention to marry was to be published fourteen days, including three Sabbaths, before the union, and was then to be consummated only on the consent of the parents or guardian of the lady, if she were under "parental covert."§

Denial of the Scriptures as the rule of life, was an indictable offence, and was punishable by whipping; so were violations of the Sabbath, the neglecting of public worship, and slander.‖ Once a Miss Boulton, on conviction of slander, was condemned to the humiliating punishment of sitting in the stocks, with a paper fastened to her breast on which were written the details of her offence in capital letters.¶ At another time, two men were similarly dealt with for having disturbed a meeting;** and this same court also "sharply reproved John Whitson for writing a note on common business on the Lord's day."†† Women who abused their husbands or who struck their fathers-in-law, were fined or whipped at the option of the magistrate.‡‡

---

* Thatcher's New Plymouth, Banvard.
† Charter and Laws of New Plymouth.   ‡ Ibid., Banvard.
§ Ibid.   ‖ Ibid.   ¶ Ibid.   ** Ibid.   †† Ibid.   ‡‡ Ibid.

Very odd and very arbitrary all this seems to us; but it came naturally from the theocratic idea, which subordinated every other interest to religion. And with all its singularities, it must be confessed that the Pilgrim code was, as a whole and at that time, adapted to secure a higher moral character to the community than would have been attained by the naturalization of the then existing laws of any other people.*

Occasionally, "whales used to be driven ashore, whereupon the Pilgrims would obtain oil from them. Ere long it was ordained that when such an incident occurred, or when any whale was cut up at sea and brought into port, one full hogshead of oil should be paid to the state;"† and this was the first impost, from which have grown the custom-houses of our age.

The court which framed this law also proposed, "as a thing very commendable and beneficial to the towns where God's providence cast whales, that all should agree to set apart some portion of such fish or oil for the encouragement of an able, godly ministry."‡

But the chief strength of New England lay in the Puritan homes. These were the nurseries of Christian freemen. Good could hardly fail to result when "parents were required to see that their children were taught to read the Scriptures and to recite some short orthodox catechism, without the book;

---

* Banvard, p. 211.   † Charter and Laws, etc.
‡ Banvard, ut antea.

and when they 'brought up' their families to some honest calling that made them useful to themselves and to the commonwealth."

The New England towns were perfect democracies. "Their formation was promoted by the dread of, and danger from, Indians, and also by the demand for churches and schools. The settlers, therefore, did not scatter widely upon large plantations, but collected in villages, with their farms around them. The town-meetings were held annually—usually in the spring—and every voter was expected to be present to take his part in the direction of affairs; this was looked upon as a chief duty; and it was held that a man who would not use his liberty and do this duty was no good citizen. The roll of voters was often called, and the absentees were each fined eighteen pence. At first they met in the church; but eventually each town provided itself with a town-house, in which to conduct its business and hold its courts. When the meetings came to order, some grave and good citizen was chosen moderator. Then the town business was brought up in order. Motions were made, briefly debated, and voted upon. Matters passed at one meeting were often reversed at a subsequent one, and the minutes read, 'Undone next meeting.' The voters granted lands, established and repaired mills, roads, and ferries, and took order as to clearing commons, paying the schoolmaster, raising the salary of the minister, and electing deputies to the General Court. In every town from three to seven 'prudential men,' afterwards called 'select men,' were appointed to administer the town affairs between the annual meetings; and these held petty courts, decided minor cases, and acted as referees in most disputes. Such was the nursing on which these states grew up a congeries of towns, true and strong and free."*

Among the many peculiarities of the Pilgrim Fathers, perhaps the oddest trait was either their lack of ambition or their sober sense of the responsibilities of office, whose honors and emoluments so little tempted them, that even the position of governor went begging. Indeed, they had to be pricked up to their duty by statute; for in 1632 it was provided that if any one should refuse to sit in the gubernatorial chair, after election, he should be fined twenty pounds.† Winthrop, under the year 1633, makes this record: "This year, Mr. Edward Winslow was elected governor of Plymouth, and Mr. Bradford, having been governor about ten years, *now got off by importunity.*"‡

How much happier we are in our age, for now-a-days thousands of devoted patriots are perfectly willing to lay their privacy upon the altar of their country by accepting any office, from a snuggery in the custom-house to the presidency of the Republic. They only beg to be used. Men no longer cite that speech of the father of Themistocles, who, in attempting to dissuade his son from government, showed him the old, discarded oars which the Gre-

* Elliot, vol. 1, pp. 183, 184. † Chap. 12, p. 151.
‡ Winthrop, vol 1.

cian mariners had thrown away upon the sea-shore, and said: "See; the people will certainly treat their old rulers with the same contempt."

But if the Pilgrims did not accept office readily, they did not hold it lightly. No; they were real rulers, not cockades masquerading in the garb of authority. They took high views of their duties, and believed with Agapetus, that "the loftier the station one reaches in the government, the truer should be his devotion to the service of God;"* and they were sensible of what Cotton Mather styles that "great stroke" of Cicero: "*Nullâ re propius hominas ad Deum accedunt, quam salutem hominibus dando*"—men approach nearest to the character of God in doing good to mankind.

"The word *government* properly signifies the *guidance of a ship.* Tully uses it in that sense; and in Plutarch the art of steering a vessel is called *government.*† New England is a little ship that has weathered many storms, and it is but fair that those who have stood at the helm of the ship should be remembered in its story." Let us mention one or two of these honored pilots.

With William Bradford, the eldest of the New England governors, we are already acquainted. Born in 1588, he had come to America in the prime of his life, and devoted himself to God and the commonweal. He was "looked on as a common blessing and father to all," and he lived long enough to see

---

* Quo quis in republicâ majorem dignitatis gradum adeptus est, eo Deum colat submissius."   † Τεχνη πυβερνητικη.

those high hopes with which he had embarked in the "Mayflower" more than realized; for the wilderness refuge was thronged and prosperous beyond his wildest dreams.* He was fully appreciated at Plymouth; and with the exception of five years' respite, when he "got off" by his "importunity," he was reëlected governor with annual regularity until death promoted him to a higher station.†

Bradford's administration of affairs as connected with the many vexatious questions arising from the difficulty with the Merchant-adventurers and with the English partners of the "Undertakers," was a model of firmness, wisdom, patience, forbearance, and energy. So also in his benevolent determination to bring over the rest of the Leyden exiles at whatever cost, he showed the fineness and beauty of his character. "Under the pressure of misfortune, his example was a star of hope, for he never yielded to despondency; and while, with Brewster, he threw the Pilgrims upon God for support and provision, he never neglected to set in motion every possible instrumentality for procuring supplies."‡ Patient, sagacious, devout, heroic, he was the very ideal of a Christian ruler.

We are assured by Cotton Mather that Bradford was "a person for study as well as for action; and hence, notwithstanding the difficulties through which he passed in his boyhood, he attained a notable skill in languages. The Dutch tongue was almost

* He died in 1657, in his sixty-ninth year.
† Thatcher, Wilson, Mather, etc.   ‡ Plymouth Pilgrims, p. 227.

as vernacular to him as the English; the French he could also manage; the Latin and the Greek he had mastered; but the Hebrew he most of all studied, 'Because,' he said, 'I would see with my own eyes the ancient oracles of God in their native beauty.' He was also well skilled in history, in antiquity, and in philosophy; and for theology, he became so versed in it, that he was an irrefragable disputant."*

But the crown of his shining life was not his genius in executive affairs, or the journal which he has bequeathed to us as a record of the cost at which he built at Plymouth Rock; it was "his holy, prayerful, fruitful walk with God," and this made him, in a better sense than Plato meant,

> "The shepherd-guardian of his human fold."

Bradford's immediate successors at Plymouth were Edward Winslow and Thomas Prince, men of the same mould, and whose lives exhaled the self-same fragrance. "Where the rulers are Christians the state prospers," was the old proverb, and in their case it was once more verified.

John Winthrop was the foremost man in Massachusetts. He was educated, he was gentlemanly, and he had been rich, but he spent his fortune "in the furtherance of God's work," bidding his son not mourn for it, but "certainly expect a liberal portion in the prosperity and blessing of the future."† He was a man of much gentleness and amiability; and

---

* Magnalia, vol. 1, pp. 113, 114.

† Letter to John Winthrop the Younger, cited in Magnalia, vol. 1, p. 161.

"his private life was charming" as it crops out in his exquisite letters to his wife, who remained for a time in England.*

He carried his admirable temper into public life. He had always an open hand of charity. When Roger Williams was banished, he wrote him privately to sustain and encourage him, and even suggested Narragansett Bay as a safe asylum.† He was always inclined to lenient ways; and when in his later days he was asked to sign an order for the banishment of an offending minister, he declined, remarking: "No, I have done too much of that already."‡ With this natural bent towards liberality, it was only with extreme reluctance that he yielded to the imperious spirit of intolerance which then reigned.

As governor, he was prudent, patient, courageous, and energetic—traits which made him the successful pilot of the ship of state in the unchartered waters on which he floated.

Winthrop never disdained to share equally with his brother Pilgrims. It is related of him that once, in a famine, he divided his last peck of meal with a hungry man, and was only not gnawed by hunger himself, because a ship entered Salem harbor ere night with a well-stocked larder, and changed the fast which had been appointed for the next day into a thanksgiving.§

* Elliot. Life of J. Winthrop, by R. C. Winthrop, Boston, 1866.
† Williams' Letter to Mason.   Knowles, Elton.
‡ Wilson, p. 494.   § Hutchinson, vol. 1, p. 23.

He knew how to conquer hearts by kindness. One hard winter, complaint was made to him that a man stole regularly to his woodpile and abstracted fuel. "Does he?" asked Winthrop; "send him to me; I'll cure him." The quaking wretch was brought in and expected to hear a rigorous sentence. "Friend," said he, "it is a cold winter, and I fear you are but poorly provided with wood to meet it. You are welcome to supply yourself at my pile till winter is over."*

Winthrop's "religion shone out through all his life, and gave a higher lustre to his character. He was zealous for truth and righteousness. Often he bore witness to the minister in the midst of the congregation; and frequently he visited the neighboring towns to prophesy, as it was called, or as we say, exhort. He had admirers not only in America, but in England and at court. ' 'Tis a pity,' remarked Charles I., ' that such a worthy gentleman should have banished himself to the hardships of a wilderness life.' "†

In Massachusetts the colonists believed in rotation in office; consequently, Winthrop was often displaced from the gubernatorial chair, and then replaced again. He always filled the post with dignity and with untarnished honor; so that on his death at sixty, worn out by toil and care, he might have torn his books of account, as Scipio Africanus did, and said: "A flourishing colony has been led out and settled under my direction. I have spent

---

* Wilson. † Shawmut; or the Settlement of Boston, p. 86.

my fortune and myself in its service. Waste no more time in harangues, but give thanks to God."*

Winthrop's great rival in influence and position was stern Thomas Dudley. His views corresponded far more completely with the theocratic formulas than did those of his mild and somewhat pliant friend. Dudley was bold, aggressive, and dogmatic; and he frequently quarrelled with Winthrop, because that statesman would not hack dissenters with his harsh hatchet, but was cautious, and temporizing, and conciliatory, alike from temperament and from discipline. He was always chosen deputy when Winthrop was elected governor; and on several occasions he held the chief office himself. "He was a man of sound sense, sterling integrity, and uncompromising faith. He was rigid in his religious opinions, and urged the strictest enforcement of the sedition laws. He considered that the various opinions that were struggling to manifest themselves from time to time tended to licentiousness; and he was desirous that his epitaph should be—'I died no libertine.'"† To paint him in a word, Dudley was an upright and downright man—a "piece of living justice."

Sir Harry Vane did not tarry long in New England; arriving in 1635, he went home in 1637 to lend his name and brains to the dawning revolution, and to carve his spirit on the marble of the ages. But short as was his sojourn on the west of

* Hutchinson, vol. 1, p. 40.
† See his Sonnet in Magnalia, vol. 1, p. 134.

the Atlantic, he stayed long enough to achieve wide honor and to leave plain traces of his genius. He, too, was a Pilgrim, and "it is a singular fact in the history of New England, that, among her pioneers, were such men as Vane, well born, well bred, and able to command a splendid career at home."*

"Sir Henry Vane the younger," remarks Bancroft, "was a man of the purest mind, and a statesman of the rarest integrity, whose name the progress of intelligence and liberty will erase from the rubric of fanatics and traitors, and insert high among the aspirants after truth and the martyrs for liberty. Almost in his boyhood he had valued the 'obedience of the gospel' more than the successful career of English diplomacy, and he cheerfully 'forsook the preferments of the court of Charles for the ordinances of religion in their purity in New England.'"†

While here he was the warm friend of Roger Williams and Anne Hutchinson; and when he went home he carried back with him the same ardor for Christian truth which had impelled him to grasp hands with Winthrop in the wilderness. He had a heart, and "he was happy in the possession of an admirable genius, though naturally more inclined to contemplative excellence than to action. He was happy, too, in the eulogist of his virtues; for Milton, ever parsimonious of praise, reserving the majesty of his verse to celebrate the glories and vindicate the providence of God, was lavish of his encomiums on the youthful friend of religious liberty. But

---

* Elliot, vol. 1, p. 170. † Bancroft, vol. 1, p. 383.

Vane was still more happy in attaining early in life a firmly-settled theory of morals, and in possessing an energetic will, which made all his conduct to the very last conform to the doctrines he had espoused, turning his dying hour into a seal of witness, which his life had ever borne with noble consistency to the freedom of conscience and the people. 'If he were not superior to Hampden,' says Clarendon, 'he was inferior to no other man;' 'his whole life made good the imagination that there was in him something extraordinary.'"*

Bluff John Endicott was another of the famous characters whose names and fame are impressed on the vellum of colonial history. He is said to have been perhaps the finest specimen of the genuine Puritan character to be found among the early governors. "He was quick of temper, with strong religious feelings; resolute to uphold with the sword what he had received as gospel truth; and feared no enemy so much as a gainsaying spirit. He tore the cross out of the English flag, cut down the Maypole at Merry-Mount, rakish Morton's sometime den, published his detestation of long hair in a formal proclamation, and set dissenters in the pillory. Inferior to Winthrop in learning—in comprehension to Vane—in tolerance even to Dudley—he excelled them all in the keen eye to discern the fit moment for action, in the quick resolve to profit by it, and in the hand always ready to strike."†

* Bancroft, ut antea.
† Hubbard, cited in Elliot, vol. 1, pp. 173, 174.

These are a few of the central figures, the pivotal men, of the first half dozen Pilgrim decades in New England. There are many more almost equally eminent and worthy of immortal honor—Bradstreet, and Hopkins, and Eaton, and the younger Winthrop. Here is an *embarras des richesses*, and neither time nor space serves to name the lengthened list of worthies who lent lustre and dignity to the colonial annals. The best of them were the peers of the first men of any age or country; and the worst more than met the requirements of the Latins in their rulers: "The Roman people," says Cicero, "selected their magistrates as if they were to be stewards of the republic. Proficiency in other departments, if it existed, they gladly tolerated; but if such additional accomplishments were lacking, they were content with the virtue and honesty of their public servants."*

The Pilgrim governors were at least all honest, and virtuous, and true; and they would have pleased those Thebans who made the statues of their judges without hands, importing that they were no takers, for these men too were guiltless of handling bribes. God blessed colonial New England rarely when he sent her such men as a benediction. But they are gone—Bradford, and Winthrop, and Carver, and Dudley, and Vane, and Endicott.

———"Woe the day!
How mingles mightiest dust with meanest clay."

* Cicero, Orati Pro. Plan.

CHAPTER XXXII.

EUREKA.

"Like one who had set out on his way by night, and travelled through a region of smooth or idle dreams, our history now arrives on the confines, where daylight and truth meet us with a clear dawn, representing to our view, though at far distance, true colors and shapes."

MILTON, History of England.

WHEN Great Britain, looking through the eyes of the Long Parliament in 1641, glanced across the Atlantic, she was surprised to see that the despised bantling of 1620 had, against all discouragements, staggered to its feet, and stood a nation, self-sustaining, robust, independent.

Already twenty-one thousand Pilgrims were permanently seated in New England;[*] fifty prosperous villages[†] peeped from the openings in the long unbroken forests. The steeples of forty churches pointed their white fingers to the sky.[‡] The rude log-cabins of the first months of settlement had been replaced by well-built houses.[§] Agriculture climbed the hill-sides. Commerce played by the sea-shore. Trade laughed and chaffed and dickered in the market-place. The spindle and the

---

[*] Hutchinson, vol. 1, p. 91. Mass. Historical Coll., vol. 1, 23. Neale's New England.   [†] Johnson, Mather, Bancroft.
[‡] Mass. Hist. Coll., vol. 1, p. 246, et seq.
[§] Ibid., Bancroft.

loom nodded merrily to each other over their work, as they labored side by side in the fabrication of "cotton and woollen and linen cloth;" for manufactures were even thus early established in New England.*

And the Pilgrims had a foreign influence. When a Madeira merchant visited Boston in 1642, he told Winthrop that the West Indian Jesuits taught that the "New-Englanders were the worst of all heretics, and that they were the cause of the civil war in the British island, and of the downfall of Archbishop Laud."†

The Pilgrims in England cordially recognized their kinship to the exiles. When the Parliament held regal prerogatives, in 1641, the colonists were urgently advised to solicit the admission of their delegates to its floor. "But upon consulting about it," says Winthrop, "we declined the motion, for this consideration, that if we should put ourselves under the protection of the Parliament, we should then be subject to all its laws, or at least to such as the Commons might be pleased to impose on us; which might be inconvenient, and prove very prejudicial to us."‡ And when, a twelvemonth later, "letters arrived inviting the colonial churches to send representatives to the Westminster Assembly of Divines, the same sagacity led them to neglect the invitation. The love of political independence declined even benefits. New

---

* Winthrop, vol. 2, p. 119. † Felt, vol. 1, p. 481.
‡ Winthrop, vol. 2, p. 25.

England spoke almost as one sovereign to another."*

The Pilgrims were singularly jealous of their franchises, and they never neglected an opportunity to consolidate and enlarge their liberty. And now, since the days had come when England was rent by the demon of war, when the throne tottered to its fall, when exultant republicanism, speaking through the lips of Cromwell, shouted, "*Sic semper tyrannis!*" as the head of a royal despot was struck off, the colonists had ample time in which to develop and define their rights.

Thus, exciting and momentous as were the scenes enacted on the European stage, and deeply as the Forefathers were interested in the issue, they were not won to overlook their own home drama. They were busy at this very time in reaping the benefits of secure and liberal domestic legislation. A bill of rights was promulgated; and under this, "though universal suffrage was not established, every man, whether citizen or alien, received the right of introducing any business into any public assembly, and of taking part in its deliberations. Then Massachusetts, by special law, offered free welcome and aid, at the public cost, to Christians of any nationality who might fly beyond the Atlantic 'to escape from wars or famine, or the oppression of their persecutors.' Thus the fugitive and the downtrodden were, by statute, made the guests of the commonwealth. Pilgrim hospitality was as wide as misfortune."†

* Bancroft, vol. 1, pp. 416, 417. † Bancroft, ubi sup.

This noble legislation was but the forerunner of a yet more significant act. In 1643, after several prior ineffectual essays, the four chief colonies of New England clasped hands in a confederacy.* Massachusetts, Connecticut, New Haven, and Plymouth, by solemn and free agreement, became the "UNITED COLONIES OF NEW ENGLAND."† The Dutch Republic was the model of this union;‡ and the reasons which impelled the Pilgrims to cement it are recited in the preamble to the twelve Articles of Agreement:

"Whereas, we all came into these parts of America with one and the same end and aim, namely, to advance the kingdom of our Lord Jesus Christ, and to enjoy the liberties of the gospel in purity and peace; and whereas, in our settling—by a wise providence of God—we are farther dispersed upon the seacoasts and rivers than was at first intended, so that we cannot, according to our desires, with convenience communicate in one government and jurisdiction; and whereas we live encompassed with people of several nations and strange languages, which may hereafter prove injurious to us or our posterity; and forasmuch as the natives have formerly committed sundry insolences and outrages upon several plantations of the English, and have of late combined themselves against us; and seeing, by reason of these sad distractions in England, which the Indians have heard of, and by

---

* Mather's Magnalia, vol. 1, p. 160. Palfrey, Hubbard, etc.
† Hutchinson, Winthrop, Felt.
‡ Ibid., Palfrey, Elliot, Bancroft.

which they know we are hindered from that humble way of seeking advice or reaping those comfortable fruits of protection which at other times we might well expect; we hereby conceive it our bounden duty, without delay, to enter into a present consociation for mutual help and strength in all our future concernments; that, as in nation and religion, so in other respects, we be and continue one."*

The old Hindoo dreamed that he saw the human race led out to its varied fortune. First, he saw men bitted and curbed, and the reins went back to an iron hand. But his dream changed on and on, until at last he saw men led by reins that came from the brain and ran back into shadowy fingers. It was the type of progress. The first was despotism; the last was a government of ideas, of morals, of the normal forces of society.† The New England Confederation was the forerunner of a mightier union; and when Liberty saw it, she cried, "Eureka!" and thanked God.

The machinery of the league was very simple, very sensible, and very effective. The colonies were co-equal. Each appointed two commissioners, who formed a directory, which was to hold an annual session. The commissioners were empowered to assemble more frequently if necessity pressed; and they could deliberate on all matters which were "the proper concomitants or consequents of confederation."‡ "The affairs of peace and war exclusively

---

* Hubbard, p. 466. Col. Rec., etc. † W. Phillips.
‡ Records in Hazard, vol. 2. Winthrop, Hubbard, Morton.

belonged to them. They were authorized to make internal improvements at the common charge, assessed according to population. They too were the guardians to see equal and speedy justice assured to all the confederates in every jurisdiction; but each colony carefully reserved its respective local rights, as the badges of continued independence; so that, while the commissioners might decree war and levy troops, they had no executive power, but were dependent on the states for the execution of the plans they matured and voted."*

Two bodies of colonists were rigidly excluded from this union. Gorges' pioneers, beyond the Piscataqua, were not admitted, because "they ran a different course" from the Pilgrims, "both in their ministry and in their civil administration." Providence and Rhode Island were shut out, partly because they were not esteemed sufficiently strong and settled to add strength to the league, and also because they were regarded as the haunts of heresy and fanaticism.† It was thought that the confederacy, in order to be effective, should be homogeneous. On that basis it was launched; and, surviving "the jealousies of the Long Parliament, it met with favor from the Protector, remained safe from censure at the restoration of the Stuarts," and walked buoyantly on, scattering its benefactions on the right hand and on the left, until James II. vacated the New England charters, in 1686.‡

* Bancroft, ut antea.
† Hubbard, Hazard, Hutchinson, Morton, Bradford.
‡ Hist. Coll., Col. Records, Elliot.

The colonial union was the crowning service of the founders of New England to humanity. Now they began, one by one, to descend into the grave, worn to early death by a toilsome grapple with the rough and grinding forces of nature. But in their footsteps trudged their sons, succeeding to the same blessed inheritance of faith, and love, and godly energy.*

* The half century which succeeded this act of union was singularly checkered. In this time four momentous events occurred. The first of these, in point of time, was the persecution of the Quakers. The early advocates of this sect in New England displayed little of the mild philosophy and statesmanlike benevolence of Penn and his modern disciples; and, indeed, "the first and most noisy exponents of any popular sect are apt to be men of little consideration." To this rule the first Quakers of Massachusetts were no exception. They knew the public opinion of the province; they knew the laws which were put into the statute-book to curb heresy; yet they broke through the restraints of sentiment, and contemned the laws—not mildly, but with harsh, violent, and often indecent obstinacy. Persecution, under any circumstances, is wrong, and the theocratic principles of the Massachusetts colonists were far from being either just or necessary. Yet granting all this, and it has still been well said that, "if the essential guilt of persecution would be aggravated when aimed against the quiet, patient philanthropist of to-day, it does not follow that it would be attended with like aggravation, however wicked else, when the subject was the mischievous madman of two centuries ago, who went raving through the city reviling authority, inveighing against the law and order of the time, running naked in the streets, and rudely interrupting divine service in the churches, as many called Quakers, of both sexes, did in 1656 and onwards. The duty of toleration stops short of the permission of such indecency; nor does it suffer men, for conscience' sake, or to gain a name like Abraham, to sacrifice their sons, as one of these Friends was proceeding to do in 1658, when the neighbors, alarmed by the boy's cries, broke into the house in time to balk the fanatic." Still, it must be confessed that there was a better way than the magistrates of Massachusetts took, and one more efficient in curb-

Travellers tell us that at Florence there is a rich table, worth a thousand crowns, made of precious stones neatly inlaid, in whose construction thirty

ing this fanaticism, than the pillory, mutilation statutes, and the death penalty; and this Roger Williams proved in Rhode Island, and the younger Winthrop demonstrated in Connecticut—in both of which colonies there was freedom of religious opinion, and yet there were few Quakers.

That furious Indian war, known as "King Philip's war," occurred in 1675. It originated in the same deep-rooted feeling of jealousy and hatred—begotten of dispossession and imagined wrong—that caused the Pequod war. Massasoit died about 1661. He was succeeded by his son Alexander, who was, on his death, succeeded by his brother Philip, the hero of the struggle. This sagacious chieftain saw that the whites were grasping; that his corn-lands and hunting-grounds were rapidly being usurped; that rum was poisoning his warriors; and he panted for revenge. So he gave his days and nights to the organization of a conspiracy. "He spared no arts; he lived but for one purpose, and that was to unite the Indians, split into numberless clans, into one body, for the destruction of the encroaching pale-faces." Philip was largely successful, and the ensuing conflict was bitter, doubtful, and prolonged. But eventually civilization and discipline triumphed. The great sagamore was slain, and peace once more brooded over mutilated and wailing New England—peace insured by the definitive subjection of the Indian tribes.

In 1683, James II. abrogated the Massachusetts charter; three years later, Sir Edmund Andros arrived, armed with the king's commission to take upon himself the absolute government of New England. Andros at once commenced to play the despot. He shackled the press; he imprisoned men for their religious opinions; he endeavored to get possession of the charter of Connecticut—which, however, was hidden in the "charter-oak" at Hartford, a circumstance which has made the tree immortal; He denied the colonists the most common civil rights, and asserted the highest doctrines of arbitrary taxation. The colonies were ripe for insurrection, when, in 1688, news came of the landing and coronation of William of Orange. Instantly Andros was deposed, and flung, broken and dishonored, out of New England. In 1691, King William granted Massachusetts a new charter; but in this

men were employed daily for fifteen years. The Pilgrim Fathers were twice that time in carving out and inlaying New England with churches, and

...e reserved the right of appointing a colonial governor, allowed appeals to be made to the English courts, freed all Protestant religions, and confirmed the annexation of Plymouth to Massachusetts—an annexation which Plymouth had decreed in 1690. This charter robbed the colonists of several prerogatives which had betokened independence, and was continued in substance until the dawn of the Revolution. The same policy was pursued throughout New England.

It was in the years 1691-2 that what has been called the "Salem witchcraft epidemic" occurred. In that age the belief in witches was general and strong. In 1644, '5, and '6, England hanged fifteen persons accused of witchcraft in one batch at Chelmsford, sixteen at Yarmouth, and sixty in Suffolk. In Sweden, in 1670, there was a panic about witches; and in one town, Mahra, seventy persons were charged with this offence, and spite of their protestations of innocence, most of them were executed. Fifteen children were hung on their own confession; and fifty others were condemned to be whipped every Sunday for a twelvemonth. Even so late as 1697, five years after the Salem troubles, seven persons were hung in Scotland as witches, and that too upon the unsupported testimony of a single child eleven years old.

New England, then, was not alone in her belief in witches, or in her punishment of them. She merely shared the opinion of such consummate scholars and noble thinkers as Sir Thomas Browne and Sir Matthew Hale. Many things combined to increase this belief. James I. had published a book on demonology. Books containing rules for binding witches were in wide circulation. The practice and the opinion of centuries substantiated these phantoms. And the recent excitement in Sweden and England was certain to cause a ripple in America. Men's minds were thus prepared for an epidemic. As early as the year 1688, a case of supposed witchcraft occurred in Boston. An old half-witted Irish woman was charged with having bewitched the children of John Goodwin, and she was soon hanged. The witches then quit Boston, and in 1691-2 appeared at Salem. Children began to act oddly, getting "into holes, creeping under chairs, and uttering foolish speeches"—all of which were esteemed as tokens of be-free schools, and printing-presses, and manufactures. Think of their task. "That gore of land, a few hundred miles wide and long, which lies between the St. Lawrence and the Atlantic ocean, and seems to have been formed of the leavings and fragments after the rest of the continent was made, whose ribs stick out past all covering; which has

witchment. Inquiries were at once and everywhere made for witches. The children accused at random. This woman was said to be a witch, and that man. Salem was aghast. Startled women passed from house to house, repeating and enlarging every idle tale. Soon the excitement was unprecedented. Fasting and prayer failed to exorcise the "spirits." Then the witches were imprisoned, tried, condemned, executed. A reign of terror commenced. All lived in fear; accusation was equivalent to proof; there seemed no safety. Many, spurred by fear, acknowledged themselves to be witches when accused, thinking thus to save their lives; others hastened to complain that they were bewitched; and only those who avowed themselves to belong to one of these two classes could be sure of life. Still the panic spread. Andover was infected. New England at large began to shudder. The executioner was busy. And it was not until January, 1692, that the panic began to abate. Nineteen persons had been hung; one had been pressed to death; many had been condemned; hundreds had been imprisoned. So remorseless, so cruel is panic. But the excess cured itself; the reaction was great; men began to lament the part they had played; and some made open confession in church of their grievous fault and weakness. The infatuation grew perhaps from the tricks or the craziness of the "bewitched" children; perhaps from the folly or the superstition of their parents. Whatever its cause, its effects were sad, and they are pregnant with warning.

It is sometimes said that these doings sprang naturally from the theology and temper of New England. Rather, they were directly counter to both. They were a weak and foolish importation from Europe; and they prevailed in New England only for a short season. Soon her sons outgrew such folly; and nowhere in Christendom was the popular revolution against witchcraft so speedy and complete as in the Puritan colonies.

sand enough to scour the world; where there are no large rivers, but many nimble little ones, which seem to have been busy since the flood in taking exercise over rifts and rocks. This was their field of action. The only indigenous productions were ice, Indians, and stunted trees. Trading and commercial adventurers had essayed to effect a settlement in vain. The soil was too hard even for Indians and rovers. It was apparently set apart for a wilderness, and it had peculiar aptitudes for keeping man away from it. Its summers were short, its winters were long, its rocks were innumerable, its soil was thin." Yet the Pilgrims entered and subdued this waste, making it to bud with churches and to bloom with schools; cultivating it to the sterile hill-tops; dotting the landscape with neat farm-houses, factories, mills, the evidences and the tokens of a ripe, full civilization.

But the fierce struggle with nature left its scars upon the Pilgrims, and it has marked their children. They had to seize and impress into their service every help. This begot the inventive faculty, and the habit of looking at every thing from the angle of its utility. This it was which strung factories on every stream-side, as gold beads are hung on a silver cord; which used every drop of water a dozen times over in turning wheels before it was suffered to run, weary and fretted, to the sea; which sent the little feet toddling to the woodpile to pick up chips; which made labor-saving machines, those gnomes whose cunning fingers were to work up the black earth and the hard rock into golden grains.

"Looking, therefore, at civilization in New England, we see a people beginning without aristocracy or hierarchical forms. We see the leading men among them educated and honorable; the working men devoted to agriculture and owners of the soil. We see all resisting the incoming of a state church, persistently opposing a distant but domineering court; and, singularly enough, through nigh two centuries of savage and civilized war, steadily refusing to organize a standing army, trusting to the native valor of the mass. Thus the commonalty educated themselves by daily practice in self-government, until, at this present time, rulers there are simply lay-figures for show-days."

"The Pilgrims were readers. Drunkenness, pauperism, filth, and dilapidation, nowhere abounded. They were thrifty, and industrious, and frugal; and so, though the land was poor, they lived in comfort. Money was hard to get, and carefully spent; no man lavished it, or lent it except on good security; yet nowhere else was there such a constant contribution for the relief of suffering or the cure of secular and religious ignorance; nowhere else would men more quickly risk life and health to serve a fellow. As there was no aristocracy, so there was no inferior or pariah class, except when, at an unguarded moment, negro slavery crept in for a time. But servitude was so palpably contrary to the genius and principles of the Pilgrims, that it was banished as soon as the mind and conscience grappled with it;" for the corner-stone of New England was religion, and the top-stone was honest, self-respecting, well-paid, and skilled labor. Religion and labor begot that spirit which has tamed the continent, cheered it with churches and schools, set the busy spindles humming and the shuttles flying, plunged into the earth and into the sea, run over the prairies, talking by lightning from the Atlantic to the Pacific, until the whole land where men are intelligent, industrious, and free, seems singing and smiling at its daily work.

The Pilgrim Fathers literally obeyed the injunction of the great German poet—they knew the aim and reason of yesterday; they worked well to-day for worthy things, calmly trusting the future's hidden season, and believing with unquestioning faith that their children would eat of the fruit of the tree which they had planted in a sterile soil and under wintry skies. Patient in waiting, they never hurried; they did not dig up their seed every twelve hours to see whether it had sprouted. Without haste, they were also without rest; and in their treatment of causes, they never paused to worry and fret about effects; for they knew that justice was the best policy, and that the steady every-day bravery which vaunteth not itself is more than a match for the Hotspur valor which presumes that any cause is good which is desperately defended.

The Pilgrims were men of conscience; and this they carried with them into work and into statesmanship. Quincy Adams once, in a happy moment, called New England "the colony of conscience." It was a religious plantation, not an essay for trade. "He that made religion as twelve and the world as thirteen had not the spirit of a true New England man." "Religion was the object of the Pilgrims; it was also their consolation. With this the wounds of the outcast were healed, and the tears of exile were sweetened."

Puritanism has been finely called religion struggling for the people—evoking, in the logical sequence of events, political equality. "Those peculiar outward emblems, which were its badges at first, were of transient duration; like the clay and ligaments with which the graft is held in its place, made to be brushed away as soon as the scion is firmly united. The spirit of the Pilgrims was a life-giving spirit; activity, thrift, intelligence, liberty, followed in its train; and as for courage, a coward and a Puritan never went together. 'He that prays best and preaches best will fight best;' such was the judgment of Cromwell, the greatest soldier of his age."

From any enumeration of the elements of the early colonial felicity, purity of morals must not be omitted. "As Ireland would not brook venomous serpents, so would not that land vile livers." One might dwell there "from year to year, and not see a drunkard, nor hear an oath, nor meet a beggar." The consequence was wide-spread health, one of the chief promoters of social happiness.

As for the soil, it was owned by the colonists. It was bought and paid for. The little farms, the straggling villages, the slowly-growing towns, were the absolute private property of their occupants; and in a time of unusual commotion, when their settlements, for which they had done and dared so much, seemed menaced with subversion—seemed liable to be converted into a receptacle for all the spawn of England—the Pilgrims assumed to decide, standing on their own grounds, who should be welcomed among them as fellow-citizens, who should be treated as guests, and who should be bidden to depart, never to return under the heaviest penalty.

Yet "on every subject but religion, the mildness of Puritan legislation corresponded to the popular character of the Puritan doctrines. Hardly a European nation has as yet made its criminal code as humane as was that of early New England. The Pilgrims brushed a crowd of offences at one sweep from the catalogue of capital crimes. They never countenanced the idea that the forfeiture of human life may be demanded for the protection of material interests. The punishment for theft, burglary, highway robbery, was far more mild than the penalties imposed even by modern American legislation. Domestic discipline was highly valued; but if the law was severe against the child who was undutiful, it was also severe against the parent who was faithless. The earlier laws did not decree imprisonment for debt, except when there was an appearance of some estate which the debtor would not produce.

Even the brute creation was not forgotten; and cruelty to animals was a civil offence. The sympathies of the colonists were wide; a regard for Protestant Germany was as old as emigration; and during the Thirty Years' war, the Pilgrims held fasts and offered prayers for the success of the Saxon cause"— crowned with the gospel.

But the glory of the Pilgrim Fathers was their faith. They trusted God, and acted. The secret of their strength and success was the open Bible and the family altar. They were men, and therefore not infallible. They sometimes erred grievously, and walked limping and awry; but they always meant right, and with God's word as a lamp to their feet, they could not stray and grope far or long from the sunlight. To much that the Pilgrim conscientiously believed, and with his whole heart accepted, the present age has grown careless; we are lukewarm or indifferent upon some points which he esteemed vital; but it is small credit to us, if we are tolerant of error simply because we care little for truth. In former times New England was not latitudinarian; and, clad in her sparkling snow, crowned with her evergreen pine, the glory of her brow was justice, the splendor of her eye was liberty, the strength of her hands was industry, the whiteness of her bosom was faith; for the Pilgrims were men of absolute conviction. Moral earnestness was the key with which they unlocked the treasure-house of success. They were always true to their highest conceptions; and they could say as Paul said to Agrippa, "I obeyed the heavenly vision."

Yet they were not visionaries, but they made that fine distinction between material nature and spirituality: "giving to Cæsar the things which are Cæsar's, and unto God the things which are God's." Thus it was that, though they were the most practical of men, they were also the most spiritual—wedding a paradox.

The curse of our age is materialism. We kindle only within the sphere of material interests and pursuits. On higher subjects we are as cold as an ice-field on the breast of Alp. There is an apotheosis of dirt. Men do not half believe in what they cannot see, and feel, and handle. They group about them the tokens of their skill—steam-engines, and telegraphs, and sewing-machines—and worship these as the ultimate good, saying, "See, these are the realities of life."

The Pilgrim spirit protests against this tendency. It comes to remind us that the controllers of the present, the moulders of the future, are not the babblers who plead for an unreal realism; that they are not the heaviest brains of the epoch, but the heroes of religious earnestness, men inspired by drinking from the spiritual springs, men who go forth to fight like the red knight of Odessa, with the cross emblazoned on their shield, and with Christ buried in their hearts. Behind intellect there must be a ground-swell of religious earnestness, else brains are a snare, and useless. Rousseau, and Voltaire, and Pascal, do not mark the ages. Name them anywhere, and scores of vacant eyes will ask you, "Who are they?" The Luthers, the Calvins, the Ridleys, the Brewsters, shake the world, seize all hearts, and educate the centuries, because they were fired by conviction, and built for God.

This is the lesson which the story of the Pilgrims teaches us. Let us heed it; and then, clasping hands with the martyrs and apostles, we too may press forward with our "garlands and singing-robes about us," and by battling for Christ, insure for ourselves in the long hereafter a blessed rest and a fragrant memory.

www.ingramcontent.com/pod-product-compliance
Lightning Source LLC
Chambersburg PA
CBHW020739020526
44115CB00030B/561